crystal energy

crystal energy

150 ways to bring success, love, health and harmony into your life

Mary Lambert

CICO BOOKS
LONDON NEW YORK

First published in 2005 by CICO Books
This edition published in 2010 by CICO Books
an imprint of Ryland Peters and Small
20–21 Jockey's Fields, London WC1R 4BW
www.cicobooks.com

10 9 8 7 6 5 4 3 2 1

A CIP catalogue record for this book is available from the British Library.

ISBN: 978 1 907030 35 2
(Previous ISBN: 978 1 904991 06 9)

Design: Jerry Goldie
Project editor: Liz Dean
Photography: Geoff Dann
Illustration: Trina Dalziel

Printed in China

Safety Note
Please note that while the descriptions of the properties of some crystals refer to healing benefits, they are not intended to replace diagnosis of illness or ailments, or healing or medicine. Always consult your doctor or other health professional in the case of illness.

Contents

Introduction

For centuries, crystals have fascinated people. Prized for their beauty, these special stones adorn royalty and the rich and powerful, and continue to be revered for their spiritual and healing properties.

Crystals were formed millions of years ago when hot gases and mineral solutions rose to the surface from the molten layer of the earth. As they cooled, the atoms merged into patterns and three-dimensional lattices to become the crystals we know today. The special structure of a crystal lets it absorb, strengthen, and transmit electromagnetic energy that can heal and energize.

Crystals in ancient times

In the mythical city of Atlantis the colored rays from crystals treated physical and emotional illness. A great healing temple was thought to have existed in Atlantis, with a large circular room and domed ceiling made of interlocking crystals. These crystals were arranged to form ancient symbols that created patterns of color when illuminated by light. Around the room were separate healing rooms for illness and emotional healing, with vast crystal doors that were energized with the color needed for the patient.

Egyptian remains indicate that this ancient race also had rooms in their temples for treating patients with healing gemstones. The ancient Egyptian people understood the power of crystals, and their rulers, the pharaohs, wore stones such as malachite in their headdresses to bring wisdom. Tiger's eye, carnelian, and turquoise were shaped into amulets; shields, hearts, and scarabs were buried with the owner in their tomb to guide them on their last journey.

Crystal skulls

One of the most fascinating crystal finds was the discovery of anatomically perfect natural quartz crystal skulls, estimated to be at least 20,000 years old. One of the best-known skulls was discovered by Anna Mitchell-Hedges with her father, Frederick Albert Mitchell-Hedges, an archaeologist, in 1924 in the Mayan ruins of Lubaantum (however, others say that they purchased it at a London auction). No one knows why the skulls are here, but they incite mystical and spiritual happenings, and reportedly many people's lives have changed after contact with a skull. Quartz doesn't decay and because of its amplifying ability, some believe that the skulls are a kind of storage device for important cosmic knowledge.

Crystals today

In this book are 150 practical tips showing you how crystals can heal and energize the many different areas of your life. Both rough and polished crystals (see below) are used. They can look quite different, so choose the type that appeals to you.

In the home, crystals give you protection from any negative energies existing there. Lepidolite is a versatile stone to position in the living room as it absorbs electromagnetic emissions from electrical equipment or other sources. Different crystals stimulate the atmosphere and energy flow, making your home a more sociable place. Even an ailing house-plant responds to the special vibration of a piece of green tourmaline. At work, you can achieve success with the crystal energy of golden topaz and keep internet viruses at bay by circling malachite around your computer. Personal power is important and comes via our seven energy centers: the chakras. The unique vibration of a sodalite crystal, for instance, can stimulate your Third eye chakra, improving your intuitive abilities.

Everyone wants romance in their lives, and crystals with a loving vibration draw in a partner or improve a relation-ship. Rhodochrosite, a pretty pink and black stone, can help attract that desired soulmate. Crystal jewelry can also work on desires. Wearing a crystal pendant or earrings daily for a week or so allows the gems' intrinsic properties to make your dreams come true or resolve a current unhappiness.

When you use a crystal for physical and emotional healing, the crystal's vibration tunes in to the malfunctioning emissions of the organ or energetic area and gently corrects them, making you feel healthier and re-energized. Placing blue calcite on the skin, for example, is thought to help relieve the inflammation and itching of eczema, while natural quartz's strong energetic field releases long-held emotional fears.

Finally, our astrological star signs will always fascinate us, and many of us live up to some of the less pleasant traits associated with them. So if you know you are an impatient Gemini, use a sunny citrine to keep your restlessness under control or, as a Capricorn, you can dispel depressive tendencies with chalcedony.

These nurturing, beautiful companions heal and enhance your life and, if necessary, may leave you and move on when their job is done. Treasure your crystals while they are with you, and let them bring you joy and happiness.

Types of crystal

Pointed: crystals with a point
Polished: rough crystals that have been abraded to create a polished surface
Rough: crystals in their natural, mined state
Rutilated: crystals, normally quartz, containing gold/red/black mineral strands
Striated: scratched, patterned, or grooved crystals
Terminated: crystals with a point
Tumbled: the same as polished, often placed in a large drum with grit to create smooth crystals

Silencing noisy neighbors with white moonstone

Polished, translucent

CRYSTAL FACTS

Crystal to use: white moonstone, translucent

Availability: commonly available

Qualities of stone: soothes stress, calms emotions and overreaction to problems

Where to place the crystal: place by outside fence or internal wall in an apartment

You may be amazed at what a crystal can do to help you, even in the most intractable of situations. If noisy neighbors develop selective deafness whenever you ask for peace and quiet, try using a white moonstone, whose very name seems to suggest tranquility.

Moonstone is sacred in India because it is associated with the Third eye chakra, which relates to inner vision and the ability to take charge of your life. A symbol of love and confidence, moonstone will spark your intuition, helping you to find creative ways to solve potentially insurmountable problems. These qualities can inspire you to take a new view on an old or long-running dispute with a neighbor, breaking the cycle of annoyance and intolerance that has become established.

Crystal cure

Hold a white moonstone in your hand for several minutes and ask it to silence unwanted noise and disturbance. Place the stone outside, next to your neighbor's boundary; let it rest on the ledge of a fence or tuck it in a crevice in the mortar of a wall. If you are in an apartment, place the crystal on the floor next to the offending wall where it will not be disturbed.

Try this moonlight ritual to give your wish for peace more power. Wait until dark when the moon is in the sky, and pick a day when the moon is waning—the time between a full moon and a new moon, which symbolizes natural endings. Hold the stone as you look up at the moon in the night sky and simply ask for help. Repeat three times.

Trust in the stone's power. Within a few days, see how intrusive noise lessens and serenity takes its place.

ALTERNATIVE PROBLEM-SOLVING CRYSTALS TO USE

Sugilite: brings about compromise in difficult situations

Snowflake obsidian: a calming stone that can release negative thinking

Chrysoprase: a soothing stone that encourages positive solutions

Protecting your boundaries with agate

Rough

Agate is a brilliant crystal to use whenever you need a security guard for your home. Whether you call upon agate's powers of protection to deter unwanted visitors or intrusive neighbors, this crystal is renowned for keeping boundaries intact. It is a particularly grounding stone, bringing a sense of security and sanctuary.

Some traditions believed that agate made a person invisible to others. You can harness this gift by using the stone to help you go about your business with discretion, and without feeling constantly observed or overlooked by neighbors. Agate is therefore a great antidote to the "goldfish bowl" syndrome of many modern homes, and will help you any time you need privacy.

CRYSTAL FACTS

CRYSTAL TO USE: agate (clear/milky white, gray, blue, green, pink, or brown); use small pieces

AVAILABILITY: commonly available

QUALITIES OF STONE: very grounding stone that creates a feeling of safety and security. Harmonizes yin and yang: the positive and negative forces of the universe

WHERE TO PLACE THE CRYSTAL: on either side of the gate and at boundary corners

Crystal cure

To make you feel secure in the area surrounding your home, you need to bury a handful of small agate crystals on each side of your gate or driveway, and then bury one at each corner of the boundary of your garden or yard. This will literally activate the grounding quality of the stone. As you place the agates in the earth, ask the stones to help solve your problem and give you the peace and safety you desire in your space. Let the crystals do their work, and notice how happy you feel as you walk through your space as you sense the protective shield the agates have cast around the perimeter of your property.

ALTERNATIVE PROTECTIVE CRYSTALS TO USE

Hematite: a grounding and protective stone that dispels negativity

Jet: protects against violence, alleviates fears

Smoky quartz: neutralizes negative energy, blocks geopathic stress

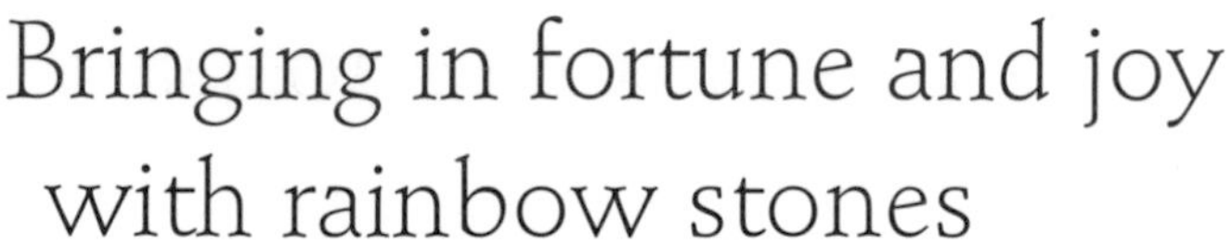

Bringing in fortune and joy with rainbow stones

Tubs of flowers that bloom year-round on each side of your front door are a welcoming presence for visitors. Sprinkling rainbow-colored tumbled stones over the tops of your flower pots creates a sense of peace, harmony, and joy around your entrance, and sets up a symbolic rainbow bridge of protection between your home and the spirit world. The color of the crystals—red, orange, yellow, green, turquoise blue, indigo, and violet—also links to the chakras, your spiritual energy centers, so you will benefit from an energy boost every time you enter your home.

Crystal energizing

Choose your rainbow stones, place in a bowl, and leave them to energize in the sun for 24 hours (see also page 154). Wait for a showery, sunny day, when the crystals will be exposed to the powerful energy of a rainbow. Now hold the stones in your hands individually and ask each one to prevent any unwanted intrusions in your home. Ask them to surround you with their unique love and compassion. As you touch and gaze at each one, let their rainbow colors inspire you and your family with creativity and success at school and work, continued prosperity and health, and ask that they instill in you peace and hope for the future. Now scatter your seven stones evenly over the top of each pot and leave them to do their work.

CRYSTAL FACTS

CRYSTALS TO USE: choose two of the same tumbled stone from each rainbow color

Red: garnet, red jasper, ruby

Orange: carnelian, orange calcite

Yellow: amber, golden beryl, topaz

Green: aventurine, chrysoprase, malachite

Turquoise, blue, blue/green: aquamarine, celestite, turquoise

Indigo: lapis lazuli, sapphire, sodalite

Violet: amethyst, lavender (purple) jade, sugilite

QUALITIES OF STONES: using a selection of these crystals protects your home and brings purifying energy, joy and happiness, love and devotion, creativity and vitality, trust and peace, compassion, success, positive health and wellbeing, good fortune inside

WHERE TO PLACE THE CRYSTALS: place seven of the same stones in each flower tub on either side of the door

Creating a party atmosphere for alfresco dining with red calcite

Rough red calcite

An opaque, soft stone, red calcite is an effective energizer. It has the ability to cleanse the environment of any unpleasant feelings, as well as injecting an appealing vitality into the atmosphere. It is the perfect stone to use for a picnic, barbecue, or alfresco dinner party because it links to the stimulating element of Fire, and projects the heat of the sun. Your guests will find themselves feeling happy and sociable as they respond to its warm, red, enigmatic vibrations.

Crystal energizing

Place the crystal in the middle of a designated dining table and watch how your friends mingle as they are drawn to stand around it happily sipping their aperitifs. The joy and happiness that emanate from the crystal are infectious, enlivening everyone within its radiance. To increase the buzz and to keep people staying for a while, scatter some chips of natural quartz, a great energizer, around the edges of the barbecue or picnic area. String some small, pretty, white lights along the ground where you have placed the crystals, as they are also associated with the Fire element and will lift the energetic vibrations.

CRYSTAL FACTS

CRYSTALS TO USE: red calcite: translucent, may be banded (sometimes treated with acid to increase color); small pieces of rough or tumbled quartz

AVAILABILITY: commonly available

QUALITIES OF STONES: **red calcite:** cleanses negative vibrations from the environment, increases energy and vitality for a party, creates a serene and joyful atmosphere; **natural quartz chips:** lift energy, bring a sparkling ambience

WHERE TO PLACE THE CRYSTALS: place red calcite on table. Scatter natural quartz chips around the perimeter of your dining area—your yard, garden, or deck

Polished quartz

Shielding your entrance with hematite

Rough

CRYSTAL FACTS

Crystal to use: hematite (metallic silver/gray, red/brown when rough), also known as volcano spit; shiny appearance when polished, or use hematite chips

Availability: commonly available

Qualities of stone: dissolves negativity, protects and prevents bad energies entering the home

Where to place the crystal: by your outside doormat, or under the mat

Polished

In its rough, natural state, hematite is a reddish brown color. The crystal contains iron oxide and, because iron was associated with Mars, the Roman god of war, legend has it that Roman soldiers pressed the stone to their bodies for protection before battle. An environmentally grounding and supportive crystal, hematite, when polished, is metallic silvery gray, and produces such a high sheen that in the past it was used as a mirror, in much the same way as obsidian (see page 14).

Hematite's mirror effect can deflect the unpleasant attitudes of unwanted visitors at your front door. Although this area may feel good generally, people who unsuccessfully sell you goods or disgruntled visitors can all deplete the positivity of your entrance. Placing hematite by the front door can smooth the flow of energy. A powerful protector, the stone builds a healing shield around the entrance. This shield connects to the earth's beneficial properties, neutralizing any bad energy that people bring with them, so that even those who come to the door feeling upset go away happy.

Crystal cure

Place a hematite crystal outside the door by the doormat, or in an apartment you may prefer to scatter some hematite chips under the mat. Hold them and ask that they protect your entrance and heal all the people that call there. Trust in their curative powers.

ALTERNATIVE PROTECTIVE CRYSTALS TO USE

***Selenite*:** creates a peaceful space, keeps out bad influences

Obsidian: very protective, shields negative forces

Polished

Increasing luck and good fortune with green jade

Jade is a stone of prosperity and luck that will draw money and good things into your life, and so is perfect for placing by your mailbox. Two types of this beneficial crystal are available: the creamy nephrite is the "older" dark leafy-green jade, which was carved into many treasured pieces in ancient China from as early as 2950 BCE, while the "newer" translucent, vivid green jadeite originated in Burma in the 13th century. As jadeite took over in popularity from nephrite in China, it was worshipped for its life-extending and erotic properties.

Jade bestows tranquility and wisdom, transmitting a sense of wellbeing and friendship that welcomes people into your home. It is also protective, so will act as a deterrent to burglars or unsavory visitors.

CRYSTAL FACTS

CRYSTAL TO USE: green jade, translucent (jadeite) or creamy (nephrite)

AVAILABILITY: generally available but can be rare; nephrite is more easily available

QUALITIES OF STONE: encourages peace and unconditional love, protects and nurtures, creates harmony, brings good luck

WHERE TO PLACE THE CRYSTAL: stick next to mail box, or put inside

Crystal energizing

To bring good fortune and abundance into your home, take hold of your jade crystal and tune in to its lucky vibrations. Using reusable adhesive putty, stick the crystal to the side of your letterbox or mailbox (inside the front door) or if you have an outside mailbox, place it inside. Let this joyous stone protect you, and ask it to attract success and many lucky opportunities.

Harmonizing the hallway with magical obsidian

Rough

Formed from volcanic lava, obsidian was used by the Aztecs as the equivalent of flint, to make knives and arrowheads. When finely polished it is deeply reflective, and the stone's magical reputation is perhaps due to its mirrorlike qualities; Dr. Jon Dee, spiritual adviser to Queen Elizabeth I, prized an Aztec "magic mirror" of obsidian for scrying, or future-gazing. As everyone who lives with you or visits can bring the mixed emotions of their day to your door, you can use this ancient stone as a symbolic mirror to deflect incoming frustrations and upsets.

Crystal cure

Place a black obsidian crystal, either tumbled or raw, in your hallway—the best position is on a small table or on a corner shelf by the front door. Bear in mind that poor lighting and clutter can inhibit your crystal's abilities, so keep your hall's surfaces clear and the whole space bright. Hold this crystal tightly and ask it to do its work for you, and soon this grounding stone will neutralize any negativity that has been brought in, and restore a more harmonious ambience.

CRYSTAL FACTS

Crystal to use: black obsidian, opaque, shiny, similar to glass, sometimes tumbled

Availability: commonly available

Qualities of stone: a very grounding stone that repels or transforms negativity, blocks geopathic stress, encourages optimism for the future

Where to place the crystal: on hall table, to the side of the front door

ALTERNATIVE HARMONIZING CRYSTALS TO USE

Citrine: brings in the feeling of sunlight, brightening dull areas

Clear topaz: helps to clear stagnant or stuck energy

Brown jasper: brings stability and balance; relieves environmental stress

Encouraging good energy flow on stairs with natural quartz

Polished

CRYSTAL FACTS

CRYSTAL TO USE: six 1/2in (12mm) small quartz pieces, polished or rough

AVAILABILITY: commonly available

QUALITIES OF STONE: amplifies energy, regulates energy flow

WHERE TO PLACE THE CRYSTAL: glue crystals to the side of four stair treads, equally spaced up the stairs, or stick to the underside of the banisters

Versatile natural quartz can increase energy or transmute any negative influences, and is easily programmed to suit your needs. This crystal can transmit electrical energy under mechanical pressure, creating the piezoelectric effect. To see this in action, rub the flat sides of two quartz crystals together in a darkened room and see how the friction makes the stones light up. You can also "lighten up" your home by placing slivers of natural quartz on the stair treads or under banisters to create a vibrant pathway between floors, enlivening the energy flow from the downstairs rooms.

Polished

Crystal cure

If you sense the energy in your home is dull and lacking in vibrancy due to building work or if you have cleared out a lot of clutter, you can improve the flow of energy between floors by gluing or fixing 1/2in (12mm) pieces of rough or polished quartz to the sides of the stair treads. Mount one each side to the bottom tread, one each side to the top, and then place one each side of a tread in between. Alternatively, glue two slivers in the same places but under the banister rail. These crystals are wonderful energizers and will take the energy frequency higher, which will then impact on you and your family, making you feel happier and more content in your home.

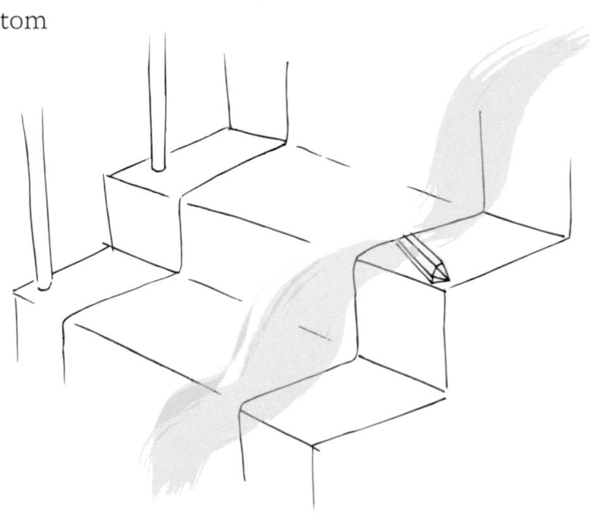

Purifying house energies with rose quartz

Polished

In chakra healing, rose quartz is traditionally used to purify the heart, the place of deep emotion and, in some ancient cultures, the soul. Associated with love, this sensitive stone dispels the bad atmosphere that most arguments bring, and clears the air after an illness, children's tantrums, or a string of minor domestic problems. Pure and uplifting, rose quartz can be used to clear residual negativity and bring happy harmony to your home.

CRYSTAL FACTS

Crystal to use: rose quartz (pink), translucent, use a medium-size raw chunk

Availability: commonly available

Qualities of stone: removes negative energy, replacing it with loving vibrations

Where to place the crystal: make a crystal essence by soaking the stone in mineral water

Crystal cure

For an immediate energy lift in your home, and to restore its loving vibrations after an argument or another energy-depleting incident, you can spray all the rooms with a rose quartz essence.

Crystal essences are often compared to flower essences as an energetic imprint of the crystal is believed to be left in the water in which it is soaked. They are simple to make. Rinse your rose quartz crystal under running water, then place in a glass container or jar. Fill the container with still mineral water until the stone is covered. Cover the container and place on a table or windowsill where it is bathed in sunlight. Ideally leave for 1–12 hours: the longer you leave it the stronger the essence will be. Pour off the liquid in to a mister bottle. Hold the bottle in your hands and ask the essence to use its soothing and healing vibrations to remove any unhappiness in your home. Hold this thought in your head as you spray in each room, moving around clockwise from the doorway. Use regularly after upsets or other disruptions.

Promoting harmony with a water fountain and stones

A mini water fountain enhanced with crystals will bring harmony and balance to your living room. The stones, which individually possess the gifts of love, peace, and compassion that we want to attract into our lives, collectively create a sacred object—the font. "Fountain" is derived from the Old French word *fontaine* and the Latin *fontana*, meaning font, indicating baptism and purification by water. A crystal water fountain purifies negativity, instilling good energy flow and feelings of calm and relaxation. The trickling water also emits negative ions, giving off a positive, stimulating vibe.

Crystal energizing

Buy the polished crystals detailed below, searching out colors and shapes that most appeal to you. Place this chosen assortment of stones in the pebbles so that their emanations soothe, foster tranquility and purity, and induce a balanced and harmonious atmosphere.

Position the fountain on a dining table, a prominent shelf, or to give your Wealth corner a boost, in the southeast corner of the living room. Notice how people are drawn toward this inspiring feature as soon as they enter the room.

CRYSTAL FACTS

CRYSTALS TO USE: polished tiger's eye, brown jasper, carnelian, jade or aventurine (green), turquoise or sodalite (blue) plus a pump-operated water fountain with pebbles

AVAILABILITY: commonly available

QUALITIES OF STONES: using this selection of stones creates serenity, peace, stability, balance, harmony, friendship, empathy, calmness, and a passion for life

WHERE TO PLACE THE CRYSTALS: in the water fountain on a table or shelf, or in the southeast of the living room

Balancing emotions with a crystal tree

A crystal tree in your living room can soothe the fluctuating emotions of your family. The three crystals on the tree—sodalite, amethyst, and rose quartz—have the special qualities of peace, love, and tranquility that all of us in our stressed, modern lives crave. Placing these stones on a tree evokes a grounded feeling, of putting down deep roots into Mother Earth: trees protect and reassure. The ancient Greeks talked to trees, believing they contained all the wisdom of the gods. Just looking at this pretty tree will bring a sense of hope and optimism; destructive moods such as irritability or anger have no place around this evocative symbol.

Crystal cure

Place your tree on a prominent shelf or on a side table where it catches people's attention. Or, place it in the east to get the benefit of the inherent family and good health energies that exist there. Notice how the interaction of your family improves around this tree, and how a visitor's demeanor softens as they are influenced by the pacifying and spiritual elements of the crystals.

CRYSTAL FACTS

Crystals to use: sodalite, amethyst, and rose quartz tree or individual trees of these crystals

Availability: commonly available

Qualities of stones: **sodalite:** stills and cleanses the mind, increases relaxation, releases stress, boosts self-esteem; **amethyst:** dispels anger and anxiety, balances emotions, increases intuition, calms or stimulates as appropriate, brings tranquility and peace, aids spirituality and meditation; **rose quartz:** attracts love, peace, happiness, promotes self-love, heals the emotions, removes negative energy, strengthens empathy and sensitivity

Where to place the crystals: living room shelf or side table and/or in the east of the room

Dowsing for geopathic stress and neutralizing it with amethyst

Polished

Natural quartz and amethyst are both piezoelectric, which means that they have a positive and negative polarity and can emit electromagnetic energy. These highly sensitive stones can be used in dowsing to identify and neutralize negative earth energies, or geopathic stress, which can cause lethargy and general tiredness.

The human body adapts to normal earth energies (or radiation waves) that come up through the ground. Geopathic stress occurs when these energies become distorted, often due to the presence of a stream, tunnel, or old mine under your property. Another cause of energetic discomfort may be ley lines—the strong energies that run along a fault or strata—particularly if your home sits on a ley-line junction, where two intersect.

CRYSTAL FACTS

CRYSTAL TO USE: natural quartz pendulum; 2 large or several small pieces of amethyst

AVAILABILITY: commonly available

QUALITIES OF STONE: amethyst: a powerful protective stone that blocks geopathic stress or negative environmental energies

WHERE TO PLACE THE CRYSTAL: in the places where negative energy registers

Crystal cure

To find if you have any negative energy areas in your living room you need to dowse for them. Take your natural quartz pendulum and ask it to indicate which is the answer "yes": it normally spins in a clockwise direction. Then ask for "no": it normally spins counterclockwise, but these can be reversed. Then walk around the room, stopping at different points, and ask the pendulum, "Are there are any negative earth energies here that are affecting my health?" Note down any areas where it swings positively. Place two large pieces of amethyst in the affected areas, or place several small pieces under the carpet, asking for their help in neutralizing the negative vibrations that are adversely affecting your health.

ALTERNATIVE PROTECTIVE CRYSTALS TO USE

Rose quartz: soothes away harsh energy

Smoky quartz: gently neutralizes unhealthy earth vibrations

Obsidian: creates a shield against negative energy

Reviving houseplants with green tourmaline

Also known as verdelite, green tourmaline is associated with the Heart chakra, or love center, and it is renowned as a healing stone. Associated with Venus and the element of Earth, this crystal also represents fertility, which is why you can use it to revive your houseplants and encourage their healthy growth.

Houseplants are wonderful energizers in a living room as they lift the atmosphere and help to increase the oxygen content, and many of them improve humidity, filter the air, and cleanse it of pollutants such as formaldehyde, which is often present in new carpets and some furniture. So if you have any houseplants that are not growing well or look sickly, it is essential to give them some care to help them thrive again and keep the living room's ambience positive and vibrant.

Polished

CRYSTAL FACTS

Crystal to use: green tourmaline, shiny, opaque, long or hexagon stone

Availability: easily available from specialist stores

Qualities of stone: wonderful healer; brings balance and aids growth

Where to place the crystal: in the soil of the plant pot

Crystal cure

If you have a plant (or several) that are in need of some love and attention, remove any dead leaves or flowers and trim back any dead stalks. Now take your green tourmaline and hold it in your hands for a few minutes. Tune into its emanations and ask for its loving help to make your plant healthy and vital again.

Place the stone on the soil by the plant stem, and see how in a few weeks your plant starts to come back to life. To aid growth leave the crystal in the pot for a while, but cleanse it regularly (see pages 149–153).

ALTERNATIVE HEALTH-GIVING CRYSTALS TO USE

Aventurine: a balancing stone that can regulate growth

Natural quartz: an energizer that increases growth and expansion

Turquoise: helps plants to recover from disease or infestation

Prolonging cut flowers with quartz crystal

Like green tourmaline (see opposite) you can also use quartz and smoky quartz to heal and sustain plants. A natural energizer, quartz can purify water, so it is the perfect choice for prolonging the life of cut flowers, which soon lose their life force.

Crystal cure

Use quartz crystals with a point or terminated end rather than a cluster, because the point will channel focused energy toward the flower stems and help them stay vital. Hold the crystal in your hands for a few minutes and ask for its help in extending the life of your beautiful flowers, then let it sink gently into the vase's water. Alternatively, if you have a large vase of flowers, dedicate three pointed crystals (see page 155) and then place them, with their points inward, in different positions facing the vase. Alternatively, use a quartz crystal or smoky quartz wand (see below, right). In this way the flowers will receive an amplified energy force to keep them looking fresh and lovely for longer.

CRYSTAL FACTS

CRYSTAL TO USE: quartz or smoky quartz pointed (terminator) crystals and/or wands

AVAILABILITY: commonly available

QUALITIES OF STONE: energy amplifier, powerful healer, also cleanses water

WHERE TO PLACE THE CRYSTAL: in the vase, or put several around the vase

Smoky quartz wand

Getting sociable with five-element crystals

In feng shui—the art of furniture placement and good energy flow—the five Chinese elements of Water, Earth, Fire, Wood, and Metal work together to produce harmony in a space. By choosing crystals from each of the element groups and displaying them together, you create a symbol of perfect balance and happiness. By placing your bowl in the east of the living room, you activate the properties of that sector—in feng shui, the east represents harmonious relationships with family and friends.

Crystal energizing

A bowl of five-element crystals creates a balanced ambience in a room that needs a relaxed yet convivial atmosphere. As well as providing an aesthetic talking point, your chosen crystals will create a scintillating buzz, inspiring stimulating conversation with friends and plenty of joy and laughter.

Buy both natural clusters and polished crystals that look good together, and display in a clear glass bowl so that you can see them from every angle. Remember to cleanse the stones every few weeks (see pages 149–153) to keep their energies vibrant.

CRYSTAL FACTS

CRYSTALS TO USE: choose at least one crystal from each of these element groups:

Water crystals (blue, purple, black): amethyst, aquamarine, jet

Earth crystals (yellow and brown): citrine, tiger's eye

Metal crystals (white): opal, selenite, snow quartz

Wood crystals (green): jade, moss agate

Fire crystals (red, pink): red calcite, red jasper, rose quartz

QUALITIES OF STONES: using a selection of these crystals energizes, cleanses, and protects the atmosphere, encouraging peace, love, and spontaneity, good communication, harmony, and balance.

WHERE TO PLACE THE CRYSTALS: on a coffee table, side table, or shelf in the east of the living room. Don't place on a windowsill as sunshine can overstimulate them.

Attracting prosperity and success with citrine, rose quartz, and aventurine

The combination of citrine, aventurine, and rose quartz can attract the money and success you want in your life. Aventurine is an all-round good luck stone, and in ancient magical rites was used to heighten perception and intelligence (after all, you need your wits about you as you wheel and deal your way to wealth!). Along with its wealth-creating properties, citrine fights the fear that holds you back, so you create the prosperous future that you desire. Rose quartz instills a loving atmosphere receptive to success, balancing existing yin and yang energies.

Crystal energizing

In feng shui, the southeast represents your corner of wealth and prosperity. To boost the energy in this area of your living room, place citrine, rose quartz, and aventurine crystals in the southeast on a table or shelf. The combined qualities of these crystals raise the vibrations in this area to attract the prosperity and success you want.

A crystal wishing spell

Write down your wish on a piece of paper. Hold it for a moment, meditating on your desire. Fold and place under the crystals so that positive energies go into your wish and help make it come true.

CRYSTAL FACTS

CRYSTALS TO USE: citrine (yellow), commonly a geode or cluster; rose quartz (pink), natural or polished; aventurine (green), opaque with shiny particles, usually tumbled

QUALITIES OF STONES: this trinity of stones brings the following benefits: ***citrine:*** brings energy, inspiring you to manifest and create wealth and success, also has a reputation as a "psychic" stone, helping you hear your intuition; ***rose quartz:*** evokes self-trust, self-love, and self-worth; ***aventurine:*** associated with prosperity, it has been known as a gambler's talisman, also enhances creativity

WHERE TO PLACE THE CRYSTALS: in the southeast corner of your living room

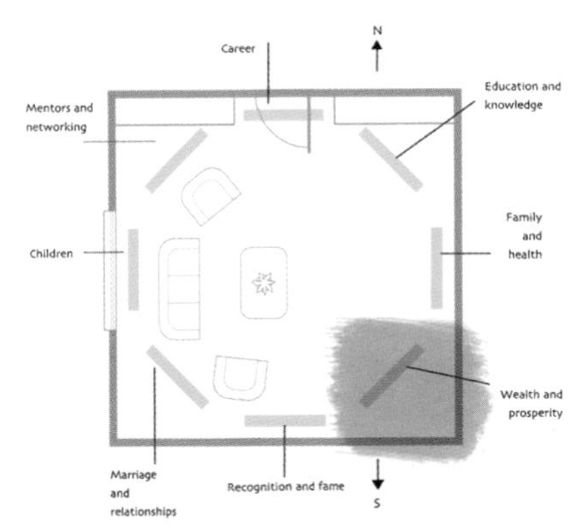

Display rose quartz, citrine, and aventurine in the southeast of your living room.

Check the orientation of the room with a compass and mark all the directions on a room plan.

Reducing TV electromagnetic stress with lepidolite

Lepidolite is a purplish fragile mineral that is a type of mica, rich in the silvery metal lithium. A very calming crystal, it can soothe an overstressed nervous system. The rough mica form of the crystal has greatly amplified properties that absorb any negative energies in a room, and its high vibratory rate also neutralizes artificial electromagnetic fields (EMFs) generated by televisions and other electrical equipment in the living room. Our bodies are used to the natural electromagnetic emissions that come up through the earth's surface, although they can be affected by distorted energy (see page 19). However, we have not adjusted to artificial EMFs, which can upset our immune systems because of the excessive electrical radiation that makes us more vulnerable to illness.

Rough

CRYSTAL FACTS

Crystal to use: lepidolite (lavender, but may be pink), shiny surfaced, grainy stone. The rough (mica) form amplifies its properties.

Availability: commonly available

Qualities of stone: can clear or absorb electromagnetic pollution; dispels negativity

Where to place the crystal: by side of your television, on the TV cabinet, or stick to shelf

Crystal cure

Children in particular can often sit too close to televisions, so encourage them to move back (as you should do) to at least 6–10ft (1.8–3m) from the set as the EMF reduces the farther away you sit. To help protect you from this radiation, take a lepidolite crystal in your hands for a few minutes and ask it to use its cleansing abilities to reduce the harmful EMFs emitted from your television. Now place it next to the set or, with reusable adhesive putty, stick it to the TV cabinet or the shelf it sits on. Over the next few days, observe how you feel more grounded and energized as the crystal acts to purify your space.

ALTERNATIVE EMF-REDUCING CRYSTALS TO USE

Fluorite: highly protective, dispels electromagnetic stress (right: blue purple fluorite)

Kunzite: shields you from unwanted energies, disperses negative forces

Deflecting negative chi with a lead-faceted crystal

Spherical lead-faceted hanging crystal

Lead-faceted crystals, made from glass, are wonderful energizers to have in your living room. They are not as powerful as natural quartz, but amplify and lift the energy, or chi, that filters through the window, making the atmosphere come alive. A round (spherical), multifaceted crystal is the most holistic one to hang, and is regularly used by feng shui consultants. As the crystal spins in front of the window it refracts the sunlight through the cut-glass ball, making prisms of color and letting the full spectrum of rainbow colors flow into the room. These colors are also linked to the chakras (spiritual energy centers) so basically the world is your oyster—you are bringing the maximum potential into the room. Hanging in the window, the crystal moves gently in the air currents, stirring up the energy flow in the room so it feels fresh and bright, or newly spring-cleaned.

CRYSTAL FACTS

Crystal to use: lead-faceted, spherical hanging crystal, 1in (25mm) for average-size room; 2in (50mm) for a large room

Availability: commonly available

Qualities of stone: amplifies energy, creates a vibrant and happy atmosphere

Where to place the crystal: hang it from the top of a window frame or the ceiling

Lead-faceted hanging crystal

Crystal cure

The best place to display this crystal is toward the top of the window. Position it so that it hangs in the middle of a pane of glass, suspended by a pin or nail from the wood above, or possibly the ceiling. Before you hang the crystal, hold it in your hands briefly and ask it to bring wonderful energy and color into your room. Notice how the energetics of the room take a step upward over the next week or so as the crystal starts to do its sparkling work. Cleanse weekly by dipping in spring water and leaving to dry in the sun.

Promoting happy relationships with amethyst and citrine

Cut and polished citrine

CRYSTAL FACTS

Crystals to use: amethyst cluster (violet/purple), transparent; faceted or smooth tumbled citrine, or citrine cluster (golden, yellow, yellow/brown)

Availability: commonly available

Qualities of stones: these two crystals bring the following benefits: **amethyst:** promotes love, spiritual wisdom, and intuition. It enhances memory and improves motivation. The crystal lends courage to the wearer and is a protective amulet for travelers; **citrine:** a crystal that encourages happiness and generosity, it imparts joy in love and raises self-esteem and self-belief, while also attracting money into your life. Placed under the pillow it ensures a goodnight's sleep.

Where to place the crystals: in the southwest of the living room

In feng shui, different combinations of crystals can strengthen the energetic forces in your aspirational areas. The pairing of amethyst and citrine lifts the harmonics of your marriage and relationship space in the southwest of your living room, raising the love vibes here and increasing your chances of meeting a new partner or strengthening an existing liaison. Amethyst is a supreme healing crystal that lets you get in touch with your feelings. Pure and true love comes out of this stone, making lovers want to exchange the crystal in the shape of a heart to show how committed they are. Citrine has a special affinity with amethyst, as it can be formed by heat-treating amethyst to achieve the yellowy citrine color and vibration. A stone of prosperity, citrine fills you with joy and makes you feel good about yourself. Meditating with citrine increases your spiritual connection, giving you more mental clarity about how to progress with your relationship or find that desired new partner.

Crystal energizing

Display chunks of these crystals together on a shelf or in the southwest of your living room and see how they raise the energetics, improving your relationship luck. Keep them away from too much sun as they may fade, particularly dark amethyst. Putting them with red candles, happy partnership pictures or photographs and a paired statue says to the world that you want a current, or desired, relationship to work.

Amethyst cluster

Aiding sleep with hematite

Hematite is an extremely grounding crystal, inducing feelings of safety and comfort. It has the reputed ability to help the regeneration of body tissue—one of the prime purposes of sleep—which may explain the connection between hematite and sleeping well.

The ancient Egyptians used hematite to quell hysteria and anxiety, which often cause sleep disturbance; during difficult emotional times, or when the mind and body are overactive, insomnia may strike. If you regularly suffer from disrupted sleep, you will often feel fatigued and irritable throughout the day. Using hematite promotes deep, healing sleep and will calm a grasshopper mind, allowing you to recharge at every level.

Polished

CRYSTAL FACTS

CRYSTAL TO USE: hematite (metallic silver/gray) tumbled and polished

AVAILABILITY: commonly available

QUALITIES OF STONE: induces a deep restful sleep, dissolves negativity and protects the soul

WHERE TO PLACE THE CRYSTAL: under the pillow

Crystal cure

Use a tumbled hematite crystal and experience its grounding and revitalizing properties. Choose a stone that you know wants to help you and feels pleasing to you when you turn it over in your hand. Go into your bedroom and sit on the bed, holding your crystal. Light a candle and sit with your eyes closed, tuning in to the stone's nurturing energies. When you feel ready, ask for better sleep and help in resolving any crisis you may be experiencing. Before bed, place the crystal under your pillow, where your head rests.

ALTERNATIVE SLEEP-INDUCING CRYSTALS TO USE

Chrysoprase: induces peaceful and relaxing sleep, unlocks blocked emotions

Aventurine: promotes emotional tranquility and positive attitudes

Golden topaz: recharges the spirit and relieves nervous exhaustion

Boosting passion with ruby

Rough

A stone of love, ruby is believed to open up the Heart chakra—the heart's spiritual energy center—to joy and bliss. In ancient Egypt the stone was held in high regard, and anyone who acquired the ruby was thought to gain beauty and good fortune. In Hindu culture, it was given the name the "king of precious stones," because of its magnificence. Legend says that an everlasting flame burned in the jewel, which is probably why today its fiery qualities are believed to instill passion and sexual allure into the person wearing it. This is the ideal stone to bring some passion back into your love life, as the dynamism of this crystal will charge up your enthusiasm for making love and increase your sex appeal.

CRYSTAL FACTS

Crystal to use: ruby (red), uncut, opaque

Availability: commonly available

Qualities of stone: charges up passion, attracts some sexual activity, stimulates the Heart chakra, and increases potency

Where to place the crystal: hold to heart, then place on your bedside table

Crystal energizing

Keep your ruby safe in a drawer and bring it out only when you want to feel sensual with your partner; otherwise, the stone may emit energy that is intense and stimulating, and not conducive to sleep and relaxation. To connect with your crystal, hold it right next to your heart for a few minutes, close your eyes, and ask it to restore any lost or waning passion and romantic feelings in your life. Now place the crystal on the bedside cabinet or nightstand and go to bed, knowing that it will lift the loving vibrations between you and your partner.

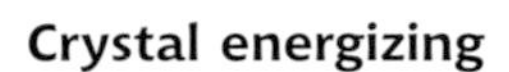

ALTERNATIVE PASSION-INDUCING CRYSTALS TO USE

Carnelian: restores vitality, overcomes reserve, increases fertility

Garnet: revitalizes energy, bringing passion and sexual potency

Smoky quartz: enhances sexual fervor, helps acceptance of body

Releasing worries at night with sodalite

Polished heart

This deep-blue crystal, colored like the sky at twilight, can clear your mind of upset, bringing objectivity and solutions to problems that may be keeping you awake at night. If you regularly go to bed plagued by all the day's problems, or you have worked late into the evening to try to resolve financial or family concerns, your brain will not rest and peaceful sleep may elude you.

Sodalite is associated with insight and wisdom—this "true blue" stone, associated with the Third eye chakra of inner wisdom, can help you discover the truth behind a troubling situation. It is also thought to help you remember your dreams, which can give you valuable insight into the type of problems you are experiencing.

CRYSTAL FACTS

CRYSTAL TO USE: sodalite, dark blue, blue/white variegated stone

AVAILABILITY: commonly available

QUALITIES OF STONE: helps to eliminate mental confusion, calms and clears mind, and brings new perceptions, alleviates fear

WHERE TO PLACE THE CRYSTAL: hold to forehead, then leave on bedside table

Crystal cure

To prepare for better sleep, it is always best to release worries or alleviate them before going to bed. Sit on your bed, close your eyes and breathe deeply, then hold your crystal to your Third eye chakra in the middle of your forehead for about five minutes, focusing on your problems, and let the crystal do its work to calm your mind. When you feel relaxed, place the crystal on your bedside cabinet or nightstand and lay down to sleep. Remember to cleanse your stone regularly (see pages 149–153).

ALTERNATIVE WORRY-RELEASING CRYSTALS TO USE

Onyx: reduces overwhelming worries and fears

Azurite (or azurite with malachite): clears worries, bringing solutions

Apophyllite: calms, and ameliorates negative thought patterns

Encouraging good study with gold calcite

Gold calcite is an ideal mind-boosting crystal. Associated with mental empowerment, it may amplify your child's efforts toward academic success. Its legendary powers of focus and concentration may be due to the reputation of one of its cousins, optical calcite, which visually duplicates whatever it touches: placed over a symbol such as a star, it will literally appear double. Gold calcite is also associated with creativity, so it will stimulate and support your child in their artistic pursuits and encourage a creative approach to projects.

Rough

CRYSTAL FACTS

Crystal to use: gold calcite, translucent, waxy, sometimes tumbled

Availability: commonly available

Qualities of stone: stimulates insight, boosts memory, helps mind retain important information

Where to place the crystal: on child's desk

Crystal energizing

To focus your child on their studies at home, place a gold calcite crystal on his desk close to where he reads and writes. This stone helps keep him alert mentally, giving him extra motivation and increasing his memory skills. If he is struggling with a difficult task, get him to hold the crystal for a while and ask for its help to solve his homework problems.

In feng shui, the education and knowledge sector is located in the northeast of a room, so, ideally, place your child's desk here so that he can benefit from the supportive education and knowledge energies. If this is not possible, place the gold calcite in the northeast sector of his desk so that he can still benefit from the good energies.

ALTERNATIVE STUDY CRYSTALS TO USE

Blue chalcedony: stimulates learning skills, promotes mental flexibility

Fluorite: encourages quick thinking, helps to assimilate information (right: purple fluorite)

Howlite: increases memory and engenders a desire for knowledge

Balancing children's energies with pink or blue crystals

Traditionally, blue clothes were bought for baby boys and pink for girls. It is not known how this tradition originated, but it does link in with feng shui principles. In feng shui, boys (or men) are considered to be yang people. Yang is associated with positive actions, the sun, heaven, vigor, light, fire, and warmth. Girls (or women) are yin people and are thought to be more passive, linked to darkness, the earth, negativity, cold, the moon, stillness, and water. To thrive, children need a balance of both these forces. To calm boys, paint their rooms in blue or green, but to energize girls decorate their rooms in pinks and oranges. Positioning some pink and blue crystals on the bedside cabinet or nightstand will also harmonize these energies.

Crystal energizing

For a girl, choose one of the pink crystals below for some yang (warm) energy to develop their passion for life, their self-expression, willpower and energy, and empathy and sensitivity. For a boy, choose a blue stone for some yin (cool) energy to quieten their minds, bring inner strength for change, calm mental confusion, and balance the nervous system. Let your child choose the crystal with you. They may feel a slight pulsating sensation as they find the "right" one. Explain how it can help to calm (boys) or energize (girls), and place the crystal by their bed so that its embracing and energies are with them all the time.

Rough kunzite

Rough rose quartz

Rough sodalite

Rough turquoise

CRYSTAL FACTS

CRYSTALS TO CHOOSE FROM:

Pink (girls): rhodochrosite, kunzite (above), rose quartz (above)

Blue (boys): sodalite (right), aquamarine, chrysocolla, turquoise (right)

AVAILABILITY: commonly available

QUALITIES OF STONES: pink: increases energetic vibrations and motivation; blue: calms energies, cleansing the body and quietening the mind

WHERE TO PLACE THE CRYSTALS: on bedside cabinet or nightstand

Stimulating creativity with quartz

Polished quartz

Natural quartz is perfect for stimulating creativity and focus in a child's room. You can bring in this energy in the form of rough quartz or polished crystal birds or animals, such as a quartz owl or cat, which are easy to find, or go for rough or polished pieces of rutilated quartz. With pretty golden or coppery fibers, rutilated quartz has a slightly different energy from that of clear quartz—it is associated with stirring the spirit, and can help heighten the natural creativity that is so free-flowing in a child.

As children grow up, the artistic side of their personalities flourish; activities such as drawing, painting, or playing a musical instrument may appeal. With either art they can express the mixed emotions of their day and become immersed in the pleasure of a stimulating hobby. The special qualities of quartz crystal can support a budding talent, developing a sense of potential and skill in their chosen pursuit.

Crystal energizing

The play area of a bedroom is generally the place where children will lose themselves in drawing or practicing a favorite musical instrument. Screen off this stimulating area from the sleep space and place the quartz crystal on a work table or on a nearby windowsill. Let this stone release its energizing and inspiring aura so that it surrounds your child, increasing their concentration and flair.

CRYSTAL FACTS

Crystal to use: natural or polished clear quartz, and/or rutilated quartz (clear or milky with silver, gold, copper-colored, brown, red, or black strands); also known as angel hair

Availability: commonly available

Qualities of stone: helps inspiration, magnifies positive energy, gives creative insight, focuses and directs the mind

Where to place the crystal: place on table or on windowsill of play area

Polished rutilated quartz

Rough

Alleviating nightmares with lepidolite

Lepidolite is a delicate mineral that is incredibly soothing, associated with easing many painful emotions such as anger, hate, irritability, or sadness. An alternative name is "peace stone," because the caring properties of the crystal take away tension and anxiety, which often create the vivid imagery of nightmares that many young children experience. Breathing problems from a cold or anxiety over school problems can trigger the nightmares.

CRYSTAL FACTS

CRYSTAL TO USE: lepidolite (lavender, may be pink), layered tone, can be shiny or grainy

AVAILABILITY: commonly available

QUALITIES OF STONE: calms sleep disturbances, reduces emotional fears, brings deep inner healing

WHERE TO PLACE THE CRYSTAL: on bedside cabinet or nightstand

Crystal cure

If your child is frightened to go to sleep because of recurring nightmares, take the lepidolite crystal in your hand and explain to your child how this comforting stone takes away their anxieties, and will soothe their mind when they are asleep; you can both make up a story about it, if you choose to. Let your child feel the crystal and connect with its gentle energies, then place it on their bedside cabinet or nightstand to let it form a worry-free zone around their bed. Leave the crystal there each night until the nightmares stop. Cleanse the crystal well to keep it vibrant (see pages 149–153).

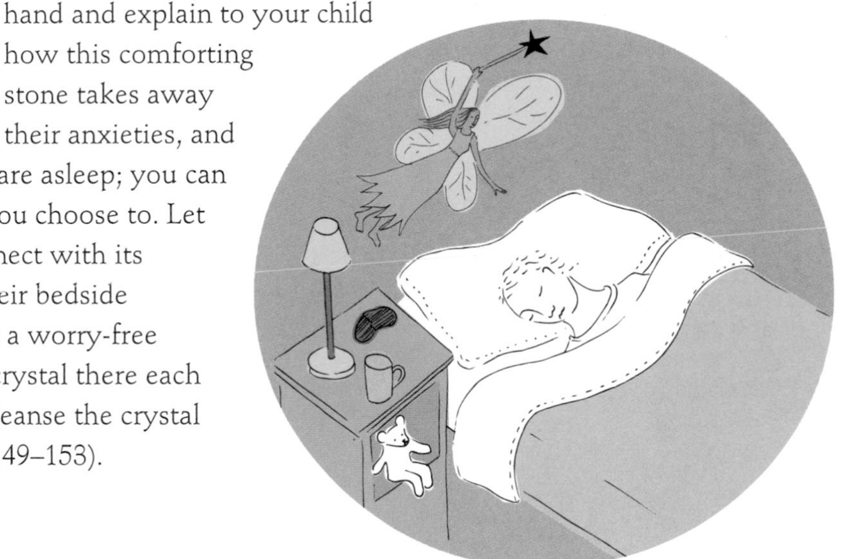

ALTERNATIVE NIGHTMARE-RELIEVING CRYSTALS TO USE

Amethyst: dispels fear and anxiety, soothes an overactive mind

Purple fluorite: removes and purifies negative energies

Lapis lazuli: releases stress and brings deep serenity

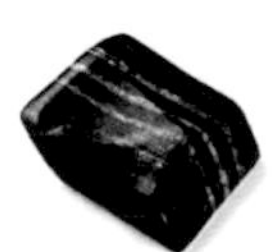

Restoring energy with jade in the bath

Polished egg

Known in ancient China as the "stone of heaven," jade has adorned temples, promoted longevity, and defended the Mayans and Maoris, who had it hewn into arrowheads and axes. Yet beneath its literally hard exterior jade has a softer side, as it is a stone associated with healing and love. The Chinese crushed it to a powder for ingestion as a remedy, and it is the crystal of Kuan Yin, the Buddhist Madonna and goddess of compassion. Bathing with jade restores depleted energy, reenergizes the nervous system, and brings inner peace.

CRYSTAL FACTS

Crystal to use: jade (green), opaque to translucent, often polished or tumbled

Availability: commonly available

Qualities of stone: cleanses, restores emotional balance, disperses negative thoughts, gently energizes

Where to place the crystal: in the bath or a footbath

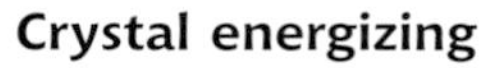

Crystal energizing

Placing a crystal in the bathwater or in a footbath will bring the energy boost that your body is seeking. Fill your bath or a large bowl with warm water; if bathing, surround the tub with lit candles to bring in some extra, positive energy. Hold your stone briefly and connect to its nurturing energies, asking it to help you let go of the stress of the day. Place it in the bath and leave for a few minutes, then step in. Feel the water embracing you and the soft vibrations of the stone revitalizing your physical body and energetic field. Relax in the bath for about 10 minutes. Afterward remove your stone, and thank it for its help.

ALTERNATIVE ENERGIZING CRYSTALS TO USE

Amazonite: reduces worries and fears, alleviates negative energy

Peridot: acts as tonic for body and mind, dispels stress

Onyx: lessens stress, promotes vigor and stamina

Lifting the atmosphere in the bathroom with citrine

Cluster

Citrine is a lovely, generous, and beneficial stone that is believed to take its name from the French *citron,* for lemon, as many of the crystals have a bright, lemon color. It is a member of the quartz family, and because of its connection to the sun, it projects pleasure and optimism. Its warming and energizing qualities are perfect for the bathroom, where the atmosphere can be humid with a sluggish energetic flow. It also has the ability to transmute and dissolve negative energy, and because of this never needs cleansing. Often known as the merchant's stone, citrine attracts prosperity and abundance into your life with its happy and generous aura.

CRYSTAL FACTS

CRYSTAL TO USE: citrine (yellow, yellow/brown), transparent, often a cluster

AVAILABILITY: natural citrine can be rare; citrine produced by heat-treating amethyst is commonly available

QUALITIES OF STONE: powerful cleansing stone, lifts and warms atmosphere, encourages mental clarity and optimism, heals any negativity

WHERE TO PLACE THE CRYSTAL: on a shelf or by the bath

Cut and polished

Crystal energizing

In the bathroom a lot of steam and condensation is generated, which can make the atmosphere feel rather heavy or oppressive. Placing a chunk of citrine on a bathroom shelf to sparkle in the sun, or by the bath, can reverse this sensation and brighten the ambience. Hold the stone in your hands and feel its vibrancy raising your self-esteem; it is a stone that always makes you feel good about yourself. Ask it to spread its natural enthusiasm into the room and to keep the atmosphere light and airy, then place it in position.

ALTERNATIVE ENERGIZING CRYSTALS TO USE

Carnelian: energizes a room and gives it increased vitality

Red jasper: gently stimulates energy, absorbs any negativity

Green fluorite: dissolves any negativity, cleanses, purifies, and helps re-energize the atmosphere

Polished

Harmonizing energies with aquamarine

CRYSTAL FACTS

Crystal to use: aquamarine, (green/blue), clear or opaque, can be faceted, although often tumbled

Availability: commonly available

Qualities of stone: brings peace, surrounds and fills a room with feelings of love and inspiration, purifies and calms the atmosphere, encourages emotional balance

Where to place the crystal: on the side of the bath, or on a shelf where you can see it while bathing

Aquamarine is a semiprecious member of the beryl family. Its lovely greeny-blue, sparkly color instantly reminds you of the soothing waves of the sea. It was once believed to be the stone of sea goddesses such as Amphitrite, wife of the Greek sea-god Poseidon, and Aphrodite, the Greek Venus, who was born from the foam of the sea. In the past, sailors carried the stone as a talisman to protect them when they were away from home, and to save them from drowning. With its special connection to water, cleansing the stone in the ocean in the full moon can be a very powerful process.

Aquamarine's vibration resonates with water energy, so this is a lovely stone to use in the bathroom to create an oasis of calm and harmonize the existing energies there.

Crystal energizing

As the bathroom needs to be a sanctuary, a retreat where you can cleanse and soak away the worries of the day, it is good to place a peaceful crystal here that can also purify the atmosphere and keep it balanced. Take your aquamarine in your hands and ask it to let its peaceful and uplifting emanations fill the room at all times and remove any pollutants there. Place the stone on the side of the bath so that you can admire it and enjoy its comforting qualities and let it release your stress and worries while bathing. If you have had a tough day, you can rub the stone over your body to cleanse you of all irritations.

ALTERNATIVE HARMONIZING CRYSTALS TO USE

Turquoise: an empathetic stone that removes any pollutants and equalizes room's energies

Blue lace agate: its cooling and calming vibrations bring relaxation

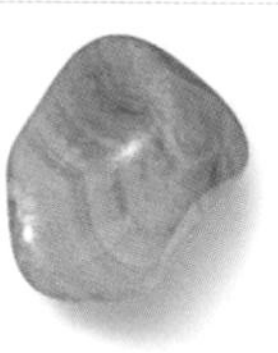

Bathing with rose quartz to heal and soothe emotions

Rough

Rose quartz cleanses the emotions, promotes inner healing, and allows self-love to flow freely. When used in crystal divination, rose quartz can signal a time of healing, or indicate the presence of our ability to heal ourselves and other people.

A rose quartz can help whenever you are dealing with emotional problems that leave your mind disturbed and your feelings fragile. A major argument at work, coping with a demanding elderly relative, or falling out with a friend can all make you feel vulnerable, upset, and demoralized. It is essential to take some time out to review your feelings. Using a healing crystal in your bath can help you regain your self-worth and support the healing process.

CRYSTAL FACTS

CRYSTAL TO USE: rose quartz (pink), translucent, sometimes tumbled

AVAILABILITY: commonly available

QUALITIES OF STONE: takes away negative energy and replaces with loving vibrations, reduces tensions, aids forgiveness

WHERE TO PLACE THE CRYSTAL: in the bath

Crystal cure

After a traumatic day, a long soak in the bath with a nurturing crystal can be just what you need the most. First set the scene: light an aromatherapy oil burner and add a few drops of lavender or geranium essential oil to the water bowl to relax you (remember, don't leave the burner unattended). Run a warm bath, then place the stone in the water for a few minutes before getting in. Step into the bath and sense the loving energies that are surrounding you. Take your stone and hold it to your heart for a few minutes. Place it back in the bath and rest there for another 5 minutes. Step out of the bath emotionally renewed, remove your crystal, and thank it for its loving work. If you have used an oil burner, extinguish the flame.

ALTERNATIVE SOOTHING CRYSTALS TO USE

Rhodochrosite: heals emotional wounds, encourages acceptance

Tiger's eye: grounds and balances emotions, enhances insight (right: red tiger's eye)

Moonstone: lessens overreaction, soothes emotions (right: polished opaque moonstone)

Focusing concentration with lapis lazuli

Rough

Lapis lazuli is a spiritual crystal that opens up your intuition and psychic abilities. People call it the "eye of wisdom" or the "stone of the gods," as it activates the Third eye chakra: the place of inner learning. The healing power of lapis is well documented in references to jewelry over 3,000 years ago in ancient Egyptian papyri. The ancient Egyptians also appreciated the protective power of the stone, crushing it to make a vivid blue eye powder to guard against the evil eye.

As a beautiful deep blue, opaque stone, lapis lazuli often has inclusions of pretty gold pyrite that catch the light. Mental clarity and objectivity come to you when you handle it, giving the necessary focus and concentration needed when studying for an examination, or assimilating complex information for a diploma course.

CRYSTAL FACTS

Crystal to use: lapis lazuli (blue with gold flecks; may be blue and white [white is calcite]; may have black spots of lazulite)

Availability: commonly available

Qualities of stone: brings objectivity and mental clarity, boosts self-confidence, stimulates the mind's faculties, helps to express opinions, amplifies your thoughts

Where to place the crystal: place on desk in front of you

Polished

Crystal energizing

Taking an examination can mean expressing acquired knowledge. Using your lapis stone can focus your attention and give you easier access to your inner wisdom. To get the crystal to work with you, take it in your hands and connect to its psychic emanations, asking for its help to stimulate your learning and to amplify your thoughts. Feel the crystal firing up your mental concentration. Now let the stone nurture you as you start to assimilate more text. For essay writing, feel it helping you to find the words to write persuasively.

ALTERNATIVE STUDYING CRYSTALS TO USE

Calcite: stimulates memory, helps to retain important information

Fluorite: helps absorb new information, aids concentration (right: green fluorite)

Creating new ideas with purple fluorite

Rough

Fluorite is an attractive transparent crystal that is coming into its own once again, and is considered one of the "New Age" stones. One variety of this colorful crystal resembles two pyramids fused together. In magic spells, fluorite is an amplifier, strengthening the effects of all the crystals used. A powerful cleanser of the environment, purple fluorite also works on the mind, stimulating mental powers, regulating thought patterns, and revealing new ideas. It is an ideal crystal to spark off a productive brainstorming session at home, pitching new topics as a lecturer or self-employed writer.

CRYSTAL FACTS

CRYSTAL TO USE: purple fluorite, transparent, cubic or octahedral

AVAILABILITY: commonly available

QUALITIES OF STONE: helps you come up with abstract ideas, focuses energy, expands mental capabilities, enhances creativity, promotes fast thinking

WHERE TO PLACE THE CRYSTAL: in your hands and by computer

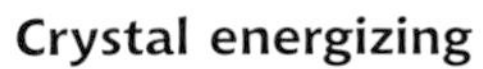

Crystal energizing

Purple fluorite helps get you out of a mental rut. So when creativity is diminishing, pick up your crystal and hold it in your hands to tune into its mental powers. Sense how the stone is clearing and energizing your mind. Now say an appropriate affirmation 20 times, such as: "My mind is full of original feature ideas," or, "I am brimming with many interesting subjects for my lectures." Let your stone work with you mentally, fixing this affirmation in your subconscious. Now turn on your computer and put your crystal beside it. Feel its vibrations increasing your vision, and start typing out the new angles or approaches that are beginning to flow through you.

Polished

ALTERNATIVE CREATIVITY CRYSTALS TO USE

Aventurine: offers alternatives, increases perception and creativity

Bloodstone: enhances creative decision-making, strengthens intuition

Citrine: revitalizes the mind, stimulates creativity

Aiding difficult self-expression with blue celestite

Rough

Celestite is a stunning, light blue crystal that is associated with the goddess Venus. The crystal clusters can be quite brittle, so it is not often used to make jewelry. A versatile gem, when ground it is used to make caustic soda, and the salts of red celestite are used to add the color red to fireworks and flares, and in the preparation of iridescent glass and porcelain. Blue celestite is, however, a soothing stone, bringing harmony to a troubled mind and easing stress. Its gentle blue rays open the Throat energetic chakra, easing any of your current communication problems. Running a home office can involve resolving problems with plumbers or electricians or may involve querying your bills. When this happens, use your celestite crystal to express what you truly want to say.

CRYSTAL FACTS

Crystal to use: blue celestite, transparent, medium to large cluster, or geode

Availability: commonly available

Qualities of stone: expands the consciousness, opens Throat chakra, heightens telepathic abilities, soothes nerves, creates honesty, sharpens the mind, promotes good communication, cools fiery emotions

Where to place the crystal: on Throat chakra in the middle of your throat and in your pocket

Crystal energizing

Blue celestite deals with speaking the truth, helping you to speak your mind in a subtle but positive way. To resolve a communication problem, hold the crystal and feel its cooling energy. Place it on your throat chakra for 5–10 minutes or so, feeling how these pure vibrations are dissolving any blockages and harmonizing the energy here. You may find yourself coughing a bit as the energy shifts. Now keep the crystal in your pocket as you prepare to deal with the trades-person who has been causing a problem. Let the crystal's calming vibrations help you to make your point assertively.

ALTERNATIVE DIFFICULT SELF-EXPRESSION CRYSTALS TO USE

Blue lace agate: helps expression of thoughts without anger

Blue kyanite: lessens fear and encourages speaking difficult truths

Sodalite: helps with rational thought and saying true feelings

Crystal first-aid for phone stress

If you work from home, your main form of communication with the outside world, aside from email, is by phone. As pressure builds on busy projects, some calls can become tense as you are asked to do several things at once. Keeping a special mix of carefully chosen de-stressing crystals by the phone can give you some protection from the debilitating vibrations of negative people or emotional vampires, helping you handle difficult situations without losing your temper.

Crystal cure

Placing these colorful healing crystals by the phone can act as an emotional first-aid kit. The grounding qualities of these stones can give you emotional support when you are doing too much, and create a harmonious atmosphere that will influence your work area. Buy the crystals as smooth tumbled stones so that when you feel yourself getting upset or angry during a difficult phone call, you can turn over the relevant crystal in your hand. The green healing qualities of aventurine will take away your anger, leaving a feeling of wellbeing. When a tricky client is frustrating you, pick up a stone such as amethyst and feel its high spiritual vibration protecting you from their emotional debris, or use bloodstone to repel their negative vibes or undesirable comments. Always cleanse your crystals every few weeks (see pages 149–153), particularly if you have experienced several fraught conversations.

CRYSTAL FACTS

CRYSTALS TO USE: choose two crystals from each of the groups below:

Calming: agate, aquamarine, howlite, selenite

Stress-relieving: amber, blue kyanite, smoky quartz

Anger-defusing: blue lace agate, green aventurine, peridot, red garnet

Protective: amethyst, bloodstone, brown jasper, carnelian

AVAILABILITY: commonly available

QUALITIES OF STONES: using a selection of these crystals brings emotional balance, calms the mind, alleviates stress, reduces frustration, neutralizes anger and irritation, protects against psychic attack, forms a protective barrier, grounds energies

WHERE TO PLACE THE CRYSTALS: in a bowl by the phone

Fostering a nurturing atmosphere with rhodonite

Polished

This pretty pink stone, mottled with black, can enhance the nurturing vibrations in the kitchen, the heart of the home. Family disputes will not last long in a kitchen that contains a rhodonite crystal, because rhodonite grounds energy, balancing yin and yang—the opposing passive and positive forces in the universe. This in turn helps balance any emotional outbursts, and thankfully encourages a spirit of forgiveness. Rhodonite and other pink crystals, such as rose quartz and rhodochrosite (see pages 78 and 104), are also associated with generating physical love and affection, and this stone radiates a warm, caring vibration that instil a nonconfrontational ambience wherever it is placed.

CRYSTAL FACTS

Crystal to use: rhodonite (red or pink), mottled effect, sometimes flecked with black and/or white

Availability: commonly available

Qualities of stone: reduces stress, increases energy levels, stimulates a peaceful and loving atmosphere, balances emotions, encourages good interaction between people

Where to place the crystal: on kitchen table or shelf

Crystal energizing

Pick up your crystal and connect with its emissions of unconditional love. Ask it to make your kitchen a comfort zone, a place of conviviality and laughter where meals are lovingly prepared and eaten. Now place the crystal in a glass bowl in the center of the kitchen table, or put it on a prominent shelf above the countertops to let it do its tender work.

ALTERNATIVE NURTURING CRYSTALS TO USE

Jade: protects the room, creates a serene, harmonious atmosphere (right: polished egg)

Green tourmaline: energizes, bringing a balanced and joyful ambience

Rose quartz: creates an empathetic and loving energy

Preventing accidents with moss agate

Known as the most powerful of the agates, moss agate was the chosen talisman worn by warriors going into battle. It is a highly protective crystal that can stabilize the fiery energy associated with stovetops and kitchen cookers, giving out a lovely healing aura. The wonderful color of the stone is also associated with maternal love, reminding us that special care needs to be taken in the kitchen, where most accidents in the home happen. The deep green color of moss agate also reduces any stress when cooking meals and creates a strong feeling of security.

Polished

CRYSTAL FACTS

CRYSTAL TO USE: green moss agate, transparent or translucent, has foliage-like markings

AVAILABILITY: commonly available

QUALITIES OF STONE: very protective, encourages a long life, reduces sensitivity to any environmental pollutants, soothes emotions

WHERE TO PLACE THE CRYSTAL: place near stovetop or cooker, or other accident hot spot

Crystal cure

Take hold of this attractive crystal in your hands and connect to its grounding earth energies. Ask the stone to protect your kitchen, keeping negative influences out, and preventing accidents such as cuts and burns. Place the stone close to your cooktop and food preparation area, so that its healing green rays span out around the space where you do your food preparation and cooking. Cleanse the crystal regularly (see pages 149–153) to keep its energies vital.

ALTERNATIVE PROTECTIVE CRYSTALS TO USE

Bloodstone: grounding and protective stone, revitalizes atmosphere

Lavender (purple) jade: protects from harm, brings harmony

Malachite: protects and absorbs negative energies and pollutants

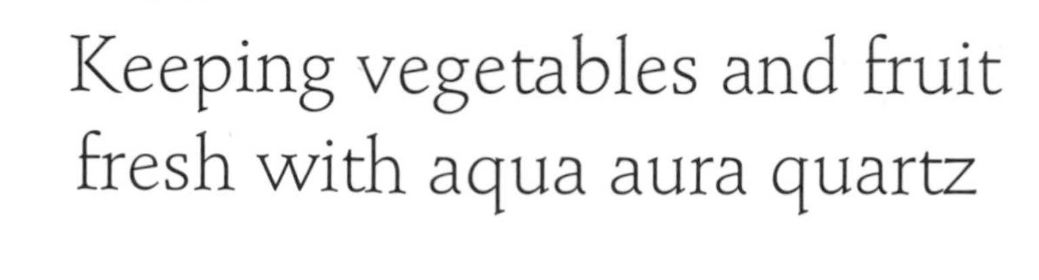

Keeping vegetables and fruit fresh with aqua aura quartz

This beautiful crystal is artificially made; a secret alchemical process bonds a quartz crystal with pure gold, resulting in the striking color of aqua aura. The color is similar to aquamarine, and has an opalescence that flashes wonderful shades of blue (or purple, if the crystal has been overheated during the process). The combination of a crystal and a precious mineral makes a high and intense energetic vibration that is ideal to increase the life force and preserve the vitamin and mineral content of fresh fruits and vegetables. The high electric charge of quartz has been proven through Kirlian photography, where an infrared image of the crystal is taken, showing its energetic field.

Crystal energizing

Use aqua aura crystals with a terminated point or a cluster with obvious points so that you can direct the energy toward the food you want to preserve. Pick up your crystals one by one and hold them in your hands briefly, asking them to keep your food fresher for longer. Now place the crystals permanently at each corner of your fruit bowl, with the points facing inward or around your vegetable basket and see how bright and vibrant the food stays. If you are preparing a meal, point one crystal toward the ingredients as you chop them up to boost their freshness.

CRYSTAL FACTS

Crystal to use: Four blue aqua aura quartz, terminated points, or a cluster. Aqua aura is artificially bonded with gold to create varying strong color

Availability: commonly available

Qualities of stone: powers of gold and quartz greatly amplify energy, help to preserve and heal, work at the vibrational level needed, preserve food and plants

Where to place the crystal: around vegetables and fruit

Purple aqua aura

Enjoying convivial dining with a crystal centerpiece

Although technically not a true crystal, lead-faceted glass crystal has been known as a powerful energizer. As the light refracts through the cut glass, it brings a charge of energy. The round shape, or circle, of the bowl is universally revered. It symbolically represents eternity, unity, and the universe, the goddess and female power, and Mother Earth. In Chinese traditions a round bowl signifies abundance, so by placing this vibrant centerpiece on your dining table you are making a statement of abundance, saying that there is plenty of food and fun in store for your guests.

CRYSTAL FACTS

CRYSTAL TO USE: wide and shallow lead-faceted crystal bowl

QUALITIES OF BOWL: amplifies and regulates energy in a similar way to natural quartz

WHERE TO PLACE THE BOWL: in the center of the dining table

Crystal energizing

To make your table centerpiece really stand out, buy a shallow, wide bowl with an attractive pattern, so that the facets will catch the light from every angle, making the room feel vibrant and vital.

On the night of the dinner party, fill the bowl with water, add a sprinkling of pretty flower petals, and place some white floating candles on top. The strong fire energy from the candles will also encourage a lively atmosphere. Light the candles just before the guests sit down for dinner to create the maximum effect.

Romantic dining with lead-crystal candlesticks and red stones

If you are in a new, ardent relationship or have been together for some time, a romantic dinner can reinforce your feelings for each other. Placing lead-faceted glass candlesticks on the table creates a *frisson* as the facets of the glass catch the light, lifting and expanding the chi, or energy, in the atmosphere. Scattering stimulating red and pink crystals around the candles helps to open up your Heart chakras, or centers of love, bringing in empathetic and passionate vibrations that will make it a meal where you only have eyes for each other.

Crystal energizing

Place the lead-crystal candlesticks in the center of the table. Use pink candles, because pink inspires unconditional love, or white candles, which represent purity. Choose red and pink crystals to symbolize your love, energizing them before dinner for 24 hours in the moonlight (see page 154), calling on the beautiful Roman moon goddess Diana to bless your love and make it last. You can use heart-shaped stones, if you can find them.

Just before dinner, pick up each chosen crystal individually: they all link to the stimulating Fire element. Feel each one's caring and affectionate pulsations: red garnet will stir up passion and feelings of devotion, while pink rhodochrosite strengthens a burgeoning relationship and boosts sexuality. Ask each stone to use its special powers to surround you with a loving and tender embrace for the whole evening.

CRYSTAL FACTS

Crystals to use: lead-faceted crystal candlesticks and choose three from the following red and pink crystals:

Red for passion: opal with red inclusions (pure red opal is rare in most countries), red garnet, ruby

Pink for love: rose quartz, pink agate, rhodochrosite, rhodonite

Availability: commonly available

Qualities: the candlesticks lift the vibrancy of the room. Red and pink crystals inspire love and devotion, romantic inclinations, increase passion and sexual potency, and inspire the emotions

Where to place: in the center of the table

Deflecting negativity from colleagues with smoky quartz

Smoky quartz wand

Smoky quartz is a protective crystal with a brownish hue. Its dark color is normally caused by radiation and the presence of carbon, iron, or titanium impurities. The stone is said to lose its dark color and become almost clear as you work through the negativity and problems in your life. Its unique vibration helps you cope with difficult times, and it has the ability to block any unwanted vibrations around you—so it's a potent stone to use at work when you need to deflect any backbiting or unpleasant gossiping from colleagues.

Crystal cure

As many office environments today are open-plan, it is inevitable that you will be influenced by the energies of the people sitting close to you. To deflect any negativity, take hold of your smoky quartz crystal for a few minutes, feeling its reasssuring aura. Ask it to form a protective barrier around you so that your energy field is not depleted by any malicious talk or action. Place the crystal on your desk and turn its protective point toward the people with the most negative attitudes. Always cleanse the crystal regularly (see pages 149–153) so that it works at its highest level.

CRYSTAL FACTS

Crystal to use: a long, pointed smoky quartz crystal (brown/black), transparent

Qualities of stone: protects and dissolves negativity on all levels, grounds and centers, aids meditation, cleanses and protects the aura (energetic field), lifts moods, relieves stress, blocks geopathic and electromagnetic stress, alleviates fear and depression

Health benefits: aids functioning of the kidneys, adrenal glands, and pancreas, balances sexual energy, increases fertility, relieves problems in abdomen, hips, and legs, good pain reliever, eases headaches, reduces cramps, strengthens the back

Where to place the crystal: on your desk

ALTERNATIVE ANTI-NEGATIVITY CRYSTALS TO USE

Fire agate: grounds and protects, forms a shield around body

Amber: protects, absorbs any negative forces, and cleanses environment

Labradorite: deflects unwanted negativity, gets rid of fear and insecurities (right: polished egg)

Dispelling computer stress with fluorite

Polished yellow/green banded

Polished green/blue purple banded

Polished purple

CRYSTAL FACTS

Crystal to use: fluorite (clear, blue, green, purple, yellow, brown), transparent

Availability: commonly available

Qualities of stone: removes negative energies, dispels electromagnetic stress from computers

Where to place the crystal: by or on your computer

Although little is known of its ritual use, fluorite, which was found in the ruins of Pompeii, has been with us since ancient times. Today, crystal healers use it as a stone of purification and protection. You can use fluorite at home or the office to absorb electromagnetic radiation from computers, and also to lift the overall energy levels in your work space.

Computer screens emit electromagnetic radiation, most of which is filtered by the screens, but this efficiency decreases as computers age. This radiation can make you feel lethargic, tired, and debilitated. The screen also gives out positive ions that can make your eyes very dry and sore. If you're suffering from any of these symptoms, fluorite may help; this stone is strongly protective, and it will remove any existing negative energies.

Crystal cure

Hold the crystal in your hand briefly and ask it to improve the atmosphere of your working environment before placing it on top of your computer or close by it. The fluorite will be hard at work every time you use your computer, so cleanse the stone regularly (see pages 149–153). You can also place a plant such as a peace lily or peperomia next to your computer to filter the air, increase negative ionization, and protect you from daily radiation emissions.

ALTERNATIVE COMPUTER STRESS-RELIEVING CRYSTALS TO USE

Smoky quartz: detoxifies and soaks up electromagnetic radiation

Black tourmaline: protects against negative energies and electromagnetic emissions

Amazonite: powerful filtering stone, removes electromagnetic pollution

Encouraging career achievement with natural quartz cluster

Natural quartz is a wonderful amplifier, stimulating brain activity, helping to formulate action and support your career needs. A quartz cluster, comprising many mini points and facets, has the ability to transmit positive energy while absorbing negative vibes—so if you have a tendency to doubt your abilities, this sparkling crystal formation can remove your indecision and instill you with confidence.

If you are finding it difficult to be recognized for your achievements, you can add a little feng shui to help you gain the success you desire.

Cluster

CRYSTAL FACTS

CRYSTAL TO USE: natural quartz cluster (clear or milky)

AVAILABILITY: commonly available

QUALITIES OF STONE: powerful energizer, tunes in to the person using the stone, boosts concentration

WHERE TO PLACE THE CRYSTAL: in the northeast section of your desk

Crystal energizing

The northeast of your desk is the best place to position your natural quartz cluster. It is your Education and knowledge area, so the crystal will support the earth energies existing in this space. Spend some time attuning to your crystal's vibrations before you place it. Program it for what you desire next in your career. Be very specific in your aims and the stone will work with you to lift the energetic frequency around you so that you gain what you want.

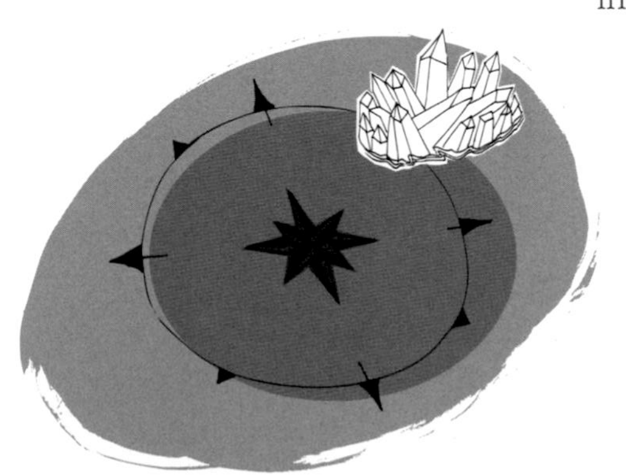

If you can, place your telephone in the south area of your desk—this is your Fame area, which again can enhance your chances of doing well.

Rough

Bringing success in meetings with green agate

An agate is a wonderful crystal for increasing mental powers and improving your perceptive skills. Its talent for aiding analysis was well known in Asia in the past, where a scryer would gaze into the stone to try to discover future trends.

If business meetings are a regular part of your working life, and making a positive impact or handling a presentation successfully is important to your career, an agate can give you the confidence to handle yourself well. Using it can increase your resolve and business acumen, keeping you "on your toes" so that you have ready answers to any tricky questions.

CRYSTAL FACTS

Crystal to use: green agate. Can be sold artificially colored, which is often banded

Availability: commonly available

Qualities of stone: boosts ego and self-esteem, increases energy, strengthens mind, improves concentration and brain function, gives mental flexibility

Where to place the crystal: in your pocket, or hold in your hand

Polished

Crystal energizing

Before your meeting starts, sit at your desk and pick up your green agate. Hold it tightly for about 5 minutes, tuning in to its vibrations as the stone gives you courage and self-respect. Feel the soothing green color calming your nerves and stabilizing your heart rate. Ask the stone for its help to make you speak eloquently at your meeting. Let it work on increasing your self-worth so that your meeting is a success. Put your green agate in your pocket, and enter your meeting positively with a relaxed smile.

ALTERNATIVE SUCCESS CRYSTALS TO USE

Tiger's eye: recognizes inner resources, promotes clarity of intention

Carnelian: encourages vitality, motivation and business success

Chrysoprase: stimulates fluent speech and versatile reasoning

Keeping away computer viruses with malachite

Malachite is a transformational crystal that lets you live life more intensely under its influence. Some people believe it will become one of the most prized healing stones of this century. Malachite is reputed to help with spiritual development and inner journeying; it is also very protective—those who use it regularly say that it breaks into pieces when danger is near.

Placed on your desk, malachite will soak up some of the electromagnetic pollution emitted by your computer and other appliances. You can make it your own personal guardian against viruses that can attack your computer via the internet and email. Its healing energy can be an added repellent to any new viruses that are attacking software programs and can be used alongside your dedicated anti-virus program. The stone dispels negativity, absorbing any radiation and pollutants that leak into the atmosphere.

Crystal cure

Pick up your stone and hold it firmly in your hand to feel its power and purifying abilities. Ask it to soak up any negativity from your office space and send out strong, positive energetic rays around your computer to keep it virus-free. Circle the stone around the computer twice daily, morning and late afternoon. Cleanse the stone after each use under running water, or see pages 149–153.

CRYSTAL FACTS

CRYSTAL TO USE: malachite (green with black); when tumbled, shows light and dark bands; best to use polished malachite as dust from rough crystal can adversely affect some people

AVAILABILITY: commonly available

QUALITIES OF STONE: prevents negativity and depression, alleviates stress and tension, protects against negative energies and electromagnetic emissions, aids sleep, promotes business success, brings transformation

WHERE TO PLACE THE CRYSTAL: on your desk

Dealing with confrontation with blue moonstone

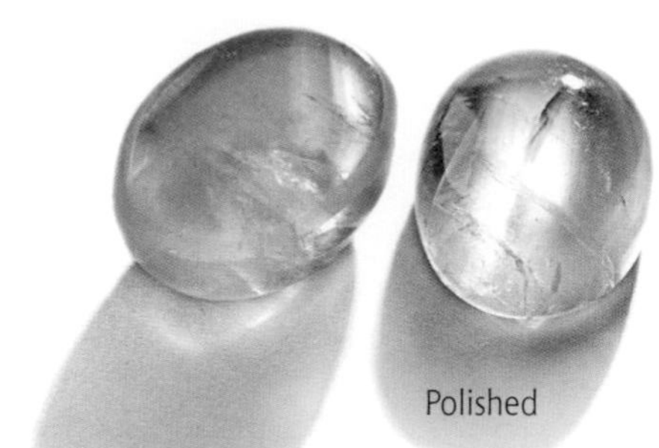

Polished

A blue moonstone, also known as rainbow moonstone, with its lovely pearly sheen may appear otherworldly—it is believed to be a stone of prophecy under a full moon—yet it is clearly a crystal for this material world. It teaches us that love is important: a message that will get through to even the hardest cynic. A stone of balance, moonstone regulates both male and female energies, letting a tough man get in touch with his feminine side and a strong woman become more empathetic. Linked to the moon's cycles, it helps to soothe your own rollercoaster of emotions and keeps stress levels down. The moonstone is also known for its conciliatory qualities, so keeping it on your desk can create a neutral zone in office politics. In fraught situations with colleagues, this sensitive stone builds an empathetic shield around you.

CRYSTAL FACTS

Crystal to use: blue moonstone, blue and cloudy-white, translucent, often with black inclusions

Availability: commonly available

Qualities of stone: helps to balance emotions, dissipates anxiety and stress, calms aggression and overreactions in arguments, encourages flexibility in attitudes

Where to place the crystal: in your pocket or on your desk, or wear it as jewelry

Crystal cure

If an office confrontation does occur, pick up your stone and hold it tightly in your hand, until you feel its passive energy stabilizing and healing your emotions, defusing your anger, and stopping you overreacting to the disagreement. Cleanse regularly to keep it vibrant (see pages 149–153).

ALTERNATIVE NON-CONFRONTATIONAL CRYSTALS TO USE

Celestite: peaceful stone that improves adversarial relationships

Jasper: gives support in conflict, encourages resolve (right: red jasper)

Pietersite: supportive stone that helps solve conflicts

Stopping constant interruptions with amethyst

Amethyst is a very spiritual crystal but has the transformational properties of natural quartz. A highly protective stone that was worn by ancient Egyptian soldiers to calm their fears in battle, amethyst can become your talisman at work. With reports to write, meetings to prepare for, and a multitude of emails to answer, the last thing you want when your time is limited is to be constantly interrupted by colleagues. A pointed amethyst crystal is wonderful to have on your desk as it supports your endeavors, soothes any worries or anxieties every time you gaze at it, while also repelling any unwanted visitors when you are desperate to meet a deadline.

Crystal cure

Hold the crystal in your hands and ask it to create a protective shield around you, then place it on your desk with the point facing the wall. Whenever you see someone approaching that you do not want to speak to, turn the point around to face them, and then watch how they stop, look a bit puzzled, and then go off in another direction. This gentle crystal will not harm them but they will not want to walk through its barrier. Cleanse it regularly to remove negativity (see pages 149–153).

Amethyst wand

CRYSTAL FACTS

CRYSTAL TO USE: amethyst (violet/purple), transparent, single point or wand

AVAILABILITY: commonly available

QUALITIES OF STONE: healing and calming, protects, soothes the mind, rebalances emotions, blocks negative environmental energies, gives focus and mental stability, strengthens memory and increases motivation

WHERE TO PLACE THE CRYSTAL: in your pocket, or on your desk

ALTERNATIVE PROTECTIVE CRYSTALS TO USE

Rose quartz: creates a loving barrier, promotes sensitivity

Natural quartz: makes a strong energetic field, works to your purpose

Black tourmaline: protects and repels negative energies

Connecting with inner wisdom with lapis lazuli

Rough

CRYSTAL FACTS

Crystal to use: lapis lazuli (blue with gold flecks; may be blue and white [white is calcite]; may have black spots of lazulite)

Availability: commonly available, but can be expensive

Qualities of stone: helps psychic development and intuition, brings mental stability and clarity, alleviates stress, balances physical, mental and emotional feelings, helps objectivity and clarity

Where to place the crystal: on your Third eye chakra in the middle of your forehead

Lapis lazuli was revered by ancient cultures such as the Sumerians, who believed it contained souls of their gods and goddesses, and that if they wore the stone they would become godlike and able to perform magical powers. A mystical crystal, lapis creates inner and outer harmony of the mind, body, and spirit.

When your life seems to be a series of setbacks, lapis helps you take charge of your life. Mentally, it stops you from feeling so stressed and gives you coping strategies when you run into difficulties at work, particularly when you feel that you have run out of solutions and ideas. Lapis lazuli's special protective wisdom shifts your mental blocks and lets you tap into your intuition to gain the guidance you need.

Crystal energizing

To source your answers, sit in a quiet space, close your eyes, and place your lapis lazuli crystal on your Third eye chakra: just touching the stone is believed to improve your mental and emotional situation. Breathe deeply and semi-meditate as you concentrate on your problem, saying mentally, "I am finding the solution I need right now." Feel this creative crystal's vibrations allowing you to access your subconscious and inner wisdom. Sit for several minutes until you sense the answers you want flowing in.

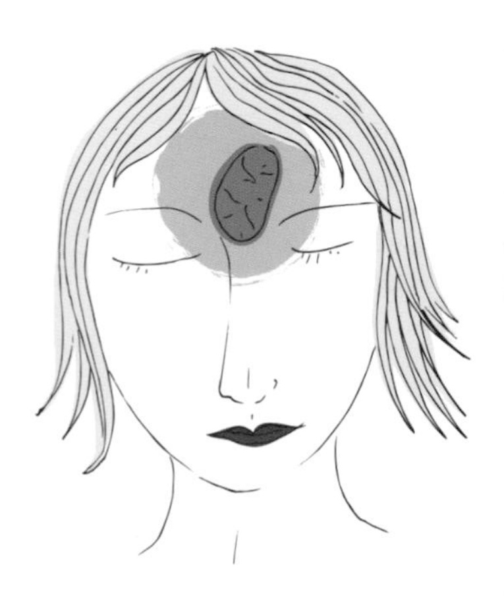

ALTERNATIVE INTUITIVE CRYSTALS TO USE

Amber: encourages wisdom and inspired self-expression

Topaz: helps tap into your inner psyche for knowledge

Onyx: helps you go inside and make wise decisions

Achieving goals with golden topaz

Polished

The word topaz may have derived from the ancient Sanskrit word *tapas*, meaning "fire." This lovely yellow crystal is an instant energizer, giving you the charisma to find the success and fame you seek. Its generosity is supposed to bring wealth and money into your life. This power of attraction can also help you attain the goals you set yourself at work. Goals are important in your working life to move you on in your career and prevent lethargy from setting in. Choosing a goal will give you focus. Everyone's goals are different: you may want promotion in a year. Other people may want to take a year out and work abroad, or need to pass an important examination. Golden topaz can connect you to your inner wisdom and help you reach your goal.

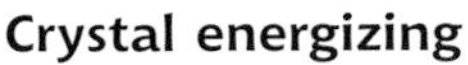

Crystal energizing

Choose your goal. If you are having problems deciding, think of each option in turn and sense which one gives you a warm sensation and feels right, even if it is a bit frightening. Use your golden topaz crystal at the full moon or when it is waxing to receive its full powers. Now pick up your stone and hold it in your hands or over your solar plexus for about 5 minutes, releasing any blockages or upsets held there, and ask for its assistance in achieving your aim. Concentrate hard on your goal, feeling the vibrations coming out of your stone as it works on boosting you physically to give you the presence you need to follow your dream.

CRYSTAL FACTS

CRYSTAL TO USE: golden topaz, transparent, tumbled, or sometimes pointed and faceted

AVAILABILITY: commonly available from specialist stores

QUALITIES OF STONE: recharges and motivates, develops intuition, strengthens nervous system, promotes self-realization and inner awareness, helps to communicate ideas and recognize own abilities

WHERE TO PLACE THE CRYSTAL: in your hands or over your heart

ALTERNATIVE GOAL-ACHIEVING CRYSTALS TO USE

Dendritic agate: brings abundance in business, aids perseverance (right: moss agate)

Carnelian: good for business success, increases motivation

Fire opal: stimulates personal power, brings progress

Reducing work frustration with blue kyanite

Rough

The word kyanite comes from the Greek word *kyanos,* meaning "blue," which is the principal color of this crystal. This flat-bladed crystal with a pearly covering is often unevenly colored, with the strongest blue tints in the middle. Its high spiritual frequencies can stimulate your psychic awareness and increase your intuition and problem-solving abilities. Psychologically, it calms and takes away trifling worries, reminding you that everything happens for a reason. Kyanite does not hold negativity, so is invaluable to keep as a soothing desk accessory to dispel the anger of a confrontation with your boss, or other stresses or difficult tasks that can build up during a normal working day.

CRYSTAL FACTS

Crystal to use: blue kyanite transparent or opaque, sometimes striated

Availability: commonly available

Qualities of stone: aids meditation, inspires loyalty, clears mind, allows new thought patterns, increases creative self-expression, increases psychic abilities and intuition, dispels energy blockages, dispels anger, frustration, and worry

Health benefits: works on thyroid, parathyroid and adrenal glands, lowers blood pressure, helps to heal infections

Where to place the crystal: hold in hands

Crystal cure

Working flat out for weeks on end can leave you mentally drained, with a tendency to overreact to any unforeseen problems that occur. Performing a short daily meditation for about 10 minutes at lunchtime with kyanite can release these frustrations, giving you increased mental clarity and perception. Sit in a quiet space holding your crystal in your hands. Breathe in deeply and as you breathe out let out all your stress and tension. Gaze into your crystal, noticing its beauty, shape, and color. As your mind slows with your breathing, feel the crystal's amplifying vibrations deepening your meditation, bringing light to your soul, and slowing you down so that you can see the right solutions to your problems. Slowly come back to the room.

ALTERNATIVE WORRY-RELEASING CRYSTALS TO USE

Amazonite: calms the brain, lets you see both sides of a problem

Onyx: relieves fears and worries, encourages wise decisions

Apophyllite: releases stress, aids decision-making process

Creating inner harmony with a natural quartz pendulum

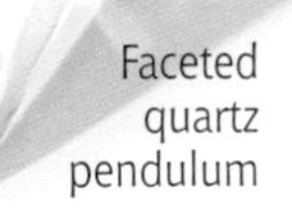

Faceted quartz pendulum

Problem

If you are out of sorts, lethargic or lacking enthusiasm, one or several chakras can be out of balance.

Solution

Dowsing with a natural quartz pendulum, a powerful energy amplifier, can find the energetic imbalance. You can then correct the chakra or chakras by using the right color of crystal for that area.

Cleansing your energy

If you are feeling run-down, here's how to test the health of your chakras:

1. Half-lie on a mat on the floor, holding your natural quartz pendulum in your dominant hand. Check the Root chakra by holding the quartz pendulum over your lower pelvis. When healthy, the crystal reacts to the normal vibration by spinning counterclockwise for a woman (clockwise for a man); if it swings from side to side the crystal has detected an energetic problem.

2. Now work up the chakras. They function like cogs in a wheel, so the second chakra, the Sacral, should spin clockwise (counterclockwise for a man) and the next one clockwise, and so on.

3. Check all the chakras, noting down any unhealthy ones, then treat them with the appropriate color of crystal (see pages 58–64).

Chakra positions

The body has seven principal chakras, or energy centers, which are situated in your etheric body, the energy-layer that surrounds the physical body.

1 Root, lower pelvic area
2 Sacral, pelvic area
3 Solar plexus, upper abdomen
4 Heart, middle of chest
5 Throat, middle of throat
6 Third eye, middle of forehead
7 Crown, top of head

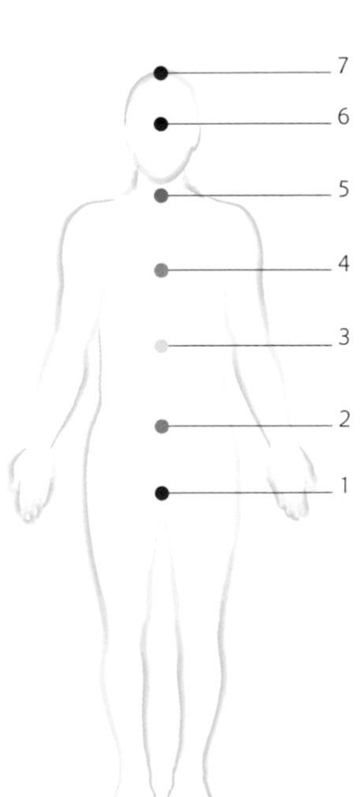

CRYSTAL FACTS

Crystal to use: natural quartz pendulum with chain

Availability: commonly available from crystal stores

Qualities of stone: powerful healer, amplifies and transmits energy, aligns the energy requirements of person needing healing, dissolves negativity in energy field, increases intuition

Working on: all the chakras

Health benefits: heals any ailment, brings body back in balance, relieves burns, soothes toothache

How a pendulum works: dowsing with a pendulum is an ancient technique that can check the vibrational frequency of the chakras. A malfunction is detected by a change in the pendulum's movement

How to be more grounded with bloodstone

Polished

CRYSTAL FACTS

Crystal to use: bloodstone, also known as heliotrope, is a type of green jasper that contains red spots of iron oxide. Although mainly green, this grounding stone resonates with the Root chakra

Availability: commonly available

Qualities of stone: links Root chakra with heart, gives vitality, strengthens idealistic views, alleviates emotional stress, increases courage to revive an exhausted mind, a grounding and protective stone

Working on: Root chakra at the base of the spine (or around pubic area on front of body)

Color needed by chakra: red

Parts of body affected by crystal: adrenal glands, lower pelvic area

Health benefits: strengthens blood circulation, corrects iron deficiencies, detoxifies liver, kidneys, intestines, and spleen, increases metabolism, helps fight against leukemia

Where to place the crystal: hold over the lower pelvis

Problem

If you are not feeling rooted in your existence, or if your instincts are down, the energy in your lower pelvis will not be up to full strength.

Solution

To feel more grounded, or down to earth, you will need to work on the Root chakra: the first energy center (see page 57).

The Root chakra and symbol

Boost your energy

The Root chakra is also the area of self-preservation, associated with our instincts to keep away from danger. To stimulate the flow of energy to this center or remove a blockage, lie on your back in a calm room. Pick up your bloodstone crystal and tune in to its power to cleanse you energetically. Close your eyes and place or hold the crystal on your Root chakra for 5 minutes by holding or resting it on your lower pelvis. Contemplate your grounding problem, allowing your stimulating red crystal to harmonize and revitalize the energies existing here, then slowly come back into the room. Cleanse the stone (see pages 149–153). Work with this crystal daily for one or two weeks until life no longer feels a burden and you feel more fixed in your own skin.

ALTERNATIVE GROUNDING CRYSTALS TO USE

Smoky quartz: solid and grounding; increases resolve, relieves fear (right: with rutiles)

Agate: grounding, healing stone that brings balance (right: brown agate)

Onyx: imparts self-control and encourages a less "airy" existence

Boosting your creativity with orange calcite

Problem

If you feel that you have lost the ability to be creative, or your life lacks fulfillment, the energy in the middle part of your body will be depleted.

Solution

To increase your creativity levels, you will benefit from doing some crystal work on your Sacral chakra: the second spiritual energy center (see page 57).

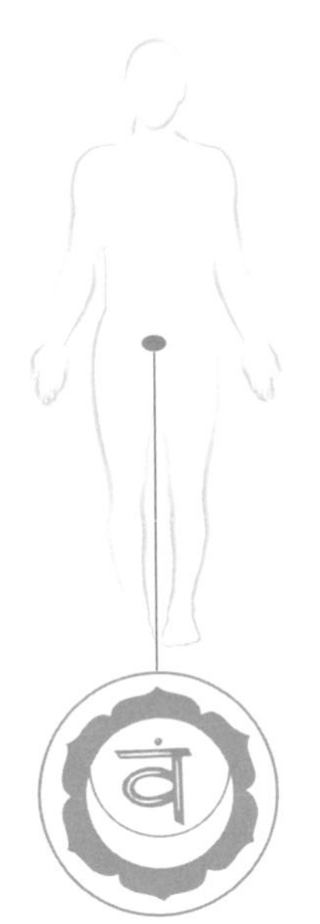

The Sacral, or navel, chakra and symbol

Boost your energy

The Sacral chakra is also the area that controls your sexuality, security, and how you see the world. To increase or balance the energy flow to this area, or to shift a blockage, lie or sit down comfortably in a quiet room, pick up your orange calcite crystal and sense your connection with this energizing stone. Close your eyes and place or hold the crystal on your Sacral chakra for 5 minutes, then focus on your creativity problem and let the crystal do its work, correcting your energetic level. Work with this warming crystal energy daily for one or two weeks until you start to feel a surge of new creativity and optimism bubbling up inside you.

Rough

CRYSTAL FACTS

CRYSTAL TO USE: orange calcite, translucent, may be banded

AVAILABILITY: commonly available

QUALITIES OF STONE: stimulates energy, can alleviate fear and stress, strengthens emotions and can build confidence

WORKING ON: Sacral chakra in the pelvic area

COLOR NEEDED BY CHAKRA: orange

PARTS OF BODY AFFECTED BY CRYSTAL: sexual organs, kidneys, bladder, and intestines

HEALTH BENEFITS: cleanses the blood, affects the kidneys, pancreas, and spleen; associated with relieving the symptoms of constipation and diarrhea

WHERE TO PLACE THE CRYSTAL: hold over your pelvic area (just below the navel)

ALTERNATIVE CREATIVITY CRYSTALS TO USE

Amber: promotes joy, takes away negativity

Moonstone: balances emotions, helps new beginnings

Carnelian: alleviates apathy and increases confidence

Increasing your personal power with citrine

Cluster

CRYSTAL FACTS

Crystal to use: citrine (yellow, yellow/brown), often a geode point or cluster

Availability: natural citrine can be rare; citrine produced by heat-treating amethyst is commonly available

Qualities of stone: brings happiness and generosity. Increases motivation

Working on: Solar plexus chakra in the upper abdomen

Color needed by chakra: yellow

Parts of body affected by crystal: pancreas, stomach, spleen, liver

Health benefits: treats digestive problems, thyroid imbalance; increases blood circulation

Where to place the crystal: hold over upper abdomen

Problem

When your ego is at a low ebb, if you are suffering an identity crisis, or perhaps you feel your personal power is lacking, the energy in the area just under your chest will be reduced.

Solution

To bring your ego up to full strength, the area to treat with a crystal is your Solar plexus chakra: the third spiritual energy center (see page 57).

Boost your energy

The solar plexus is your area of personal achievement and it relates to speaking out boldly about things that are important to you. To realign the energy flow here, or dissolve a blockage, lie or sit comfortably where you will not be disturbed. Pick up your citrine, and feel your connection to this sunny, joyful stone, then place or hold it on your Solar plexus chakra for 5 minutes. Close your eyes; concentrate on your ego problem as your yellow crystal's stimulating vibrations work on correcting the impulses in this chakra, then slowly come back into the room. Cleanse the stone (see pages 149–153). Use this crystal daily for one or two weeks and notice how your ego is strengthened and how good you now feel about yourself.

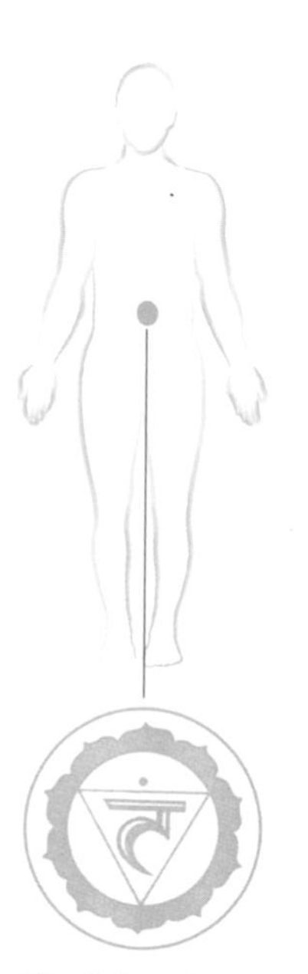
The Solar plexus chakra and symbol

ALTERNATIVE PERSONAL POWER CRYSTALS TO USE

Golden topaz: recharges trust and optimism

Golden beryl (heliodor): promotes independent spirit and will to succeed

Rhodochrosite: encourages positive feelings of self-worth

Opening up to love with rose quartz

Rough

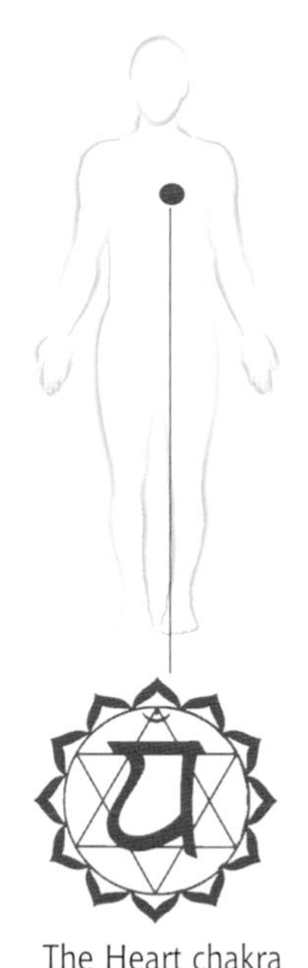

Problem

If you have emotionally shut down or you are finding it hard to maintain an intimate, loving relationship, the energy in the middle of your chest will be low.

Solution

To give and receive love once more, you need some crystal energy on your Heart chakra: the fourth energy center (see page 57).

The Heart chakra and symbol

Boost your energy

The Heart chakra is also the place of giving compassion and seeking empathy with other people. To augment, smooth out, or remove a blockage in the energy flow to this center, lie or sit comfortably in a still room and hold your beautiful rose quartz crystal in your hands and feel its gentle, loving pulsations. Close your eyes and place or hold your crystal on your Heart chakra for 5 minutes. Contemplate the lack of love in your life and sense how your purifying and reassuring pink crystal is adjusting the energetic levels here, then slowly come back into the room. Cleanse the stone (see pages 149–153). Use this soothing crystal daily for one or two weeks and see how you much more loving you feel and how much more affectionate you now are with your partner, friends, or family.

CRYSTAL FACTS

CRYSTAL TO USE: rose quartz (pink) translucent or transparent, can be tumbled

AVAILABILITY: commonly available

QUALITIES OF STONE: heals emotional trauma, stimulates friendship, brings peace and unconditional love, promotes compassion and forgiveness, restores trust and harmony, increases self-worth

WORKING ON: Heart chakra in the middle of the chest

COLOR NEEDED BY CHAKRA: green or pink

PARTS OF BODY AFFECTED BY CRYSTAL: thymus, lower lungs, and heart

HEALTH BENEFITS: benefits kidneys, adrenals, and circulatory system, strengthens physical heart, heals cuts or bruises, soothes burns, helps chest and lung ailments

WHERE TO PLACE THE CRYSTAL: hold to heart

ALTERNATIVE LOVE-INCREASING CRYSTALS TO USE

Celestite: dissolves inner pain and lets love in

Rhodochrosite: brings out repressed feelings, opening up the heart to love (rough)

Kunzite: helps to express emotions and awaken unconditional love

How to become more communicative with aquamarine

Polished

CRYSTAL FACTS

CRYSTAL TO USE: aquamarine (green/blue), clear or opaque, sometimes faceted or can be tumbled

AVAILABILITY: commonly available

QUALITIES OF STONE: stimulates self-knowledge, inspires intellect, helps with creative self-expression, balances emotions, reduces stress, stills the mind, encourages understanding of other people

WORKING ON: Throat chakra, in the middle of the throat

COLOR NEEDED BY CHAKRA: turquoise blue

PARTS OF BODY AFFECTED BY CRYSTAL: thyroid and parathyroid, upper lungs, and throat

HEALTH BENEFITS: associated with alleviating toothache, reducing fluid retention, strengthening kidneys, liver, and spleen, soothing sore throats, aiding thyroid problems, helping the body to detox

WHERE TO PLACE THE CRYSTAL: hold to throat

Problem

If you feel you cannot express your true needs or if you are not able to communicate your opinions, the energy in the middle of your throat may be deficient.

Solution

To open up your communication channels, the area that will gain from some crystal work is your Throat chakra: the fifth energy center (see page 57).

The Throat chakra and symbol

Boost your energy

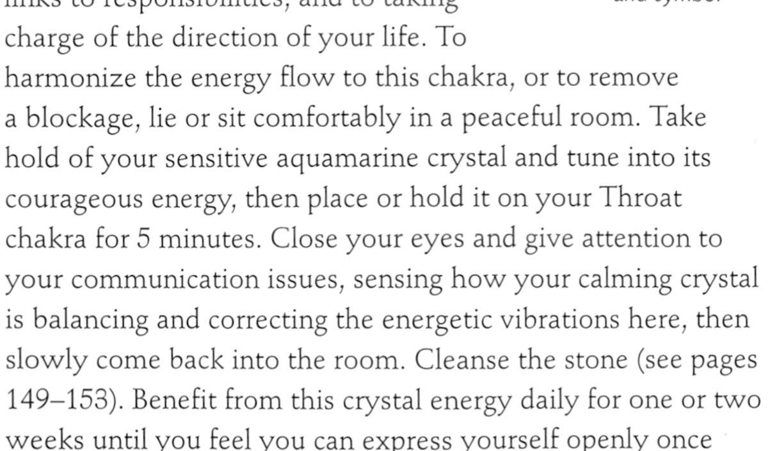

The Throat chakra is also the area that links to responsibilities, and to taking charge of the direction of your life. To harmonize the energy flow to this chakra, or to remove a blockage, lie or sit comfortably in a peaceful room. Take hold of your sensitive aquamarine crystal and tune into its courageous energy, then place or hold it on your Throat chakra for 5 minutes. Close your eyes and give attention to your communication issues, sensing how your calming crystal is balancing and correcting the energetic vibrations here, then slowly come back into the room. Cleanse the stone (see pages 149–153). Benefit from this crystal energy daily for one or two weeks until you feel you can express yourself openly once more and say, from your heart, what you truly mean.

ALTERNATIVE COMMUNICATION CRYSTALS TO USE

Turquoise: aids creative communication, helps find ultimate purpose in life

Lapis lazuli: encourages taking charge of life, aids eloquent self-expression

Kyanite: promotes speaking the truth and clear communication

Improving your intuition with sodalite

Rough

Problem

If you are finding it hard to connect with your inner wisdom or if you have lost your ability to take command of situations, the energy in the middle of your forehead will be lacking.

Solution

To tap into your inner wisdom or your intuitive powers, use some crystal energy on your Third eye chakra: the sixth energy center (see page 57).

Boost your energy

The Third eye chakra is the place where you can develop your psychic abilities—it is connected with your dreams, self-respect, and insight. To boost or harmonize the energetic flow or remove a blockage, lie or sit in a quiet room. Hold your perceptive sodalite crystal and tune in to its spiritual vibrations. Place or hold it on your Third eye chakra for 5 minutes as you think about your depleted intuitive powers. Sense how your crystal is re-aligning your energies, then slowly come back into the room. Cleanse the stone (see pages 149–153). Use daily for one or two weeks until you start receiving inner messages and have more mental clarity about your life.

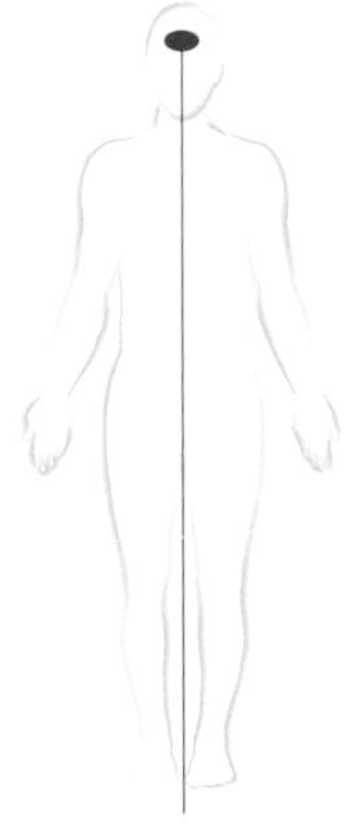

The Third eye chakra and symbol

CRYSTAL FACTS

Crystal to use: sodalite, dark blue, blue/white variegated stone

Availability: commonly available

Qualities of stone: brings clarity and truth, increases spiritual awareness, accesses higher parts of mind, helps you stand up to beliefs, releases guilt and fears, encourages rational and logical thinking

Working on: Third eye chakra in the middle of the forehead

Color needed by chakra: indigo

Parts of body affected by crystal: pituitary and pineal glands, brainstem (medulla oblongata)

Health benefits: associated with balancing metabolism, lowering blood pressure, boosting the functioning of the lymphatic system, helping digestive problems, aiding endocrine system

Where to place the crystal: hold to forehead

ALTERNATIVE INTUITIVE CRYSTALS TO USE

Aquamarine: clarifies perceptive abilities, stimulates intuition

Malachite: encourages self-expression, increases empathy and intuition

Moonstone: accesses information from subconscious, promotes intuition

Rough

Accessing your spirituality with snow quartz

The Crown chakra and symbol

CRYSTAL FACTS

Crystal to use: snow quartz (white), also known as milky quartz and quartzite, can be crystalline form or pebble

Availability: commonly available

Qualities of stone: helps you learn lessons, enhances spirituality, calms and balances, can purify and protect, can link to deep inner wisdom, raises spiritual energy to highest level

Working on: Crown chakra on top of head

Color needed by chakra: violet or white

Parts of body affected by crystal: pineal gland, brain (cerebral cortex)

Health benefits: associated with boosting the immune system, can work on any condition, activates pineal and pituitary glands, enhances brain functions

Where to place the crystal: hold to top of head

Problem

When you have lost your love for life, your spirit is down, or your artistic side is unfulfilled, the energy around the top of your head will be deficient.

Solution

To enhance your spiritual wisdom and your appreciation of the beautiful things in life, work with some crystal energy on your Crown chakra: the seventh energy center (see page 57).

Boost your energy

The Crown chakra is also the place which allows you to meditate more deeply, and show kindness and compassion to others. To open this chakra to a positive energy flow or to get rid of a blockage, lie or sit in a peaceful room and pick up your supportive milky quartz crystal and sense its tactful emanations. Close your eyes and place or hold your crystal on your Crown chakra for 5 minutes. Now concentrate on raising your spirit and your negative attitude to life, letting your gentle white crystal increase the energetic vibrations here, then slowly come back into the room. Cleanse the stone (see pages 149–153). Use this crystal daily for one or two weeks and notice how good everything looks once more and how much more in tune you feel with nature, your spirit, and your artistic side.

ALTERNATIVE SPIRITUAL CRYSTALS TO USE

Natural quartz: aids meditation, helps you realize life's possibilities

Amethyst: promotes spiritual awareness, removes negative feelings

Celestite: helps meditation, awakens spiritual desire

Cleansing your aura with amethyst

Cluster

Problem

You have had a demanding day with frustrating problems at work or children's tantrums at home, plus travel stress.

Solution

Clearing your aura of all the day's negativity can refresh your mind, body, and spirit.

Cleansing your energy

The purple color of the amethyst crystal is believed by healers to represent the merging of night and day. Its soothing, calming qualities are supposed to ease the physical conscious into unconscious: going from being awake to falling asleep. A powerful and protective crystal, it can cleanse your aura of any debris that you have picked up during the day. Stand upright in a quiet room and pick up your amethyst stone. Close your eyes and ask the crystal to remove any negativity and dissolve any unhealthy emotions from the day, replacing them with a higher spiritual vibration. Circle the stone all around your body: the front, back, and sides, feeling a wonderful warmth as your energetic field is fully restored, then slowly come back into the room. Cleanse the stone (see pages 149–153). Repeat daily.

What is the aura?

The aura is a subtle energy field that surrounds the physical body. It has several layers that constantly change color due to the light that our bodies absorb. The aura shows our emotional, mental, and spiritual wellbeing.

CRYSTAL FACTS

CRYSTAL TO USE: amethyst (purple/lavender) geode, cluster or single point

AVAILABILITY: commonly available

QUALITIES OF STONE: reduces stress and tension, inspires divine love, protects against psychic attack, dissolves negative environmental energies, rebalances spirit, increases intuition

WORKING ON: the aura

HEALTH BENEFITS: associated with increasing right brain activity and pineal and pituitary function, cleanses the blood, fights acne, neuralgia, and insomnia, balances endocrine system and metabolism, eases headaches and digestive problems

ALTERNATIVE AURA CLEANSING CRYSTALS TO USE

Fluorite: protects psychically, cleanses and balances aura (right: purple fluorite)

Rutilated quartz: heals energetic vibrations, cleanses and energizes aura (right: smoky quartz with rutiles, single terminator)

Polished

Attracting a soulmate with rhodochrosite

Rhodochrosite is a pink, passionate crystal that dares you to be adventurous. Just holding the stone, you feel the urge to seek change and bring about those things you truly want. Perhaps you are single and your heart's desire is for a soulmate to be your lover and best friend—someone with whom to share your hopes and dreams. Rhodochrosite is a powerful love crystal that vibrates at a higher level than rose quartz, so is very effective for removing any emotional blockages you have set up in your Heart chakra and increasing your sexual attraction. Legend also says that rubbing this vibrant crystal over your face improves your complexion, making you more beautiful and appealing to a new lover.

CRYSTAL FACTS

Crystal to use: rhodochrosite (pink), banded

Availability: commonly available

Qualities of stone: heals emotional wounds and upsets, inspires forgiveness, promotes acceptance of self, encourages self-expression, can bring in a soulmate, inspires unconditional love

Health benefits: purifies blood and kidneys, improves poor eyesight, aids spleen, heart, pancreas, and pituitary gland, invigorates the sexual organs, aids anorexia and bulimia

Where to place the crystal: on your Heart chakra in the center of your chest

Crystal energizing

To attract your dream partner, have a quiet night at home and sit on your living room floor. Light two pink candles, as pink links to Venus, the goddess of love. Burn some sensual ylang ylang essential oil. Now write down on paper the characteristics of the partner you desire and fold it in four. Pick up your rhodochrosite crystal and hold it with your love list to your heart for about ten minutes. Close your eyes and visualize your new lover: see you both together, holding hands and laughing; feel your love and send this emotion flowing into this potent stone and out again for it to do its romantic work; and then slowly come back into the room. Repeat this love visualization regularly until your soulmate appears in your life.

ALTERNATIVE LOVE CRYSTALS TO USE

Rose quartz: purifies and opens the heart, attracts a new partner

Celestite: alleviates pain and brings in love

Increasing your sexuality with red tiger's eye

Polished

In the past, tiger's eye was believed to be "all-seeing" because of its banded appearance. A rich, earthy stone, natural tiger's eye is heat-treated to achieve the stone's deep red color.

Ruled by the bright sun, red tiger's eye is a supportive stone that lets you go inside to find the courage and confidence to resolve your sexual problems. In a long-term relationship it is common for sexual desire to wane, or a loss of interest in sex may be triggered by too much stress or a bout of depression. This bright, stimulating crystal matches the color needed by the sexual organs to stay healthy. The vibrational level of the stone stirs up the dormant sexual energies, curing any imbalances and reawakening your sexual desire.

Crystal cure

To rebalance your sexual organs and your root chakra, lie on your bed in late evening, placing your red tiger's eye on your lower pelvis for about ten minutes. Close your eyes and let the stone's energy correct any physical imbalances, and dissolve any emotional blockages such as self-criticism or a lack of self-worth. Open yourself up to the motivational healing and ask for a return of your sexual interest, then slowly come back into the room. Work nightly for a week until your emotional barriers melt and you feel the stirring of sexual desire once more.

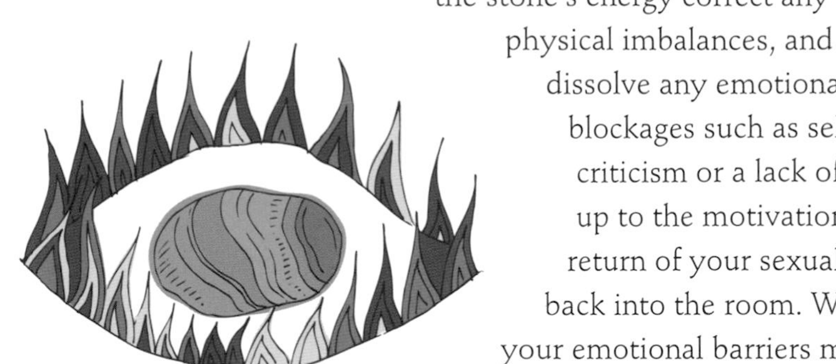

CRYSTAL FACTS

Crystal to use: red tiger's eye (a form of quartz), banded can be small and tumbled

Availability: commonly available

Qualities of stone: provides motivation, increases sex drive, balances emotions, enhances perceptions and insight; grounding and balancing

Health benefits: relieves asthma, aids the digestive system, balances spleen and pancreas, helps night vision, heals throat and reproductive organs

Where to place the crystal: on your Root chakra in the lower pelvic area

ALTERNATIVE SEXUALITY CRYSTALS TO USE

Garnet: balances sex drive and reduces emotional upset

Fire agate: ignites sex drive, stimulates vitality

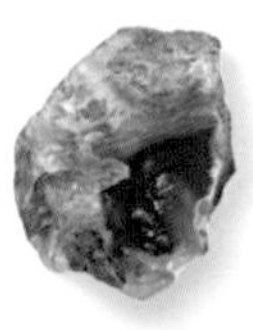

Ruby: fires up passion and enthusiasm for life once more

Healing a broken heart with agate

Polished

CRYSTAL FACTS

Crystal to use: agate (clear/milky white, gray, green, pink, blue, brown), sometimes artificially colored, usually banded

Availability: commonly available

Qualities of stone: gives strength and courage, improves ego and self-esteem, improves vitality, soothes and calms, promotes love, dissolves bitterness of the heart, helps with speaking the truth

Health benefits: stimulates digestive system, detoxes lymphatic system and pancreas, boosts circulatory system, reduces fevers, heals skin problems

Where to place the crystal: over your Heart chakra or hold in hands

In past times, an agate was worn on the arm by gardeners to encourage fertility in their plants and crops. In today's world you can use the crystal's slow energy to encourage feelings of forgiveness and overcome the loss of a great love: the gentle energy of agate is ideal for healing a broken heart. The crystal gives first aid to the shell-shocked emotions, creating a safety net, and gradually bringing acceptance of what has happened. Recovering from the break-up of an intense love affair can be traumatic. Your world can fall apart and it can be hard to keep going. Your work, sleep, and eating patterns can all be disrupted in this emotionally depleting time. Agate is a wonderful emotional aid that can release your inner anger and kickstart your coping mechanism.

Crystal cure

A crystal that is often used in spells to draw in love, agate removes any spiteful tendencies you may be harboring toward an ex-lover. To heal your wounds, sit in a still room and pick up your agate stone. Close your eyes and really tune in to the stone's energy. Hold it in your hands or place on your heart in the middle of your chest and visualize your aching heart. Now see healing rays coming out from your stone and filling your heart, releasing the anger, pain, and sadness held there, making it whole once again. Feel your joy as the crystal fills your heart with love, then slowly come back into the room. Repeat several times to let go of grief. Cleanse the crystal well to keep it vibrant (see pages 149–153).

ALTERNATIVE LOVE-HEALING CRYSTALS TO USE

Chrysocolla: removes destructive emotions, works on heartache

Lavender (purple) jade: emotional balancer, dissolves upset and trauma

Kunzite: clears out deep-rooted hurts, heals heartache

Releasing a past lover with chrysocolla

Rough

A very tranquil stone, blue chrysocolla with its tiny flecks of copper looks similar to turquoise, and some people confuse the two. An emotional balancer, this crystal brings serenity and peace into the lives of people who have suffered heartache. A love affair may be long over and you may feel that you no longer care about your ex-partner, but often the ties with them can be so strong that it is hard to let go. Chrysocolla cleanses the Heart chakra of deeply held pain, sustaining you as your past emotional hurts are banished from your life.

CRYSTAL FACTS

CRYSTAL TO USE: chrysocolla (blue, turquoise, green), opaque

AVAILABILITY: commonly available

QUALITIES OF STONE: alleviates nervous tension, brings joy, enhances connection with inner self, aids meditation, heals heartache and inner child, can release negative emotions, reduces guilt

HEALTH BENEFITS: prevents ulcers, helps stomach problems caused by stress, helps PMS and period pains, treats eye problems and skin diseases, relieves arthritis, detoxifies liver and kidneys, and increases blood circulation

WHERE TO PLACE THE CRYSTAL: hold in hands

Crystal cure

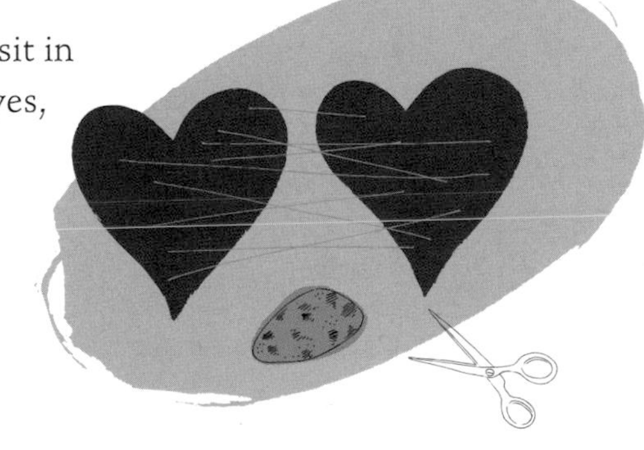

To release your past lover, sit in a quiet room, close your eyes, and clasp your chrysocolla crystal in your hands. Visualize your ex-partner and see several golden cords connecting your hearts. Mentally pick up a pair of scissors and cut these cords, saying, "Thank you for your love but now I am releasing you from my life." See healing vibrations coming from your stone, and filling both your hearts with joy and anticipation for the new lovers in the future. Slowly come back into the room. Cleanse your crystal well (see pages 149–153).

ALTERNATIVE RELEASING CRYSTALS TO USE

Obsidian: cleanses the heart of old attachments and painful memories

Kunzite: heals the heart, disperses old, upsetting emotions

Aventurine: heals the heart, brings emotions back in control

Fostering commitment with opal

Rough

CRYSTAL FACTS

Crystal to use: opal (white, black, beige, blue, yellow, brown, orange, red, purple, green, pink), milky appearance

Availability: commonly available but gem opals can be expensive

Qualities of stone: balances emotions, controls temper, absorbs feelings, increases them and sends them back to source, brings loyalty and faithfulness, strengthens self-worth

Health benefits: aids eyesight, particularly as a gem essence, treats fever and infections, helps glandular dysfunction and fluid retention, reduces PMS

Where to place the crystal: over your Heart chakra in the middle of your chest or hold in your hands

Rough

The opal, with its unique, beautiful, and flashing colors brings luck to the people who use it; the bad luck story surrounding the crystal supposedly originates from when jewelers broke the delicate stone when setting it. It is an absorbent stone that senses your emotions, amplifies them, and mirrors them back to you, revealing your hidden desires. A stone that teaches you to be responsible for your feelings, opal can show you how to resolve the emotional blockages that are preventing you from having a stable, long-lasting, and loving relationship. Commitment is a word that many people fear: you may have met the right partner but feel that he or she is not fully committing and that your relationship is stuck. Or it may be you who is holding back from finally binding yourself to that one person. The energy of a precious opal crystal can induce the loyalty and faithfulness you seek but beware of any doubts, as these can be amplified as well.

Crystal energizing

To encourage commitment from a partner or open up your heart, pick up your opal stone, close your eyes, and hold it in your hands or over your heart for several minutes while you visualize you and your partner together. See you both committing to each other. Feel how this shimmering crystal is intensifying your emotions and your partner's (it may well change color), releasing any fears, blockages, or inhibitions you both have about making a permanent relationship, then slowly come back into the room.

ALTERNATIVE COMMITMENT CRYSTALS TO USE

Garnet: encourages true love and emotional commitment

Magnetite: attracts love, long-term commitment, and a loyal partner

Making a positive relationship with green tourmaline

Green tourmaline is a delightful deep green; some forms show two or more colors when held to the light. The stone has many faces and can suit many moods, so it is no wonder that people say it has magical powers. A very fertile stone, it can stimulate growth in plants (see page 20), which you can replicate in the emotional side of your relationship.

Our relationships are often mirrors of our parents' marriage. Without awareness, we may be recreating the distant interaction that they had, and wonder why we are not happy. If there seems to be a wall of ice between you and your partner, a compassionate green tourmaline can give you the clarity to recognize what is causing your lack of intimacy, and help to bring your relationship back on track.

Crystal cure

Sit in a quiet room and hold the crystal to your heart. Closing your eyes, visualize both of you in a room ignoring each other: feel the tense emotions, then ask this nurturing stone to give you guidance and show you some way to resolve these feelings. Sense its healing rays surrounding you both and see how a positive solution to your communication problems pops into your head, then slowly come back into the room. Work daily with your crystal until you have a way to talk emotionally with your partner and to achieve the relationship you desire. Cleanse your crystal well (see pages 149–153).

CRYSTAL FACTS

CRYSTAL TO USE: green tourmaline, opaque/transparent, striated

AVAILABILITY: commonly available from specialist stores

QUALITIES OF STONE: brings in goodwill and friendship, dispels fear and negativity, balances emotions, restores enthusiasm and optimism, can help deal with problems constructively

HEALTH BENEFITS: aids sleep, balances the endocrine and nervous systems, boosts immune system, treats diarrhea and constipation, relieves migraines and asthma

WHERE TO PLACE THE CRYSTAL: hold on your Heart chakra in the middle of your chest

ALTERNATIVE RELATIONSHIP CRYSTALS TO USE

Turquoise: helps you to understand your partner

Opal: encourages you to become more emotionally responsive

Sugilite: dispels jealousy, fosters forgiveness and love

Rough

Banishing jealousy with sugilite

Sugilite is a very spiritual crystal that can cast light and love onto the blackest situations. Its alternative name is luvilite because it is a major love stone that opens the Heart chakra to unconditional love. Hostile or jealous feelings just do not survive around sugilite.

Jealousy in a relationship is a very destructive emotion. Some men, for example, can throw a jealous rage after seeing their partners just talking to another man. Women can be just as bad, secretly checking their partner's text messages or emails, if they mistrust them. Sugilite can transform these emotions before they threaten to destroy the relationship.

Crystal cure

To cure jealous outbursts, you need to look inside yourself and realize that your partner is normally doing no wrong; it is your insecurities that are causing the jealousy. To change your emotional pattern, sit in a quiet room and pick up your sugilite crystal and place it on your heart. Think of your partner and ask the stone to help release your jealous inclinations. Feel this purple crystal's spiritual vibrations cleansing your heart of negative emotion, eliminating hostility and your possessive tendencies. Let it leave just pure love and tenderness for your partner. Work with the stone until your jealous tantrums cease. Cleanse it well to restore its vitality (see pages 149–153).

CRYSTAL FACTS

CRYSTAL TO USE: sugilite (also known as royal luvilite and royal azel—mauve-pink, purple, often with black manganese inclusions; lower grades are black with purple inclusions), opaque with bands, occasionally translucent, often tumbled

AVAILABILITY: available from specialist stores

QUALITIES OF STONE: an emotional balancer that relieves stress, gives spiritual awareness, brings love and wisdom, protects the inner self from emotional disappointments, disperses jealousy

HEALTH BENEFITS: increases functioning of the pineal, pituitary, and adrenal glands, balances brain hemispheres, improves autism and dyslexia, removes toxins, clears headaches, and is good for pain relief

WHERE TO PLACE THE CRYSTAL: hold to Heart chakra in the center of the chest

Polished

ALTERNATIVE HEALING CRYSTALS TO USE

Peridot: removes negative patterns, releases jealousy and resentment

Watermelon tourmaline: helps to resolve emotional conflict

Moving on a stale relationship with malachite

Working with the right crystal can give you the energetic shift to change a stale relationship into a positive one once more. Malachite is a powerful crystal that lets you express your true feelings. Many people believe it is a stone that attracts money into your life and emotionally it can attract feelings of love that you thought were lost. When you are in a relationship for several years it can become comfortable and settled but you often lose sight of the initial passion and excitement that were a major part of your first months together. Malachite is a transformational stone that wakes up old feelings, letting you feel that love again.

Crystal energizing

The high energetic level of malachite stirs your emotional depths to revitalize your stale relationship. Find a recent photograph of you and your partner, then sit in a dimly lit room holding your malachite crystal with the photograph in front of you. Look at your photograph and remember how you and your partner were in the early, heady days of your relationship. Experience, feel, and sense that initial excitement and sexual attraction. Now ask the crystal to help you recreate those initial feelings. Let its loving vibes inspire you to make some exciting changes with your partner to reawaken your latent passion for each other.

CRYSTAL FACTS

CRYSTAL TO USE: malachite (green), light and dark bands, can be tumbled or polished. Only use in polished form as the dust can be toxic

AVAILABILITY: commonly available

QUALITIES OF STONE: reduces stress and tension, cleanses the aura, removes spiritual blocks, increases hope and happiness, brings emotional balance and harmony, can be transforming

Rough

HEALTH BENEFITS: strengthens heart, boosts blood circulatory system and pineal and pituitary glands, aids sleep, relieves menstrual cramps, alleviates toothache, asthma, arthritis, and swollen joints

WHERE TO PLACE THE CRYSTAL: hold in hands. If you experience mild heart palpitations using malachite, remove and replace with rose quartz

Polished

ALTERNATIVE LOVE-REVIVING CRYSTALS TO USE

Rose quartz: opens up heart, restores harmony, brings change

Rhodonite: transmutes resentments, helps reconciliation in love partnerships

Opal: fosters love and desire, encourages positive emotions

tting go of an unhappy relationship with aventurine

CRYSTAL FACTS

CRYSTAL TO USE: aventurine (green, red, blue, brown, peach/orange), opaque, contains shiny particles

AVAILABILITY: commonly available

QUALITIES OF STONE: relieves troubled emotions, stimulates creativity, attracts money, boosts intuition, promotes perception and decisiveness, encourages emotional recovery and living your own truth

HEALTH BENEFITS: reduces fever and joint inflammation, improves muscle tissue, equalizes blood pressure, lowers cholesterol, stimulates metabolism, alleviates migraines, helps treat skin diseases

WHERE TO PLACE THE CRYSTAL: hold to Heart chakra in middle of chest

Polished

Most aventurine bought today is green. It is a lovely healing crystal that works on attuning the mind, body, and spirit. The rough stone is dull on the surface but is speckled with pieces of hematite and mica that sparkle when you turn it in the light. In magic spells aventurine is worn to strengthen eyesight, but this ability also works spiritually, bringing a clearer insight into your current problems.

A stone that can calm troubled emotions, aventurine can give you the courage to end a relationship or marriage and cope with the sadness, and often bitter feelings that this separation brings. Making that final decision to split up because your love has died is traumatic and can be eased emotionally by this embracing savior that supports you in breaking away from a difficult and painful situation.

Crystal cure

Leaving an unhappy relationship, you can experience relief but also other complex emotions: fear, anger, betrayal, sorrow, or loneliness. To help you deal with these emotions, sit in a quiet room and pick up your aventurine crystal. Close your eyes and hold it to your heart, sensing each emotion you are experiencing, one by one. As each one surfaces, feel the crystal's responsive energy soothing and calming you and offering you a more empathetic way to handle your break up, then slowly come back into the room. Use for several days until you see a positive way forward. Cleanse the stone well (see pages 149–153).

ALTERNATIVE RELEASING CRYSTALS TO USE

Obsidian: dissolves love connections and heals barbs left in heart

Peridot: helps you let go of a relationship, eliminates negative patterns

Polished egg

Reducing bitter arguments with green jade

For thousands of years jade has been renowned in different cultures as a symbol of love, longevity, virtue, and wisdom: the superstitious Chinese wore bird images made from jade to protect and prolong their lives. The purity of the crystal soothes emotional upsets, dispelling any surrounding negativity.

Jade is also a supreme emotional balancer, taking the fire out of an argument, reducing the verbal ricochet. Arguing occasionally with a partner is a normal, healthy interaction between two personalities with different viewpoints, but constant heated arguments where cruel words are spoken can leave you both emotionally drained, damaging your feelings for each other.

Crystal cure

When you want to resolve the dysfunctional side of your relationship, jade can be your nurturing amulet and restore good communication. Take hold of your crystal and ask it to stop the senseless arguments and fill both you and your lover with unconditional love. Feel your joy as you experience this deep, intimate emotion. Cleanse the stone well (see pages 149–153) and place it by your bed so that it can carry on protecting you and promoting a harmonious relationship while you sleep.

CRYSTAL FACTS

Crystal to use: green jade, translucent (jadeite) or creamy (nephrite)

Availability: generally available but can be hard to find; nephrite is more easily available

Qualities of stone: balances emotions, calms the nervous system, releases negative thought patterns, encourages peace and unconditional love, creates inner harmony, releases irritability

Health benefits: strengthens heart and kidneys, removes toxins, eases bladder problems, improves eye disorders, aids fertility

Where to place the crystal: hold in hands, and put by bed

ALTERNATIVE HARMONIZING CRYSTALS TO USE

Emerald: increases love and promotes a balanced relationship

Fluorite: stabilizes relationships, makes you understand emotional needs (right: green fluorite)

Increasing intuition with amethyst earrings

Purple is the color of royalty, and exquisite amethyst jewels have adorned crowns, rings, collars, and bracelets for centuries. A stone of great healing, amethyst aids meditation and increases your spiritual awareness and knowledge. Following your inner guidance helps you to make the right decisions in life. But when you are busy or living a hedonistic lifestyle you can ignore these "nudgings" or "messages" and come off your true life path. Amethyst can help you to connect with your sixth sense—your wisdom or intuition—once more.

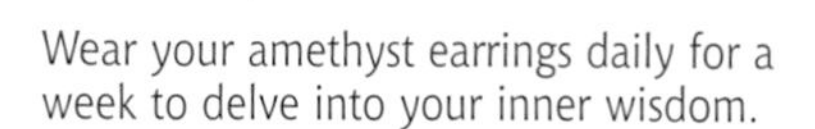

Wear your amethyst earrings daily for a week to delve into your inner wisdom.

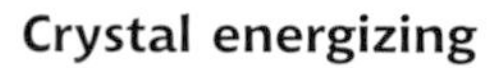

Crystal energizing

When you start listening to your intuition, your mind and spirit merge and are in accord. Wearing purple amethyst earrings helps you become more in tune with your Third eye chakra: your inner vision center. In the past, earrings were worn less for their beauty and decorative appeal and more as protection to keep away negativity and disease from the ears. When you put on your amethyst earrings, sense how you merge with these spiritual crystals, feeling how their gentle emanations are calming your active mind, making you feel less distracted, and letting you hear your deepest emotional needs.

ALTERNATIVE CRYSTAL EARRINGS TO USE

Kyanite: brings compassion, stimulates intuition and psychic abilities

Azurite: cleanses the third eye, increases intuitive knowledge

CRYSTAL FACTS

Crystal to use: amethyst (purple/lavender), polished

Works on: Third eye chakra in the middle of the forehead

Color of chakra: indigo

Qualities of stone: aids meditation, increases intuition and spirituality, reduces stress and tension, focuses decision-making, improves memory, increases motivation. Physically it heals acne and neuralgia, cleanses the blood, and releases the tension of headaches

Deities: Bacchus, Dionysus, Diana

Sacred to: the ancient Greeks, who believed it could prevent drunkenness because of the legend surrounding Dionysus, the god of wine (see page 84). Jewish priests wore it to symbolize spiritual power

Associated with: brainstem (medulla oblongata)

Jewelry: cleanse regularly (see pages 149–153). Do not wear continuously for weeks on end as the effect can be too powerful

Expressing yourself with sacred turquoise

A stone of spiritual self-expression, turquoise is sacred to many ancient religions and cultures, from ancient Egyptians to Tibetan Buddhists. This healing crystal is also associated with truth—"true blue" turquoise was once given to lovers for it signified that, if the stone faded, love faded too. Wearing turquoise can overcome a fear of public speaking. It also encourages you to tell the truth about what you want from others.

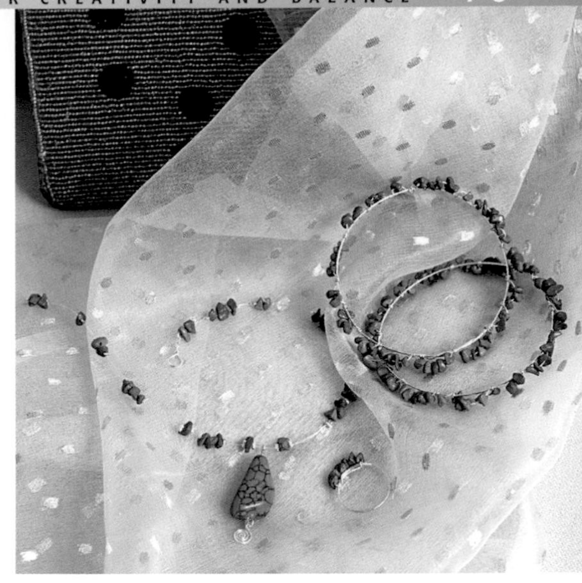

Wear turquoise every day for two weeks until you have released your speech inhibitions.

Crystal energizing

To let your inner voice and thoughts come through so that you can relate your emotions, wear a short turquoise pendant that hangs over your Throat chakra: your spiritual center of communication. To enhance the effectiveness of the crystal, wear turquoise earrings, as these will also work on the throat and help balance the energies in your head. A turquoise bracelet will stimulate the flow of energy in the body's meridians, encouraging you to express yourself well or to talk eloquently on your subject. Navajo Indians use turquoise rings to guard against the evil eye, illness, and accidents, which may be why, traditionally, turquoise was said to be the travelers' or horsemen's stone. Riders wore it for protection, and often placed a tiny stone under their horse's saddle or on the bridle to safeguard their animals. You can use it when traveling too.

CRYSTAL FACTS

CRYSTAL TO USE: turquoise (blue), opaque, often veined

ASSOCIATED WITH: upper lungs and throat

WORKS ON: Throat chakra

COLOR OF CHAKRA: blue

QUALITIES OF STONE: enhances self-expression, releases inhibitions, dispels negativity, brings courage. Physically, has been worn to prevent migraines and calm the nervous system

DEITIES: the Great Spirit, Buddha, Hathor

SACRED TO: Navajo Indians (as the stone of the Great Spirit); Buddhists; ancient Egyptians (Hathor was goddess of beauty, associated with Isis, queen of love and magic)

WEAR IT WITH: gold, its associated metal. Nepali Sherpa brides receive turquoise and gold jewelry as a wedding gift to bring marital happiness, luck, and prosperity

ALTERNATIVE CRYSTAL JEWELRY TO USE

Aquamarine: aids mental clarity, clears blocked communication, increasing self-expression

Lapis lazuli: teaches the importance of the spoken word, encourages self-awareness and speaking inner truth

Rose quartz for higher self-love

Rose quartz is the stone of joy and fulfillment. It will draw love to you whenever you need it, enhancing confidence and self-esteem, and bringing more magic and love to all your relationships. This crystal is also associated with deep healing; perhaps a much-loved partner has left, or your self-respect has been damaged.

CRYSTAL FACTS

Crystal to use: rose quartz (pink), polished or rough

Associated with: the heart and lower lungs

Works on: Heart chakra in middle of your chest

Color of chakra: pink/green

Qualities of stone: purifies the heart, brings compassion, inner healing, and self-love; releases unexpressed emotions. Physically, detoxes the body

Deity: the Great Mother

Sacred to: shamans in many cultures, particularly Cherokee shamans; Wiccans

Wear it with: silver, copper, gold, its associated metals. Do not wear continuously for weeks—the effect can be too powerful

Crystal energizing

To increase self-love and loving emanations to your heart area, you need to wear a long rose quartz pendant that hangs over your Heart chakra, your spiritual energy center of love and compassion, in the center of your chest. If you can find heart-shaped rose quartz, this enhances the love vibrations. Focus on the healing for your heart, so that your rose quartz can carry the message to your inner self.

Wear rose quartz every day for two to four weeks until your love energies are back to full strength.

A love ritual

Rose quartz also promotes fidelity. If you have suffered hurt in your partnership, place a large healing rose quartz crystal by your bed. The Chinese used a variation, where a large rose quartz geode was placed under the left side of the bed (where the woman slept). This was sure to keep a man faithful.

ALTERNATIVE CRYSTAL PENDANTS TO USE

Emerald: balances internal feelings, enhances unconditional love, promoting friendship and partnership

Aventurine: boosts emotional healing and wellbeing, brings compassion and empathy

Balancing emotional disharmony with a garnet bracelet

Wear your garnet bracelet for several days until you feel more emotionally centered.

In ancient times the deep red color of the garnet crystal was said to illuminate the night sky. Its potent qualities were recognized by the Native American Indians, who believed that the crystal's rich color increased the heat of fire and brought healing and enlightenment to their people. This purifying stone brings light into your life and heals a damaged spirit. It can show you the way out in a crisis, turning despair into a challenge after emotional outbursts with a partner at home or a work colleague.

Crystal healing

When your emotions are unstable you can feel very tired and drained. Putting on a fiery, red garnet bracelet grounds your Root chakra and improves your energetic flow. Even when your emotional problems seem insurmountable, this stone's powerful emissions increase your vigor, giving you the necessary courage to find solutions. A very protective stone, in the ancient past garnet was thought to keep away any ghosts or demons. As you put on your bracelet, notice how your ghosts start to leave, and feel you have the support and the confidence to handle anything.

Crystal facts

Crystal to use: garnet (red), transparent or translucent, polished

Associated with: lower pelvic area and adrenal glands

Works on: affects Root chakra at bottom of spine and body's meridians

Color of chakra: red

Qualities of stone: stimulates love and compassion, increases imagination, encourages self-confidence and success, cleanses and re-energizes chakras, strengthens survival instinct. Physically it protects against infection, purifies the bloodstream, boosts the heart and lungs, and stimulates the metabolism

Sacred to: Mayans, Aztecs, and Native American Indians to enhance the potency of fire

Jewelry: cleanse regularly (see pages 149–153). Do not wear continuously for weeks as the effects can be too powerful

Alternative crystal bracelets to use

Citrine: releases negative emotions, promotes joy in life

Rhodonite: emotional balancer, shows both sides of a problem

Taking control of your life with a jet necklace

Just like amber, jet is an unusual crystal that becomes electrically charged when it is rubbed. Choose carefully when buying jet as many pieces sold today are just black glass. A solid, glasslike dark crystal, jet has strong protective qualities and in the olden days was worn to protect against dark spirits. Today it can guard against unreasonable worries or fears: it evens out mood swings and can stop you feeling depressed. Jet can help in times when your life seems to spiral out of control with too many projects at work, or a demanding family to look after.

Crystal energizing

If you are starting to lose control, wearing a long jet necklace will help to harmonize the energy flow in your stressed meridians, allowing you to slow down and stabilize your emotions. Put on the necklace and sense how the crystal's properties are calming your nervous system and balancing your stress. Do not lend this stone to anyone as it is believed to become part of you, showing your personality.

Wear your jet necklace for several days to get your life back on track.

CRYSTAL FACTS

Crystal to use: jet (black), polished

Associated with: all organs

Works on: body's meridians

Qualities of stone: reduces fear and depressed feelings, protective, boosts psychic abilities, helps take control of life, emotional balancer, removes negative energy. Physically it can ease menstrual cramps, relieves stomach ache, and soothes the pain of migraines

Deity: Cybele, the goddess of growth

Sacred to: ancient Greeks who worshipped Cybele

Jewelry: cleanse regularly (see pages 149–153). Do not wear continuously for weeks as the effects can be too powerful

ALTERNATIVE CRYSTAL JEWELRY TO USE

Sodalite: calms panic attacks, brings emotional balance and self-trust

Onyx: brings self-control and a more stable way of living

Following your spiritual path with blue sapphire earrings

An eye-catching, tranquil crystal, the blue sapphire is a wisdom stone that lets you seek your spiritual truth. It focuses and stills the mind, allowing you to dismiss unwanted thoughts. In today's world, it can be hard to stay on your spiritual path: your job may pay well but suppress your creativity, or you may have a partner who discourages spiritual development. The sapphire resolves any spiritual confusion, giving you the wisdom and confidence to make the right changes.

Wearing sapphire for up to one week can help illuminate your spiritual path.

Crystal energizing

Sapphire is known as the jewel of truth and clarity, the stone of destiny that helps you achieve your dreams. To open yourself up to your spiritual desires, wear blue sapphire earrings. The energetic impulse of this beautiful stone enhances your psychic abilities and opens your Throat chakra, your communication center, more fully, so that you express your needs. In magic spells a sapphire increased the potency of the spell or brought prosperity: use it to bring the spiritual abundance you are seeking.

CRYSTAL FACTS

CRYSTAL TO USE: blue sapphire, polished or cut

ASSOCIATED WITH: upper lungs, throat, thyroid, and parathyroid glands

WORKS ON: head energies and Throat chakra

COLOR OF CHAKRA: turquoise blue

QUALITIES OF STONE: inspires imagination and creativity, gives peace of mind, attracts friendship, love, and good luck, facilitates self-expression, develops psychic abilities. Physically it stimulates the pituitary gland and complete glandular system, soothes the eyes, and relieves insomnia

DEITIES: Apollo

SACRED TO: ancient Greeks who wore the stone when visiting oracles

JEWELRY: cleanse regularly (see pages 149–153). Do not wear continuously for weeks as the effects can be too powerful

ALTERNATIVE CRYSTAL EARRINGS TO USE

Agate: encourages quiet contemplation to stimulate spiritual growth (right: green moss agate)

Topaz: helps spiritual development, connects you to inner wisdom (right: golden topaz)

Overcoming mistakes with a snowflake obsidian ring

Wear your snowflake obsidian ring for several days to clear the negative events in your life.

This delightful black crystal with its whitish crystallite snowflakes is actually volcanic glass, formed when the lava cooled. A calming, soothing stone, snowflake obsidian is also called flowering obsidian; it helps you to recognize stressful mental attitudes and teaches you that life is a learning curve. Sometimes we have to make mistakes to gain experience from them. A failed business relationship, or course can linger on in our psyches as mistakes, and this crystal of change helps you release these distorted thought patterns.

CRYSTAL FACTS

Crystal to use: snowflake obsidian (mottled black and white), polished

Associated with: all organs

Works on: body's meridians

Qualities of stone: absorbs and releases negativity, reduces mental stress, grounding, fosters inner wisdom and introspection, clears the mind of confusion, harmonizes mind, body, and spirit. Physically it aids the stomach and digestion, alleviates joint pain, helps arthritis, benefits the circulation of blood

Deities: Aztec—Tezcatlipoca ("smoking mirror" or "shining mirror")

Jewelry: cleanse regularly (see pages 149–153). Do not wear continuously for weeks as the effects can be too powerful

Crystal energizing

When emotions relating to past events or mistakes need releasing from your subconscious, wear a snowflake obsidian ring on the ring finger (third from thumb) of your left hand. In the past this finger was believed to have special powers, and herbal medicines were often applied to the body using this finger. Rings were also considered sacred and magical as the ancient gods and goddesses wore them. To allow some magic into your life and increase your energetic flow, put the ring on your finger, and, mentally run through these events, sensing and feeling the special powers of this crystal turning them around so that you see their positive aspects.

ALTERNATIVE CRYSTAL RINGS TO USE

Peridot: helps to see mistakes, accept their guidance, and move on

Rhodonite: clears past emotional wounds, encourages self-esteem

Checking for physical illness with a pendulum

If your energetic field is blocked or lacks good energy flow (see page 57) you can eventually become ill. If you are suffering from confusing physical symptoms, or are unsure what organ is malfunctioning, you can diagnose the area that needs treating with a pendulum.

Crystal diagnosing

To use your pendulum, see page 19. A clockwise swing is normally "yes," although it can be opposite. "No" is generally counterclockwise. A side-to-side swinging movement indicates "don't know." Now sit in a quiet room and test your organs from your lower pelvis to your head. Hold the pendulum over each area and ask: "Are these organs healthy?" If you get a "no" or "don't know" response to an area of your body, treat it for 10 minutes daily for a week with a relevant crystal (see box). The color of the crystal resonates with the vibrations of the organ you are treating. For example, if you are having trouble with your stomach, golden beryl's yellow vibration will help to correct the imbalance in your stomach.

ORGANS AND CRYSTALS

Organs and glands	Color	Crystals
Lower pelvis—adrenals	red	red jasper, ruby, red tiger's eye
Pelvic area—kidneys, bladder, intestines, ovaries, gonads	orange	carnelian, amber, orange calcite
Below breastbone—spleen, stomach, liver, and pancreas	yellow	citrine, golden topaz, golden beryl (heliodor)
Middle of chest—lower lungs and heart	green (rose)	rose quartz, aventurine, chrysoprase
Middle of throat—upper lungs and throat, thymus	turquoise blue	turquoise, lapis lazuli, chrysocolla
Middle of forehead—brainstem, pituitary and pineal glands	indigo	amethyst, sodalite, azurite
Top of head—brain and pineal glands	violet (white)	clear quartz, lepidolite, violet fluorite

CRYSTAL FACTS

Crystal to use: natural quartz pendulum with chain

Availability: commonly available from crystal stores

Qualities of stone: receives, transmits, and amplifies energy, increases psychic abilities and intuition, dispels negativity

Health benefits: heals any condition, stimulates pineal and pituitary glands, relieves headache and toothache

Where to place the crystal: move pendulum over body

How dowsing with a pendulum works: a natural quartz pendulum is a valuable diagnostic tool: allowing you to ask questions of your subconscious. Answers come through the electromagnetic energies emitted by your hand moving the pendulum

Curing headaches with amethyst

Cluster

In Greek mythology a young maiden called Amethyst was turned into white quartz by Artemis, goddess of fertility, after Dionysus, god of wine, tried to kill her when he realized she didn't drink alcohol. Remorseful of his deed, Dionysus cried and dropped his wine goblet, and the flowing red wine ran over the quartz crystal turning it into the stone we know today as amethyst. Since then, the crystal has been renowned for its ability to cure hangovers.

Amethyst is a purifying and protective crystal. Its color, purple is associated with spirituality and brings inner vision and psychic awareness. Well known as a healer, many years ago amethyst was often rubbed into the face with saliva to heal pimples and flaky skin. It is also believed to be a great pain-reliever, and its calming vibrations may be used to relieve the constricting tension of headaches when the muscles and blood vessels around the scalp and neck tighten, bringing pain and discomfort.

CRYSTAL FACTS

Crystal to use: amethyst (purple/lavender), geode, cluster or single point

Availability: commonly available

Qualities of stone: ideal meditation crystal, increases psychic abilities, calms and protects, relieves stress and tension, lifts the spirit, gives mental focus, promotes spiritual wisdom

Health benefits: strengthens functioning of endocrine and immune systems, alleviates acne, neuralgia and insomnia, cleanses the blood, heals respiratory disease, eases headaches

Where to place the crystal: hold to head

Crystal healing

To reduce the pain of a headache, sit in a darkened room and pick up your amethyst crystal; clasp the stone tightly to connect to its healing properties. Now place the stone on the part of your head or neck that is painful for 5–10 minutes. Let the cool crystal soothe your pain. Cleanse it well after use (see pages 149–153). If your headaches are regular, do seek medical advice.

ALTERNATIVE TENSION-RELEASING CRYSTALS TO USE

Larimar: draws out pain, relieves constricted blood vessels

Magnesite: relaxes muscle tension, eases headaches

Smoky quartz: alleviates pain, reduces muscle restriction

Easing stomach ache with amber

Nicias, an ancient Greek, wrote in the 5th century BCE that amber was the essence of the setting sun, which had congealed in the sea and been cast up on the shore. This bright, sunny stone is not actually a crystal but a fossilized resin, first formed between 360 and one million years ago. As the resin oozed from pine trees, insects and plant material were trapped in the flow that fossilized into amber. In the past, beads of amber were often worn to prevent digestive problems as the stone is thought to be able to remove disease from the body, absorb pain, and let the body heal itself. Its yellowy orange color links to the unique vibrations of the stomach so it can ease the pain of stomach ache or an upset brought on by indigestion as a result of overeating or eating spicy foods.

Crystal healing

To soothe stomach pain, sit in a quiet room and hold the stone in your hands for a few minutes to sense its warming energies. Now place it on your stomach for about ten minutes, or until your pain subsides, as this cleansing stone clears the disturbance in your stomach and rebalances your body's energetic flow. Cleanse the stone after use to restore vitality (see pages 149–153). Do seek medical advice if symptoms persist, and/or are acute.

CRYSTAL FACTS

CRYSTAL TO USE: amber (yellow, orange, golden/brown), transparent or opaque; some have insects or vegetation trapped inside, as it is actually a fossilized tree resin

AVAILABILITY: commonly available, but beware of imitations. One way to check if it is genuine is to make a saltwater solution with 1 tablespoon salt in a glass bowl of water and place the amber in it. If it floats it is amber, if it sinks it is artificial

QUALITIES OF STONE: encourages compassion, changes negative energy into positive, helps with depressive tendencies, inspires the intellect, aids self-expression, brings wisdom, can release pent-up emotions, protects from radiation from sun, x-rays, and computers

HEALTH BENEFITS: boosts endocrine system, spleen, heart, liver, and bladder, reduces earache and asthma symptoms, gives vitality, can remove disease from body, treats throat problems, heals the stomach

WHERE TO PLACE THE CRYSTAL: hold to stomach

Polished

ALTERNATIVE STOMACH PAIN-RELIEVING CRYSTALS TO USE

Yellow jasper: releases toxins and eases stomach pain

Labradorite: regulates metabolism, heals stomach pain (right: polished egg)

Rough

Relieving PMS and menstrual cramps with moonstone

Sacred to all the lunar goddesses, moonstone is a beautiful, feminine, and loving crystal. As it links to the moon in the night sky, placing a crystal under your pillow is thought to bring blissful rest. Moonstone is also a fertility talisman, and in the Arab world women often sewed moonstones into their clothing to help them get pregnant. The crystal merges with the waxing and waning cycle of the moon, so is thought to have a balancing effect on the female menstrual cycle. Its calming energy may help ease the symptoms of premenstrual syndrome (PMS), such as irritability, depression, fatigue, a bloated stomach, and headache.

CRYSTAL FACTS

Crystal to use: moonstone (white, cream, yellow, blue, brown, green) cloudy and translucent

Availability: commonly available

Qualities of stone: balances emotions, reduces tendency to overreact, increases inner wisdom and clairvoyance, relieves anxiety, increases sensitivity, attracts happiness, removes old emotional patterns

Health benefits: reduces menstrual problems and PMS, lessens fluid retention, boosts lymphatic system, good for fertility and breastfeeding, detoxes the body, an essence can help insomnia

Where to place the crystal: hold to pelvic region or wear as jewelry

Crystal healing

To lessen the effects of PMS, sit in a quiet room a week or so before your period is due and pick up your moonstone. Connect to its healing energies and hold it on your pelvis for about 10 minutes, feeling its delicate vibration evaporating any tension, tearfulness, or tiredness. Repeat daily for a week. If when your period starts you suffer from cramps, hold your stone to your pelvis. Close your eyes and visualize the pain leaving your body; keep the stone in position until you feel some relief. Cleanse the stone after treatment to keep it vibrant (see pages 149–153).

ALTERNATIVE PMS/CRAMP-RELIEVING CRYSTALS TO USE

Chrysocolla: alleviates menstrual cramps, treats PMS

Labradorite: balances hormone levels, improves PMS (right: rough labradorite)

Jet: balances mood swings, relieves menstrual cramps

Alleviating menopausal symptoms with citrine

Cluster

Citrine deposits are becoming increasingly rare, and most citrine that is sold today was once amethyst, heat-treated to a high temperature to attain the stone's yellow color and vibration. Red tints on the stone distinguish it from the more lemony, natural citrine, although in natural citrine red tints can indicate the presence of hematite. A wonderful, sunny stone, citrine is a powerful cleanser and energizer, never needing cleansing itself. It protects the aura, the body's energy field, and in ancient times was carried as a protective stone against deadly snake venom. The inspiring yellow color of the crystal has the power to stimulate the intellect and improve memory and concentration. Physically the stone can also even out the hormonal imbalances that cause some of the more unpleasant symptoms of the menopause. Drinking a revitalizing citrine essence can lessen the severity of hot flashes or night sweats, both symptoms that plague many menopausal women.

Crystal healing

Make your gem essence by rinsing the citrine under running water and placing it in a glass container or jar. Fill with still mineral water to cover the stone. Cover and place on a sunny table or windowsill for 1 or 2 hours or longer. Strain some of the liquid into a glass, keeping the rest. Drink the essence when you are feeling low or suffering a hot flash and feel how the crystal starts to lower your temperature and lift your mood. Drink whenever needed.

CRYSTAL FACTS

CRYSTAL TO USE: citrine (yellow, yellow/brown), often a geode point or cluster

AVAILABILITY: natural citrine can be hard to find; citrine produced by heat-treating amethyst is commonly available

QUALITIES OF STONE: lifts self-esteem, warms and energizes, brings hope, controls emotions, clarifies mental processes, improves memory, cleanses chakras, a beneficial stone linked to abundance

HEALTH BENEFITS: aids tissue regeneration, improves circulation, lessens anxiety and depression, alleviates digestive problems, helps heal kidney and bladder infections, works on hormonal and menopausal symptoms

WHERE TO PLACE THE CRYSTAL: make a gem essence

ALTERNATIVE MENOPAUSE-RELIEVING CRYSTALS TO USE

Lepidolite: relieves exhaustion, aids menopausal symptoms

Blue tourmaline: relieves distressing menopausal night sweats

Helping backache with rutilated quartz

Rutilated quartz is an attractive clear crystal with colorful golden rutile, copper, or blue titanium fibers that glow in the light. Like all quartzes it is a powerful healing stone that amplifies energy flow. In physical ailments it is thought to detoxify the blood of waste products, and stimulate the body's innate healing force, reducing inflammation caused by damaged back muscles—from an accident or postural problems. The crystal can also encourage the regeneration of body tissue, speeding up healing.

CRYSTAL FACTS

Crystal to use: rutilated quartz (milky with silver, gold, copper-colored, brown, red, or black strands), also known as angel hair

Availability: commonly available

Qualities of stone: alleviates depression, helps inspiration, soothes dark moods, aids transition

Health benefits: regenerates cells and repairs damaged body tissue, boosts immune system, helps chronic pain

Where to place the crystal: hold it on the painful area of your back

Cut and polished

Crystal healing

If you suffer a painful attack of back pain, lie flat on your bed and place your rutilated quartz crystal under the painful area for about 15 minutes, letting the crystal's strong energy focus on dissipating the pain and encourage healing in the inflamed tissues, muscles, or discs. Someone can also work on the pain by circling the crystal clockwise over the affected area for 15 minutes, "pulling" out the negative energy. Use the crystal regularly until the pain goes. Cleanse it well to keep vibrant (see pages 149–153).

ALTERNATIVE BACKACHE-RELIEVING CRYSTALS TO USE

Magnetite: acts as an antispasmodic and relaxes muscles

Fire opal: re-energizes, its vibrations relieve pain in lower back

Smoky quartz: alleviates pain, strengthens back muscles (right: polished)

Soothing physical pain with carnelian

Polished

CRYSTAL FACTS

CRYSTAL TO USE: carnelian

AVAILABILITY: commonly available

QUALITIES OF STONE: energizes and aids motivation and mental focus, releases negative patterns

HEALTH BENEFITS: increases fertility, helps tissue regeneration, treats sores, muscular spasms, and wounds, treats rheumatism and arthritis

WHERE TO PLACE THE CRYSTAL: hold it on affected area

The word carnelian, or cornelian, may be derived from the Latin word *carne*, which means "flesh," a reference to the orangey red coloring of the stone, which is caused by the presence of iron oxides. This high-energy stone is believed to be particularly good at removing blockages and neutralizing the pain associated with ailments such as neuralgia, fever, infection, and muscular pain, and also treating nosebleeds.

Physical pain is the result of special sensory nerve endings being stimulated and sending pain messages to the brain because of bodily injury or disease. Energetically, a blockage, an excess of energy, or an imbalance in the body's energy channels (meridians) causes the physical pain that you feel, and all energy blockages need to be removed or harmonized to restore health and wellbeing.

Crystal healing

If you experience a nagging pain that does not seem to want to go away, you can help to remove the discomfort by using a carnelian crystal. Place the stone on or over the source of your pain for about 15 minutes to let the crystal do its work. As the throbbing pain begins to improve, remove the stone and cleanse it well (see pages 149–153).

ALTERNATIVE PAIN-RELIEVING CRYSTALS TO USE

Lapis lazuli: gentle pain reliever, helps headaches, boosts immune system

Blue calcite: dissolves pains, soothes pain, and removes anxiety

Magnetite: removes blockages, is anti-inflammatory, helps muscle strain or painful cramps

Treating colds and flu with fluorite

Polished

Many healers call fluorite the "genius" stone, as they believe it opens new pathways for the mind. As it is such a tactile and spiritual stone, communing with it can bring ideas from the spirit world into our own reality. Physically, using a green fluorite crystal, or drinking a crystal essence, can relieve nasty cold symptoms such as runny nose or sore throat, or can reduce the fever, aching muscles, and debilitating fatigue of the flu virus. It is believed that the crystal draws any negativity from the body, clearing the virus. A wonderful healing color, the green of the stone is also thought to encourage tissue and cell growth, while generally restoring body health.

CRYSTAL FACTS

CRYSTAL TO USE: green fluorite, transparent

AVAILABILITY: commonly available

QUALITIES OF STONE: protective psychic stone, increases concentration, aids meditation, grounds energy, helps to focus mind and store information, cleanses aura, boosts self-confidence, clears emotional trauma

HEALTH BENEFITS: reduces dental disease, relieves pneumonia, helps viral infection, reduces inflammation, strengthens teeth and bones and cells, reduces body toxins, relieves stomach disorders, alleviates arthritis and rheumatism

WHERE TO PLACE THE CRYSTAL: hold to nose, head, or chest, or use as essence

Crystal healing

Sit in a quiet room and hold your crystal in your hands and feel its medicinal pulsations. For a cold, place the stone over your nose for 5 minutes and then on your forehead for the same time, letting the stone fight the virus and clear congestion. For flu, hold the stone to your chest for 10 minutes, and sense the crystal's vibrations lowering your fever. Alternatively, drink a fluorite crystal essence (see page 16). Use the stone every few hours until you feel better, then cleanse it well (see pages 149–153).

ALTERNATIVE COLD/FLU-RELIEVING CRYSTALS TO USE

Moss agate: boosts immune system, treats infection, lowers fever

Jet: relieves aches and pains, reduces cold symptoms

Helping eczema with blue calcite

Rough

Blue calcite is a very cleansing crystal that can absorb any negative vibrations that have become "stuck" in the physical body or the aura (our energetic field). Often used in purification ceremonies to add a brightness to the atmosphere, calcite can remove any lingering stagnancy from the environment. A well-known pain reliever, the crystal can be used to soothe the sore red skin and the itching sensations of eczema. Its healing rays are believed to cool hot and inflamed skin and act as a natural antiseptic.

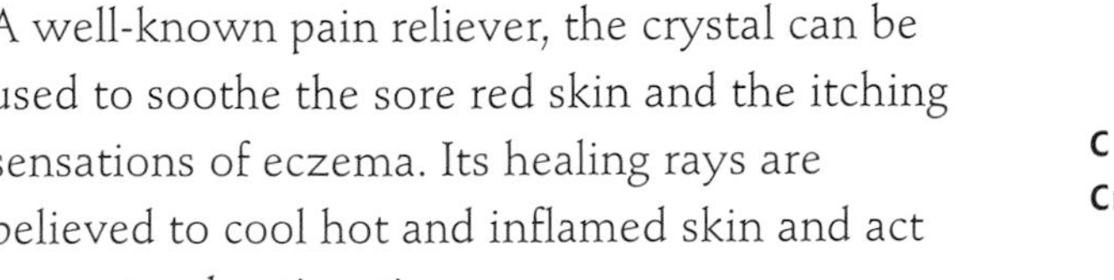

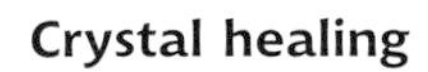

Crystal healing

To ease your eczema, sit in a quiet room and pick up your blue calcite crystal and tune in to its cleansing qualities. Place or hold the stone over your irritated skin for about 5 minutes each time. You may feel a slight tingling as this gentle crystal works on relieving the pain and healing the affected skin tissue. Alternatively, make a calcite essence (to make, see page 16) and dab it on the skin. Repeat every few hours until you feel the itchy sensations abating. Cleanse the stone regularly to revitalize its energies (see pages 149–153).

CRYSTAL FACTS

Crystal to use: blue calcite, translucent, waxy texture, can be banded (may be treated with acid to increase color)

Availability: commonly available

Qualities of stone: reduces stress and fear, balances emotions, inspires joy, speeds up spiritual development, cleanses negative energies, increases spiritual development, soothes nerves, calms anxieties

Health benefits: lowers blood pressure, heals back pain, alleviates skin conditions, aids kidneys, pancreas, and spleen, helps to strengthen skeleton and joints, boosts immune system

Where to place the crystal: hold to affected area or use as essence

Rough

ALTERNATIVE SKIN PAIN-RELIEVING CRYSTALS TO USE

Brown jasper: reduces inflammation, treats skin disorders

Moonstone: alleviates eruptions, relieves stress (right: opaque polished moonstone)

Relieving earache with rose quartz

Polished

The healing rays of rose quartz envelop the body like a soothing, cozy blanket. Emotionally this stone brings peace and forgiveness after heartbreak, a reminder that we can be happy and make our dreams come true. This lovely pink stone is also known as the children's stone, because it is thought to be effective at healing the childhood ailments and upsets that may follow us into adulthood. Earache, caused by an infection of the inner ear, is one childhood ailment which as adults we may also suffer from. The healing vibration of rose quartz is believed to help to fight the infection and give comforting pain relief.

CRYSTAL FACTS

Crystal to use: rose quartz (pink), translucent, sometimes tumbled

Availability: commonly available

Qualities of stone: can clear resentment, anger, guilt, or fear, relieves emotional trauma, opens you up to beauty, promotes romantic love, increases empathy and a sensitive attitude, supreme healer of pain

Health benefits: benefits the kidneys and circulatory system, increases fertility, releases waste products, soothes headaches, migraines, sore throat, earache, and burns, improves the complexion

Where to place the crystal: hold to ear

Crystal healing

To reduce the pain of earache, place your rose quartz crystal in a warm towel and hold it to your ear or your child's ear for about 10 minutes. Alternatively, put it inside the cover of a hot water bottle filled with warm water and hold it to the ear. Feel how the gentle emissions of this beautiful, compassionate stone are penetrating deep into the inner ear and reducing your pain. Work with the stone every few hours until the pain starts to diminish, then cleanse it well to keep it vibrant (see pages 149–151). Do consult a medical professional if symptoms continue or are acute.

ALTERNATIVE PAIN-RELIEVING CRYSTALS TO USE

Amber: can draw illness out of the body, absorbs pain of earache

Celestite: heals ear disorders, eliminates pain

Blue fluorite: amplifies healing potential, good pain relief for ear problems (right: green/blue purple banded fluorite)

Rough

Easing hay fever with blue lace agate

It is hard to feel anxious around blue lace agate. This serene crystal resonates peace and calm. In ancient home rituals, the stone was placed between two lit blue candles to reduce stress and quarrels and bring a harmonious atmosphere. The stone has a particular affinity with the Throat chakra, releasing any anger or unease that may have blocked communication, letting you calmly express your feelings. Physically, the cooling blue vibes of the gem can cool the heat of fevers. With allergic ailments, such as hay fever, it is thought to appease immune system reactions to pollen or molds, soothing irritating sneezing, itchy eyes, and nasal congestion. Using this crystal may also help when you don't have your regular remedy to hand.

Polished

CRYSTAL FACTS

CRYSTAL TO USE: blue lace agate, has white and light blue lines, banded, can be tumbled

AVAILABILITY: commonly available

QUALITIES OF STONE: helps to express thoughts and feelings, releases fears of rejection and repression, relieves stress and tension, works on Throat chakra to release blockages, neutralizes anger, and brings peace

HEALTH BENEFITS: heals throat infections, reduces inflammation and fevers, treats arthritis and bone problems, relieves shoulder and neck problems

WHERE TO PLACE THE CRYSTAL: hold to nose and face

Crystal healing

To ease hay fever symptoms, sit in a quiet room and pick up your blue agate. Hold it, connecting with its peaceful and tranquil energy. Hold the stone over your nose for about 5 minutes, letting its therapeutic emissions work on your inflamed nasal passages. Now move the crystal to your sinuses either side of your nose and hold for a few minutes on each side so that the stone's cooling energy eases the congestion and relieves your eyes. Use the crystal daily in the hay fever season, cleansing it after each session (see pages 149–153).

ALTERNATIVE HAY FEVER-RELIEVING CRYSTALS

Aquamarine: balances the reactions of the immune system in hay fever

Moss agate: an anti-inflammatory stone that boosts the immune system

Sodalite: increases functioning of immune system

Polished

Alleviating toothache with aquamarine essence

Aquamarine has a gentle and compassionate energy, and its beautiful light blue color resonates with the sea. Many legends surround this connection. One says that the stone was found hidden in the treasure chest of a mermaid.

Aquamarine's curative powers make it a lucky charm for the wearer who wants to stay healthy. Well known for stimulating and cleansing the Throat chakra, its cool energy can treat the irritation of a sore throat and swollen glands. The healing blue rays of the stone also resonate at the same rate as healthy cells in the jaw, so can correct the vibrational level of the damaged cells that are causing the dull throbbing pain or sharp twinges of toothache. When you have an interminable wait to see your dentist, an aquamarine remedy may help.

CRYSTAL FACTS

Crystal to use: aquamarine (green/blue), clear and opaque, faceted, can be small and tumbled

Availability: commonly available

Qualities of stone: clears the mind, sharpens the intellect, lessens fears, helps creative self-expression, brings peace and calm, protects the aura, increases intuition

Health benefits: strengthens kidneys, liver, spleen and thyroid, relieves throat and stomach troubles, soothes toothache, eases fluid retention, can help hay fever

How to use the crystal: make a crystal essence with it

Crystal healing

Rinsing your mouth with a curative aquamarine essence (see also page 16) may reduce pain and soothe any gum inflammation that accompanies tooth decay, a fracture in the tooth, or an abscess. It can also strengthen your immune system so that your body rallies to fight the infection. To make the essence, rinse your aquamarine crystal under running water, then place in a glass container or a jar and fill with still mineral water. Cover and leave on a table or windowsill in the sun for about 1–2 hours, or leave this stone in moonlight for 3 hours; the longer you leave the essence the more potent it will be. Strain some liquid into a glass; reserve the rest. Wash the liquid around your mouth and over your affected tooth, feeling how this cleansing essence is reducing your acute twinges of pain. Repeat every 2 hours.

ALTERNATIVE TOOTH-PAIN CRYSTALS TO USE

Amber: draws disease from the body, eases tooth pain

Lapis lazuli: great pain reliever, helps tooth discomfort and boosts immune system

Fluorite: powerful healer, regenerates gums, strengthens tooth (right: purple fluorite)

Soothing joint pain with rhodonite

Polished

Rhodonite is a peaceful and joyful pink crystal that opens up the Heart chakra to unconditional love. A "rescue" stone, it can ward off negative influences, raise self-worth and cleanse you of any limiting doubts you may have. Deeply rooted emotions can hold us back: rhodonite releases old fears or stubborn pride, emotions often held in the joints, which may manifest physically as a joint sprain, a damaged joint capsule, or the loss of protective cartilage associated with arthritis. The nurturing pink vibrations of the crystal can give some relief to the joint pain and encourage the growth of new, healthy bone and cartilage.

CRYSTAL FACTS

CRYSTAL TO USE: rhodonite (pink), mottled effect, often has flecks of black, can be tumbled

AVAILABILITY: commonly available

QUALITIES OF STONE: improves memory, reduces emotional trauma, lowers stress and calms the mind, raises self-esteem, clears out painful emotion, encourages forgiveness

HEALTH BENEFITS: balances central nervous system, improves hearing, heals wounds, aids bone growth, reduces joint inflammation and arthritic pain, can be drunk as an essence for shock or trauma

WHERE TO PLACE THE CRYSTAL: on the affected joint

Crystal healing

To reduce the swelling of a painful joint injury or inflamed arthritic joints, take your compassionate crystal in your hands and feel a tingling as you sense its healing powers. Sit down comfortably and place the stone on your painful joint, or even tape it in position. Leave for 10–15 minutes. You may feel a slight warmth as the crystal works on releasing any fear or inflexibility held in the joint, while also reducing the heat of the existing inflammation or injury. Repeat every day for a week or until you see some improvement. Cleanse your stone daily (see pages 149–153).

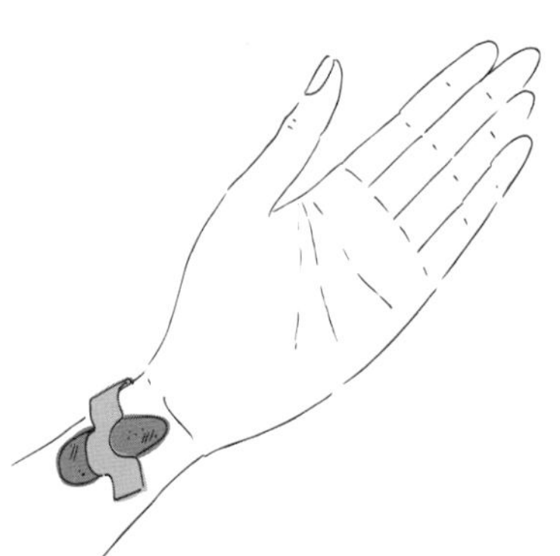

ALTERNATIVE JOINT-HEALING CRYSTALS TO USE

Malachite: reduces swelling in joints, treats arthritis (use polished stone)

Obsidian: detoxifies and reduces joint pain, relieves arthritic discomfort

Fluorite: helps to mobilize joint, gives pain relief, and treats arthritis (right: green fluorite)

Soothing a sore throat with beryl

Polished

Today beryl is associated with helping to ease a sore throat; historically, it was prized as a stone of the voice and for eloquence, yet may, equally, be used as a shield to protect against heavy persuasion or a hard sell. Some people use this crystal to help them find an item that they have lost, just as a crystal essence made with beryl may treat a sore throat, perhaps helping you to recover your lost voice.

Crystal healing

If you have a sore throat you can treat it with a crystal essence (see also page 16) made with water and a beryl crystal. This potent crystal is associated with increasing your immunity to toxins and pollutants and works on the invading infection.

A crystal essence is easy to make. Rinse your beryl crystal under running water then place it in a glass container or jar. Fill with still mineral water until the stone is covered. Cover and place on a table or windowsill to be bathed in sunlight. Ideally leave for 1–12 hours: the longer you leave it, the stronger the essence. Strain some of the liquid from the stone into a glass; keep the rest. Add half a teaspoon of sea salt, which acts as a natural antiseptic. Gargle briefly and repeat every 2 hours until you feel the crystal's potency helping your throat to feel better.

CRYSTAL FACTS

Crystal to use: beryl (pink, golden, yellow, green, white, blue) can be transparent and pyramid shape

Availability: commonly available

Qualities of stone: reduces stress, increases willpower, helps in realizing potential, relaxes the mind

Health benefits: helps heart problems and liver upsets, treats stomach and throat infections, strengthens circulatory system

How to use the crystal: make a crystal essence by soaking the stone in mineral water

ALTERNATIVE THROAT-RELIEVING CRYSTALS TO USE

Blue lace agate: reduces fever and fights throat and lymph infections

Aquamarine: great tonic, relieves sore throat and swollen glands

Improving immune system function with turquoise

Rough

Turquoise is a very supportive and strengthening crystal that is thought to give protection against environmental pollution and viral infections, and aid tissue regeneration. When we work too hard, eat unhealthily, and do not get enough sleep our immune system can become compromised, so it is vital to keep it healthy and functioning at its best.

Prized by ancient cultures, turquoise is regarded as sacred to some shamans because of its powerful healing ability. In healing visualizations, turquoise is believed to "absorb" the illness from the patient. It's also a symbol of prosperity, luck, and loyalty.

CRYSTAL FACTS

CRYSTAL TO USE: turquoise (blue), normally veined, often polished

AVAILABILITY: commonly available

QUALITIES OF STONE: aids intuition and creative thoughts, enhances communication, removes negative energy

HEALTH BENEFITS: strengthens entire body, boosts immune system, helps body to take in nutrients, helps tissue renewal

WHERE TO PLACE THE CRYSTAL: around the chest area

Crystal healing

If you are starting to feel run down, don't wait until you catch a cold or get the flu before you pay attention to the needs of your immune system. Take your crystal in your hand and connect with its healing energies, then ask it to keep you strong and free from illness. Slowly move it in clockwise circles for a few minutes around your chest area, feeling its positive emanations boosting your immunity to infection. Repeat daily to keep you well.

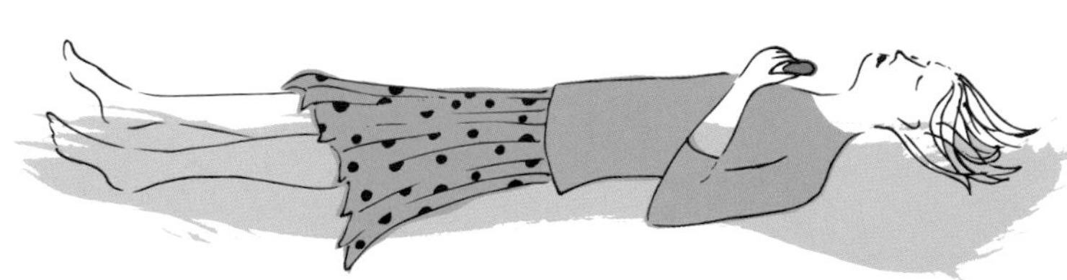

ALTERNATIVE IMMUNE-BOOSTING CRYSTALS TO USE

Moss agate: encourages removal of waste products, enhances immune system

Snow quartz: stimulates immune system, balances body

Brown jasper: clears toxins, strengthens immune system

Reducing travel sickness with yellow jasper

Jasper is available in a variety of colors. Yellow jasper occurs when the crystal is mixed with goethite, a yellow mineral of hydrated iron oxide. A powerful healer, it sustains the body during times of stress, giving the courage to attack problems head on.

Back in ancient Egypt, King Nechepsus always wore green jasper engraved with a dragon surrounded by rays to strengthen his digestive tract, and today jasper's curative properties are still used to strengthen digestion. Yellow jasper, in particular, may treat the discomfort of stomach upsets, and can relieve the nausea and vomiting of travel sickness. It may also stabilize the organ of balance in the inner ear, which gets disrupted by travel motion, bringing on the unpleasant queasy feelings.

Crystal healing

In the past jasper was worn as an amulet to keep away illness, so keep travel sickness at bay by taking out your jasper at the start of your journey. Hold it for about 5 minutes on each inner ear, then move it to your stomach for a further 10 minutes, feeling how this grounding, centered stone is balancing the functioning of the organs in these areas and making you feel better. Keep moving the crystal between your ears and stomach for the rest of the journey. Cleanse it well after treatment (see pages 149–153).

Polished

CRYSTAL FACTS

Crystal to use: yellow jasper, an opaque variety of chalcedony, can be patterned, sometimes water-worn, can be small and tumbled

Availability: commonly available

Qualities of stone: nurturing stone that supports during stress, absorbs negative energies, clears environmental pollution, inspires imagination, and promotes clear thinking

Health benefits: boosts endocrine system, strengthens kidneys and liver, protects when traveling, alleviates stomach problems, soothes travel sickness or bilious attacks, releases toxins

Where to place the crystal: hold it to ears and stomach

ALTERNATIVE SICKNESS-RELIEVING CRYSTALS TO USE

Malachite: reduces stomach cramps, helps travel sickness

Aventurine: a comforting stone; green aventurine is particularly good for settling nausea

Green fluorite: aids stomach upsets, reduces anxiety

Helping muscle cramps with hematite

Polished

Hematite is known as a protective crystal that grounds and balances the flow of environmental energies around the home (see page 12) but it is also a profound physical healer. Strongly connected to the blood and circulatory system, the stone appears to "bleed," producing a red line if you try to draw with it. Healers believe that hematite possesses special magical powers, spiriting away illness when placed on the body. This innate power can also work on muscle cramps: those short, painful spasms brought on by the contraction of muscle fibres. These spasms often happen immediately after a workout at the gym because lactic acid builds up in the muscles. Repetitive movement or lying in a fixed position for a long time can also bring cramps on.

CRYSTAL FACTS

CRYSTAL TO USE: hematite (silver/gray metallic when polished, reddish brown when rough)

AVAILABILITY: commonly available

QUALITIES OF STONE: enhances vitality and optimism, increases courage, boosts self-esteem and confidence, gives focus, takes away any self-limitations

HEALTH BENEFITS: stimulates circulatory system, helps insomnia, stimulates the spleen, aids fractures, alleviates leg cramps and stress and anxiety

WHERE TO PLACE THE CRYSTAL: hold it to affected muscle

Crystal healing

If you are prone to muscle cramps it is best to keep your hematite crystal with you at all times. This stone will increase the blood flow in the body, releasing the tightness and restriction in the muscles. When you feel a spasm starting, hold the crystal in your hand and ask for its help in removing the tension. Now place it on the affected muscle, wrapping your hands around the stone for about 5–10 minutes. Feel the crystal's restorative vibrations easing the pain and lessening the contraction. Cleanse it well after use (see pages 149–153).

ALTERNATIVE CRAMP-RELEASING CRYSTALS TO USE

Chrysocolla: strengthens blood and muscles, alleviates spasms or cramp

Amazonite: dissolves blockages in nervous system, relieves muscle cramps

Cluster

Letting go of your stress with amethyst

CRYSTAL FACTS

Crystal to use: amethyst (purple/lavender) geode, cluster or single point

Availability: commonly available

Qualities of stone: calms nervous system, heals emotions, relieves tension and stress symptoms

Health benefits: good blood cleanser, eases headaches, heals lung and digestive problems

Where to place the crystal: on your forehead or stomach

Amethyst is the perfect crystal to instill peace and calm. A mind-protector, the stone increases vigor, deflecting any psychic attacks that may be aimed at you. Many peoples and cultures appreciated amethyst's qualities. During the Middle Ages, its soothing properties were adopted by the clergy, with both priests and cardinals wearing amethyst rings to symbolize their piety and celibacy.

Many healers deem amethyst to be "nature's tranquilizer" for its ability to relax the mind and destress the nervous system. Stress can be brought on by endless work pressures and deadlines, unemployment or relationship difficulties for example. Although a certain amount of stress is good for you, if it becomes long-term and your body is on constant "fight-or-flight" alert, burn-out can become a problem.

Crystal healing

An effective way of dealing with stressful situations is to use an amethyst to calm your body and emotions. Sit in a quiet place where you will not be disturbed and hold the stone to your forehead for about 5–10 minutes; or, if you are in a public place and prefer to use the stone more discreetly, just hold it in your hand. Feel the stone's calming vibrations releasing the stress from your body and slowing down your nervous system. Work with this crystal whenever your stress levels start to soar, and remember to cleanse it regularly (see pages 149–153).

ALTERNATIVE STRESS-RELIEVING CRYSTALS TO USE

Aquamarine: reduces stress, clears communication problems

Lapis lazuli: releases stress and brings inner peace

Lavender (purple) jade: regulates heartbeat, calms the nervous system, soothes the mind, alleviates anxiety

Calming your anger with agate

Rough

Agate is a powerful emotional healer that works slowly on taking away your inner bitterness and angry feelings. In ancient times, the crystal was highly valued as an amulet to quench the thirst and to soothe a fever. Today, agate can work on emotional upsets, taking the heat out of an upsetting argument and throwing "water" on overheated emotions.

Losing your temper in a business meeting or when your children are being disobedient in a public place just draws attention to yourself. Releasing angry feelings is important, because if they stay pent-up inside, you can become bitter and repressed. Working with a crystal can help you to express your feelings before you get to boiling point.

CRYSTAL FACTS

CRYSTAL TO USE: agate (clear/milky white, gray, blue, green, pink, or brown) translucent, usually banded

AVAILABILITY: commonly available, occasionally artificially colored

QUALITIES OF STONE: removes bitter anger and transforms negativity, grounds emotions

HEALTH BENEFITS: stimulates digestion and soothes stomach, releases toxins, heals skin disorders

WHERE TO PLACE THE CRYSTAL: hold in your hands

Crystal healing

When you feel an angry outburst about to surface, use your agate to calm your emotions—keep the crystal with you at all times. When you start to get angry, take hold of the crystal and and hold it in your hands for about 5 minutes, breathing deeply as the crystal starts to soothe your anger. Use this technique whenever you feel you may completely lose control.

ALTERNATIVE ANGER-RELEASING CRYSTALS TO USE

Moonstone: soothes emotional overreaction

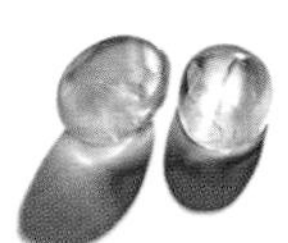

Red garnet: reduces unreasonable anger, particularly toward yourself; turns a crisis into a challenge

Dealing with fear with natural quartz cluster

Cluster

CRYSTAL FACTS

Crystal to use: natural quartz cluster (clear)

Availability: commonly available

Qualities of stone: powerful healer and energy amplifier, tunes in to vibrational energy, lets you find spiritual purpose, aids concentration, fuels memory, purifies the soul

Health benefits: heals all conditions, relieves pain, aids diarrhea, soothes headaches, boosts immune system, soothes burns

Where to place the crystal: solar plexus in upper abdomen

A natural quartz cluster is a beautiful clear crystal that looks like a piece of chiseled ice. The more you stare into the stone, the more you are supposed to see in it. Many ancient civilizations revered the crystal, using its high energetic vibration to increase the effectiveness of their religious and magical ceremonies. The ancient Japanese who worshiped the fiery dragon believed in the purity of quartz, thinking it was formed from a white dragon's breath.

Natural quartz heals the mind and spirit and can alter fixed mental attitudes, particularly fears. Fears can hold you back in life. Everyone experiences fears: fear of being left alone, fear of giving a talk, fear of children leaving home. What is important is working through the fear and facing reality. Natural quartz adjusts its vibrational level to the person using it, so it can help you see through your fears, and achieve what you want.

Crystal healing

To release a current fear, sit cross-legged in a darkened room and hold your crystal in your hands; feel it aligning with your energies. Look deeply into your stone: staring into clear quartz is believed to enhance your psychic abilities. Now place it on your fear center—the solar plexus in your upper abdomen—and see your current fear. Let your doubts about this challenge flit through your mind. Now ask your stone to give you ways to handle it. Feel the pleasing emotions as your crystal shows you positive solutions. Cleanse the crystal well after the session (see pages 149–153).

ALTERNATIVE FEAR-RELEASING CRYSTALS TO USE

Moss agate: releases fear and encourages personal growth

Apophyllite: dissolves negative thought patterns and worries

Chiastolite: calms fear, helps with facing reality

Balancing your emotions with sodalite

Sodalite is a dark blue stone, flecked with pieces of white calcite. It can be confused with the mystical lapis lazuli crystal as it also contains pyrite, but it doesn't have the gold specks that lapis often has. A stone of the mind, sodalite dispels mental clutter and promotes rational thoughts. It is a supreme balancer of the emotions, helping to bring them back under control when we lose good communication with our inner selves. Noticeable signs are becoming irrationally angry because of not dealing with a past upset or crying because of a suppressed hurt.

Crystal healing

Sodalite brings issues from your past to the surface and releases them, repairing your fragile emotions. Sit in a quiet room and take your sodalite crystal in your hands and hold it to your chest for about 5–10 minutes. Close your eyes and connect with your inner child who is about five and who holds all your shame and guilt. Ask them what past incident is causing your emotional upsets. As they tell you, focus on the event and let your crystal send blue healing energy out to release the pain and transform it into love and self-acceptance. Feel a wonderful emotional peace come over you as you slowly come back into the room. Cleanse your crystal of any negativity (see pages 149–153).

CRYSTAL FACTS

CRYSTAL TO USE: sodalite (dark blue, blue/white) variegated stone

AVAILABILITY: commonly available

QUALITIES OF STONE: disperses fear, calms the mind, enhances self-expression, increases rational thoughts, promotes courage, clears old mental patterns, soothes panic attacks, balances emotions, encourages self-acceptance

Rough

HEALTH BENEFITS: aids functioning of the pancreas, balances endocrine system and metabolism, detoxifies the lymphatic system, lowers blood pressure, treats throat and digestive problems

WHERE TO PLACE THE CRYSTAL: on the heart in the middle of the chest

ALTERNATIVE EMOTIONAL-BALANCING CRYSTALS TO USE

Chrysocolla: works on guilt and brings in joy

Citrine: releases negative traits, overcomes anger

Rhodonite: creates emotional balance and promotes love

Asking forgiveness with rhodochrosite

Polished

Rhodochrosite is a wonderful crystal for bringing repressed upsets to the surface, healing emotional scars and allowing you to move on positively. Interestingly, its alternative name, Inca Rose, may have derived from its formation in ancient Inca silver mines, where the rose-colored crystal grew as stalactites and stalagmites. Like rhodochrosite, our secrets and worries may be hidden deep within our consciousness. Holding past resentments can literally eat away at your body, and in time if they are not released, may cause physical illness. You need to forgive ex-lovers for letting you down, past friends for not supporting you enough, parents for being overcritical and yourself for not achieving everything you wanted. Sometimes we do not want to forgive, but trying starts the healing process and allows us to live more fully in the present.

CRYSTAL FACTS

Crystal to use: rhodochrosite (pink/orange), banded structure, can be tumbled, polished

Availability: commonly available

Qualities of stone: encourages change, heals emotional wounds, releases hidden feelings, inspires forgiveness, brings in love

Health benefits: helps asthmatic and respiratory problems, improves eyesight, stabilizes blood pressure, relieves migraines

Where to place the crystal: on your heart

Crystal healing

Work on deep-held resentments one at a time or you may find it overwhelming. Lie down, close your eyes, and hold the crystal to your heart. Visualize a darkened stage and put the person you want to forgive on it. Now see good things happening to him or her, and send the healing vibrations from your crystal to them. Feel the resentment lifting from your heart and being replaced with love. See this person laughing before they fade from the stage.

ALTERNATIVE FORGIVENESS CRYSTALS TO USE

Pink calcite: a forgiving stone that releases sadness

Chrysoprase: aids compassion and acceptance of others

Celestite: resolves conflict, bringing inner peace

Removing old belief patterns with green calcite

Rough

Green calcite has many different uses. It can balance the male and female polarities and ground the emotions. Many spiritualists say it improves astral projection when your soul goes traveling at night.

Belief patterns can be imposed on us in childhood from parental influence. Some are positive but many adversely affect our adult lives. Green calcite is a special healing crystal that dissolves fixed beliefs and deep inner programming. The stone's gentle green emissions can dissolve the rigidity of an old belief pattern to allow a more fulfilling one to come in. For example, a workaholic lifestyle created from a childhood criticism, "You need to achieve more," can be transformed into a career with an enjoyable work/life balance by recognizing and letting go of this unwanted belief. Green calcite gives you the strength to recognize things that no longer serve you.

Crystal cure

To do a belief-releasing ceremony, sit in a quiet room and burn two green candles. Pick up your calcite stone, hold it to your heart, feeling its balancing, calming vibrations, and gaze into the flames. Think of the belief pattern that is adversely affecting your life and sense your crystal's purifying properties helping to melt it in the flames. Now see a positive belief appearing in the flames such as, "I am successful in everything I do." Slowly come to, remembering to cleanse your crystal to keep it positive (see pages 149–153).

CRYSTAL FACTS

CRYSTAL TO USE: green calcite, translucent, waxy feel, often with bands, sometimes treated with acid to improve color, can be tumbled

AVAILABILITY: commonly available

QUALITIES OF STONE: balances the emotions, takes away fear, reduces stress, soothes anxiety, aids intuition, removes rigid beliefs and old programming, increases psychic abilities, stimulates memory

HEALTH BENEFITS: releases body toxins, boosts kidneys, spleen, and pancreas, helps arthritis and ligament problems, calms fever, soothes burns and inflammations

WHERE TO PLACE THE CRYSTAL: on your Heart chakra in the middle of your chest

ALTERNATIVE RELEASING CRYSTALS TO USE

Pietersite: removes beliefs and conditioning set by other people

Sodalite: releases old mental patterns and creates new insights

Smoky quartz: releases beliefs from the psyche that no longer serve you

Revitalizing your energy with kyanite

Rough

Kyanite is a courageous crystal that can help you to find your soul's purpose. The stone is thought to work with archangel Michael and his sword of truth, which cuts away unwanted mental or spiritual attitudes, and is a more powerful sword than King Arthur's sword Excalibur. A calming, compassionate crystal, kyanite also amplifies and transmits energy, helping to clear any emotional blockages from your energetic meridians or pathways and balancing your main energy centers, your chakras. If you are suffering from a lack of vitality after a demanding time at work meeting pressured deadlines, or are taking time out from an upsetting relationship, this stone can boost your energy field and bring its flow back into balance.

CRYSTAL FACTS

Crystal to use: blue or green kyanite, transparent or opaque, striated

Availability: blue kyanite commonly available; green kyanite can be hard to find

Qualities of stone: promotes mental clarity, calms emotions, balances chakras and clears blockages, helps meditation, dispels anger, restores energy, stimulates spiritual energy and intuition

Health benefits: relieves pain, calms fevers, treats muscular pain, stimulates endocrine system, lowers blood pressure

Where to place the crystal: on your Heart chakra (middle of chest) and Third eye chakra (middle of forehead)

Crystal healing

To revitalize your energy, lie in a darkened room and pick up your crystal and feel its vibrating emissions. Hold it to your Heart chakra for 5–10 minutes, feeling the stone clearing any emotional confusion or trauma and increasing your energy levels. Now move it to the Third eye chakra for a further 5 minutes to release any worries or anger here and to stimulate mental clarity and positive brain energy to deal effectively with your life once more. Some healers have found that kyanite does not retain negativity, so it never needs cleansing.

ALTERNATIVE ENERGY-BOOSTING CRYSTALS TO USE

Garnet: energizes, cleanses, and balances the chakras

Fire opal: reenergizes, bringing change and progress

Natural quartz: regulates and amplifies energy flow, dissolves blockages

Protecting your aura with apache tear obsidian

Polished

CRYSTAL FACTS

CRYSTAL TO USE: apache tear obsidian (black), translucent, often water-worn

AVAILABILITY: commonly available

QUALITIES OF STONE: absorbs and disperses negative energy, promotes inner growth, reduces stress, blocks geopathic stress, releases mental pain, relieves sadness and loneliness, helps to face dark side, strengthens aura

HEALTH BENEFITS: aids functioning of the stomach and intestines, reduces muscles spasms, detoxes the body, relieves arthritis, joint problems and muscle cramps

WHERE TO PLACE THE CRYSTAL: move the crystal round your aura

A sad legend surrounds apache tear obsidian. A group of Apache Indians were attacked by soldiers, and with their arrows gone, they leaped to their deaths over a cliff to avoid capture. The inconsolable women of the tribe wept below the cliff for a complete moon cycle, and the obsidian crystals in the rock absorbed their tears, forming this new crystal. The belief today is that whoever owns this stone will never cry again.

Made from volcanic glass, apache tear obsidian is a "truthful" crystal that shows your strengths and weaknesses. Many people are drawn to obsidian because it protects the aura—our subtle energetic field. The aura is a "buffer" for our bodies (see also page 65). It has several layers and changes colors to reflect our fluctutating moods: the brighter our aura's colors, the healthier we are.

Crystal healing

To shield your aura, stand by your bed in the morning holding your crystal, and feel its supportive energies. Ask the stone to create an impenetrable barrier around you, then move it all around your aura, from your head, out to the right side and down to your feet, then all around your left. Now visualize a powerful white light coming from your Crown chakra filling your body with a spiritual energy that lasts all day. Cleanse your crystal well after use (see pages 149–153).

ALTERNATIVE AURA-PROTECTING CRYSTALS TO USE

Aquamarine: balances chakras, shields the aura

Hematite: deflects negative energies from the aura

Kunzite: banishes unwanted energies from the aura

Clearing meditation with sunstone

Polished

CRYSTAL FACTS

Crystal to use: sunstone, (yellow, orange, red/brown), transparent, clear, or opaque, can be small and tumbled

Availability: sunstone from Oregon is commonly available from specialist stores

Qualities of stone: joyful stone, restores the spirit, clears the chakras, brings luck and good fortune, removes attachments, gives self-empowerment, an antidepressant, lifts black moods, promotes enthusiasm

Health benefits: good for heart and blood circulation, aids aching bones or joints, can increase sexual energy, helps organs, helps sore throats

Where to place the crystal: hold in hands in lap

A warm, joyful crystal, nowadays sunstone (a lemony, transparent stone) mainly comes from Oregon and India, where it is a golden stone, similar to moonstone. You can only feel good around this crystal. In the past it was prized as a lucky stone that attracted the influences of benevolent gods. We all have emotional hang-ups that drain our energy, and sunstone is a crystal that removes psychic attachments from our aura (energy field), sending them back with love to past partners or overbearing parents. This sunny stone can cleanse you at the end the day when you are emotionally and mentally exhausted from work stress or maybe the pain of ending a close friendship.

Crystal healing

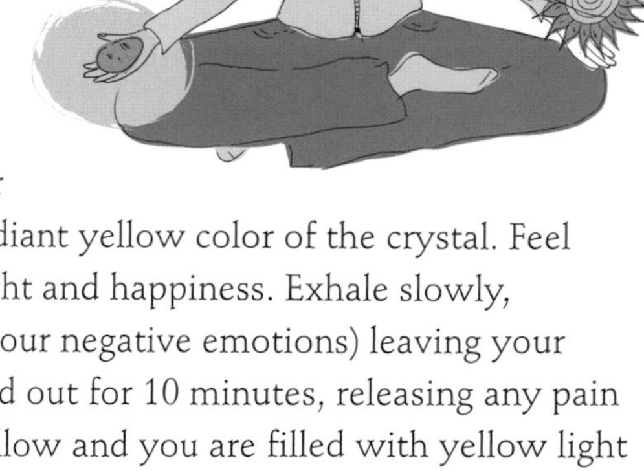

To clear your mind each evening, sit cross-legged in a darkened living room. Burn some relaxing lavender essential oil and light a candle. Hold your crystal in your lap, and take some slow, deep breaths from your diaphragm. Look deeply at your stone, then close your eyes, and breathe in the radiant yellow color of the crystal. Feel it filling your body with light and happiness. Exhale slowly, visualizing a black cloud (your negative emotions) leaving your body. Keep breathing in and out for 10 minutes, releasing any pain until the black becomes yellow and you are filled with yellow light and wellbeing. Slowly open your eyes. Cleanse your crystal well (see pages 149–153).

ALTERNATIVE CLEARING CRYSTALS TO USE

Amber: powerful cleanser, brings wisdom

Agate: clears negativity and bitterness (right: brown agate)

Fluorite: purifies and removes stress (right: green fluorite)

Letting go of sorrows with onyx

Polished egg

The name onyx comes from the Greek *onux*, meaning fingernail or claw. In Roman legend, Venus, the goddess of love, was sleeping and her son, Cupid, cut her fingernails, leaving the clippings on the ground. As no heavenly entity can die, the gods transformed the clippings into the stone we know as onyx. It is a balancing crystal that gives strength to the user suffering extreme emotional stress. A releaser of pain, it gets rid of past hurts that eat away inside you, stopping you from enjoying your current life and being fully in the moment. We all need to mourn but constantly reliving an upsetting childhood or an old love affair is only holding you back. Black onyx is a supportive stone that pushes you to take that step forward and express these hurts.

Crystal healing

To liberate past hurts, sit in a quiet room and pick up your black onyx crystal. Turn the stone over in your hands feeling its wise vibrations. Close your eyes and focus on your first hurt, feel the emotions, see that person or situation, be back in that moment. Now ask the stone for its help in releasing this trauma, to heal your hurt and to learn a lesson from it. Let the images fade and with them all your pain. Work on further hurts, or slowly come to. Cleanse your crystal well after use (see pages 149–153).

CRYSTAL FACTS

Crystal to use: green onyx, banded, often polished

Availability: commonly available

Qualities of stone: eliminates grief, encourages self-control, promotes happiness and abundance, relieves stress, helps you to become master of your own destiny, releases past trauma, encourages fidelity

Health benefits: aids hearing problems, benefits the heart, heals ulcers, strengthens teeth and bones, works on blood disorders

Where to place the crystal: hold in hands in lap

ALTERNATIVE PAIN-RELEASING CRYSTALS TO USE

Pink tourmaline: relieves emotional pain, cleanses destructive emotions

Chrysocolla: heals heartache, releases repressed emotions

Promoting self-love with pink tourmaline

Rough

Tourmalines are precious crystals that often display beautiful color. According to an ancient Egyptian legend, tourmaline traveled along a rainbow, collecting its delightful mix of colors on its way from the earth's crust to the sun. Holding up a tourmaline to the light, it is unusually transparent from the side but opaque from either end. Pink tourmaline is a wise and inspiring crystal that attracts love and friendship. You may find it easy to love other people but tend to hang onto all the criticisms received from your parents and friends and see yourself as imperfect or unworthy. This crystal teaches you that you need to love yourself before others will truly love you.

CRYSTAL FACTS

Crystal to use: pink tourmaline, transparent or opaque, often striated and hexagonal

Availability: commonly available from specialist stores

Qualities of stone: very protective stone, inspires and aids concentration, balances the chakras, promotes self-confidence, gives understanding of emotions, promotes self-love, brings peace and relaxation

Health benefits: harmonizes endocrine system, encourages sleep, aids the lymphatic and digestive systems, treats the heart and lungs, improves skin

Where to place the crystal: on your Heart chakra in the middle of your chest

Crystal healing

To love yourself, you need to reprogram the self-criticism that stems from your subconscious so that you can give and receive love freely. The pink tourmaline crystal links to Venus, the goddess of love, and it is hard not to love yourself when holding this tender stone. To work on loving yourself more, stand in front of a large mirror. Hold the crystal to your heart and say 20 times looking directly into the mirror, "I love you as you are." Feel the compassionate pink vibrations from your stone melting any destructive feelings held in your subconscious and opening your heart to love. Practice the affirmation daily until you really believe what you are saying. Always cleanse your crystal after use to remove any negative emotions (see pages 149–153).

ALTERNATIVE SELF-LOVE CRYSTALS TO USE

Rose quartz: facilitates deep inner healing and self-love

Rhodonite: transmutes self-criticism into self-love

Magnesite: opens Heart chakra and encourages self-love

Letting go of guilt with peridot

Rough

A delicate, transparent stone in varying shades of yellow-green, red and brown, peridot has legendary curative powers. As far back as Roman times, medicine drunk from goblets decorated with this crystal were believed to increase in potency. A wonderful cleanser, peridot clears the mind and lets you release things from your past. So if you have hidden guilt lingering in your subconscious, it can be affecting your adult life. You may have stolen money as a child from your mother, and now money slips through your fingers, or you may have been unkind to a child at school and now find it hard to get on with your work colleagues. This crystal clears away guilt and teaches you that hanging on to old emotion is counterproductive.

CRYSTAL FACTS

CRYSTAL TO USE: peridot, also known as chrysolite, olivine (olive green, yellow/green, red, brown, deep yellow)

AVAILABILITY: commonly available, but good crystals are hard to find

QUALITIES OF STONE: increases intuition, stimulates the mind, reduces stress and negativity, clears hurts, cleanses guilt, increases confidence and assertive behavior

HEALTH BENEFITS: increases tissue regeneration, aids the heart, pancreas, spleen, liver, and adrenals, boosts metabolism, helps digestion, improves skin texture

WHERE TO PLACE THE CRYSTAL: hold in hands

Crystal healing

To heal your inner guilt, sit in a quiet room and pick up your peridot crystal and study its wonderful green color that can heal your emotions and bring gentle regrowth. Close your eyes and see yourself in a peaceful field. Sit on the grass and ask your subconscious to join you. Ask it to show you the guilt that still affects you, then allow these images or feelings to flow through you. Now ask your crystal to release cleansing vibrations to remove this guilt, and let you admit the mistake and move on. Send love to your subconscious, and sense a deep warm glow, then slowly come back into the room. Always cleanse your crystal well (see pages 149–153).

Rough

ALTERNATIVE GUILT-RELEASING CRYSTALS TO USE

Chrysocolla: a sustaining stone that liberates inner guilt

Sodalite: transforms, and lets go of core fears and guilt

Chiastolite: clears hidden guilt, balances emotions

Increasing self-esteem with moss agate

Rough

Moss agate is believed to feed the soul. Known as the gardener's stone, this clear crystal has a deep connection with nature because of its curious plantlike markings. A prime ingredient in magic spells to promote happiness and a long life, it is a wonderful crystal to balance the emotions and bring new beginnings. A weight problem can ruin your self-image, and constant criticism from your parents can drain self-esteem. This stone works on dispelling your inner fears and feelings of inadequacy.

Crystal healing

Moss agate is a crystal of self-realization; it releases fear, making you appreciate your true worth and see your inner radiance. To work on improving your self-worth, sit in a quiet room, pick up your crystal, and hold it to your Solar plexus chakra: the place where we take all the emotional blows in life. Hold it there for about 10 minutes, feeling this stabilizing crystal boosting your positive characteristics and dispelling any depression. Use your crystal every day for a week until you feel you can take on the world once more. After healing, always cleanse your stone well to keep its energy bright (see pages 149–153).

CRYSTAL FACTS

Crystal to use: moss agate (green, blue, red, yellow, brown), transparent or translucent, has foliage or mosslike pattern, can be tumbled

Availability: commonly available

Qualities of stone: attracts money and abundance, increases strength and courage, inspires the soul, improves ego and self-esteem, brings emotional balance, reduces negativity

Health benefits: relieves exhaustion, helps neck and back problems, cleanses the blood, strengthens the immune system, reduces fever, treats colds and flu

Where to place the crystal: on your Solar plexus chakra in your upper abdomen

Polished

ALTERNATIVE SELF-ESTEEM CRYSTALS TO USE

Citrine: reduces sensitivity to criticism, raises self-esteem

Rhodochrosite: alleviates painful feelings, improves self-worth

Boosting confidence with chrysocolla

Chrysocolla, a stone of peace and wisdom, removes negative emotions—in chakra healing, using chrysocolla on the Third eye chakra (between the brows) helps promote inner knowledge and psychic vision.

You can use this bright stone to correct any subconscious imbalances or destructive programming you may be harboring. We are all very good at criticizing ourselves, but often we do not praise our good points. Our self-image can be poor and we may find it hard to be positive about our bodies. Often this negative patterning, or lack of confidence, is what we felt about ourselves as young children, perhaps unconsciously instilled by parents and contemporaries.

Rough

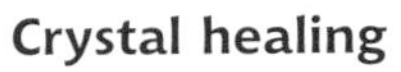

Crystal healing

Working with a chrysocolla can help to change your self-image and increase self-esteem. Take hold of your crystal and turn it over a few times in your hands to feel its energy. Lie down, close your eyes, and place the stone on your Throat chakra (see also page 62) in the middle of your throat near your jaw for about 5 minutes. Focus on letting go of what has caused your bad self-image, and visualize yourself as a happy, positive person. Feel the vibrations of the crystal working with you, releasing your old pattern, increasing your personal power and confidence. Repeat daily for a week until you feel you can take on the world.

CRYSTAL FACTS

CRYSTAL TO USE: chrysocolla (green, blue, turquoise), opaque, often with bands, generally polished or tumbled

AVAILABILITY: commonly available

QUALITIES OF STONE: takes away fears or guilt, brings balance, releases nervous tension, increases self awareness, and brings confidence

HEALTH BENEFITS: soothes digestive problems and arthritic conditions, reduces period pains and premenstrual tension, heals infections, calms burns

WHERE TO PLACE THE CRYSTAL: on your throat

ALTERNATIVE CONFIDENCE-BUILDING CRYSTALS TO USE

Agate: brings self-acceptance and builds confidence (right: brown agate)

Garnet: dissolves old behavioral patterns, increases self-confidence

Tiger's eye: heals issues of self-worth and helps recognition of abilities

Visualizing a positive future with labradorite

Labradorite is a mystical crystal that is named after Labrador, a Canadian town, which mines the stone. A plain grayish color, it shows glorious flashes of colors such as blue and yellow when held to the light. A transformational stone, labradorite works on your Third eye chakra: your intuitive center increasing your psychic abilities. It is a crystal that attracts success for its owner, so if you have what seems like an impossible dream, perhaps owning a villa abroad, becoming an artist, or training as a ski instructor, working with labradorite can make this dream a reality.

CRYSTAL FACTS

Crystal to use: labradorite (grayish with flashes of blue/yellow), also known as spectrolite (white with blue/yellow flashes), transparent, can be small and tumbled

Availability: commonly available

Polished egg

Qualities of stone: unblocks chakras, induces peaceful sleep, increases intuition and psychic vision, promotes courage, perception, and visualization techniques, dispels insecurities, inspires imagination

Health benefits: balances hormones, alleviates menstrual pain, reduces blood pressure, controls metabolism, treats colds and eye problems

Where to place the crystal: hold in hands

Rough

Crystal energizing

Living your dream as though it were already happening can give out the positive energies to attract what you want. Visualizing your dream also fixes it firmly in your subconscious, endorsing what you want. Labradorite increases your spiritual connection, strengthening your visualization techniques to bring in your desired change. Sit in a quiet room and close your eyes. Pick up your stone, feeling its wisdom and strength. Breathe deeply and visualize your dream: see yourself having a drink on the terrace in your villa in the sun, or leading a party of skiers down the mountain. Let your stone increase your imagination, helping you to be there, feeling and absorbing the sensations. Step out of the scene and observe it from the outside, then step back until you are really part of it. Slowly step out of the scene and come back into the room. Practice regularly with your crystal until your dream comes true.

ALTERNATIVE VISUALIZATION CRYSTALS TO USE

Magnesite: place on Third eye chakra on forehead for increased imagery

Ruby: helps follow dreams, stimulates pineal gland for visualization

Amethyst: has a high spiritual vibration, enhances visualization

Calming fears when flying with rhodochrosite

Polished

The pretty pink banded colors of rhodochrosite are caused by the element manganese that blends with the stone. One way the crystal is formed is when manganese is dissolved by groundwater and combines with a carbonate material that drops off the ceilings and crevices underground forming stalagmites and stalactites. Known as another powerful love stone, rhodochrosite also alleviates emotional upset or stress, and can help to ease a fear of flying. Even though statistically it is a far safer mode of transport than driving a car, it is often the lack of control, or having to put their trust in a pilot, that can make people anxious and upset when they step on a plane.

Crystal facts

Crystal to use: rhodochrosite (pink), banded, can be tumbled

Qualities of stone: heals emotional upsets or stress, encourages forgiveness, attracts love, helps to face reality and confront irrational fears, eases loneliness and heartache

Health benefits: improves eyesight, helps functioning of kidneys, pancreas, spleen, and sexual organs, aids blood detoxification, improves asthma and respiratory disease, improves skin, relieves migraine, balances thyroid

Where to place the crystal: hold in hands

Crystal healing

To cope with any anxieties about flying, such as during turbulence or going over water, take out your rhodochrosite crystal as soon as you sit down on the plane. This gentle, loving pink stone has the power to release your irrational fears, leaving you calm and centered. As the plane takes off, hold your crystal tightly and concentrate on releasing any muscular tension in your body with your stone's help. Start at your feet, breathe in deeply, and as you breathe out visualize any tightness flowing out of them. Move on to your calves, then your thighs, breathing in and relaxing any taut muscles as you breathe out. Work through your body until you reach your head. Sense your crystal's compassionate vibrations working with you, soothing mind and body and releasing your emotional upset. Leave it on your lap for the flight, holding it tightly whenever you feel distressed. Cleanse the stone after use to keep it working well (see pages 149–153).

Alternative fear-reducing crystals to use

Orange calcite: alleviates stress, takes away fear

Amazonite: calms nervous system, takes away worries

Onyx: calms mental stress, reduces overpowering fears

Dealing with jet lag with snow quartz

Quartz is the supreme healing crystal. In early Britain they were often called "star stones" and were a part of folk magic rituals. The stones were collected with some water from a stream and boiled together. The cooled water was drunk as an elixir to keep illness at bay.

Snow quartz has a more gentle vibration than clear quartz, but still works on regulating your body energy. A crystal that balances your body, it brings your biorhythms (your body's natural rhythms) back to normal after you have crossed different time zones when traveling long-haul. The symptoms of jet lag are debilitating, often disturbing your sleep patterns, making you feel tired or physically and mentally low.

Crystal cure

To restore your body's natural rhythms after crossing time zones, take hold of your snow quartz crystal and request its help to regain your normal energy levels. Place the stone under your pillow at night so that its slow vibrations can harmonize your body's rhythms throughout the night. If you still suffer during the day, carry your crystal around with you. Cleanse well after use (see pages 149–153).

Rough

CRYSTAL FACTS

Crystal to use: snow quartz (white), known as milky quartz and quartzite; can be crystalline form or pebble

Availability: commonly available

Qualities of stone: balances emotions, clears negativity from aura, gently energizes

Health benefits: aids functioning of the organs and recuperation from illness, stimulates immune system, soothes burns

Where to place the crystal: under your pillow, in your pocket or handbag

Polished heart

ALTERNATIVE JET-LAG CRYSTALS TO USE

Black tourmaline: releases toxins, reduces effects of jet lag

Amethyst: soothes nervous system, boosts memory, and aids sleeping

Coping with daily travel stress with brown jasper

Jasper is a form of chalcedony (part of the quartz family). When you look carefully at this pretty stone, it has beautiful color variations. In the past, its light and dark brown markings meant that this stone was often referred to as Egyptian marble.

A wonderful nurturing and protective crystal, jasper absorbs any negative energy and clears any environmental pollution that surrounds you. Traveling by car, train, or bus to work, meetings, or while doing the school run can be very demanding, and feelings of frustration at delays or traffic jams can build up inside you as your stress levels soar. Carrying a brown jasper crystal with you sustains and supports you during your daily onslaught with travel, slowing your nervous system and controlling your anger. This supportive quality was well known in the past when the stone was carried to drive away evil spirits and protect against venomous snake or spider bites. Jasper also brings you good luck if you wear it in the shape of an arrowhead.

Crystal cure

Your brown jasper crystal will help you get to grips with any situation that you encounter on your journey. When a problem arises, or if you start to get upset at another delay, take out and hold your stone for a few minutes until you feel your stress abating and you start to become more relaxed.

CRYSTAL FACTS

CRYSTAL TO USE: brown jasper, opaque, patterned, can be tumbled

AVAILABILITY: commonly available

QUALITIES OF STONE: absorbs negative energy, clears environmental pollution, protects and grounds energies

HEALTH BENEFITS: boosts immune system, aids circulatory and digestive systems

WHERE TO PLACE THE CRYSTAL: your pocket, purse, or workbag

ALTERNATIVE TRAVEL-STRESS CRYSTALS TO USE

Blue lace agate: dissolves mental stress, calms nervous system

Golden topaz: releases all tension and stabilizes the emotions

Celestite: calms the mind and gets rid of any worries

Harmonizing your car with amber

Hippocrates, the ancient Greek father of medicine, wrote in the 5th century BCE about the healing powers of amber, and native shamans in many cultures have used its protective qualities in rituals for years. Sometimes called the honey stone because it is so soft and warm to touch, amber generates a flowing, calming energy and is said to contain the heat and power of many suns, absorbing negativity and protecting the user from harm. It generates courage, self-confidence, and a joy of life, so placing this harmonizing crystal in your car can help maintain a supportive atmosphere, as you drive around for work or transport fractious children to school.

Crystal healing

To use in the car, first have a clear-out as the crystal will find it hard to battle against stagnant energies. Now take hold of your amber crystal, feel its loving and generous power filling your body, and ask it to become your protective talisman when driving. Place it on the dashboard or in a pocket, letting its uplifting energies form a gold ring around your car. Cleanse it every few months to keep it working at full strength (see pages 149–153).

CRYSTAL FACTS

Crystal to use: amber (yellow, orange, golden/brown), transparent or opaque; some have insects or vegetation trapped inside, as it is actually a fossilized tree resin

Availability: commonly available but expensive; beware of manmade copies (see page 85)

Qualities of stone: promotes compassion, relieves depression, cleanses the environment, transmutes negative into positive energies, stimulates a positive mental state

Health benefits: boosts the endocrine system, soothes earache and rheumatism, eases stomach problems, treats the kidneys, spleen, and bladder, has antibiotic properties as an essence

Where to place the crystal: on the dashboard or in a side pocket

Polished

ALTERNATIVE PROTECTIVE CRYSTALS TO USE

Fire agate: grounding stone that creates a secure and safe ambience

Amethyst: absorbs negative energies, calms and protects

Jasper: nurturing stone, grounds energies, provides protection (right: red jasper)

Polished

Promoting calm when driving with blue lace agate

The beautiful pale blue lace agate with its attractive striped patterns was worn in ancient times as a truth amulet to make sure that the only words you spoke were pure. Renowned as a peace-bringer, it links to the soothing element of water, so using the stone can help you relax and de-stress. In today's busy world this crystal's calming influence can defuse any fiery emotions that arise from traffic incidents when you are driving. Sitting in endless traffic jams, or experiencing road rage from another driver can make you stressed and angry. Anger can make you drive less carefully, but carrying a blue agate crystal, or leaving one in the car, can reduce tension and ensure you keep your emotions under control.

CRYSTAL FACTS

Crystal to use: blue lace agate, banded, can be small and tumbled

Availability: commonly available

Qualities of stone: improves vitality, increases ego and self-esteem, restores calm and peace and relieves stress, encourages open expression of feelings, strengthens mind

Health benefits: reduces infections, inflammation, and fever, heals thyroid, throat, and lymph disturbances, treats arthritis and joint problems, stimulates digestion, prevents gastritis

Where to place the crystal: on the dashboard or in your pocket

Crystal healing

Place your stone on the dashboard of your car or leave in your pocket. If you get angry because of a driving upset, stop the car safely, then start to gaze into the soothing depths of your blue agate crystal. Take some deep breaths and feel how this supportive stone is lowering your blood pressure, and neutralizing your irritation and anger so that you can continue driving calmly once more. If you are getting exasperated in a long traffic line, turn the stone over in your hand like a worry bead to lessen your anxieties or frustrations. Cleanse the crystal regularly after prolonged use (see pages 149–153).

ALTERNATIVE CALMING CRYSTALS TO USE

Aquamarine: quiets the mind, reduces stress, invokes tolerance

Howlite: teaches patience, cools rage and anger

Blue tiger's eye: calms mind and takes away stress

Keeping safe with jet

Polished

Jet has long been known for its protective qualities and its ability to absorb bad vibrations. In fact, in ancient times, wives of fishermen kept a jet amulet at home so that their husbands would return safe from the sea. The protective amulet of travelers, it is thought to look after you when you are out alone at night. So in today's world it can be a reassuring talisman to have with you when you are traveling on public transport late at night or if you need to walk or cycle in less populated areas on your own where you can feel a bit unsafe.

CRYSTAL FACTS

CRYSTAL TO USE: jet (black), normally small and polished, made from fossilized wood

AVAILABILITY: commonly available

QUALITIES OF STONE: reduces fears, prevents depressive tendencies, helps to grieve, protects from violence, can guard against bad dreams, looks after travelers, assists spiritual development

HEALTH BENEFITS: reduces swellings in legs and feet, relieves neuralgia and toothache, treats colds and migraines, reduces menstrual problems, alleviates stomach troubles

WHERE TO PLACE THE CRYSTAL: carry in bag or pocket or wear it as jewelry

Crystal healing

A black, glasslike stone, jet is actually made from fossilized wood. When worn continuously as jewelry it is said to absorb part of the person's soul, so if you inherit or buy some old jet, always cleanse it well before wearing.

To protect you when traveling, keep your stone in your bag or pocket or wear it as jewelry. Each time before you go out, hold the crystal in your hands and tune into its caring vibrations. Ask it to create a white protective shield around you to repel attackers, keeping you safe from violence at all times. If you suffer from nightmares, keep a jet stone beside your bed at night to soothe your troubled emotions. Always cleanse the crystal regularly to keep it vibrant (see pages 149–153).

ALTERNATIVE PROTECTIVE CRYSTALS TO USE

Fire opal: strengthens personal power, protects from danger

Garnet: a protective amulet, can warn of approaching dangers

Bloodstone: protective stone that shows how to avoid dangerous situations

Energizing a hotel room with natural quartz

Cluster

Many past civilizations, such as the ancient Christians, revered the healing power of quartz, making their relics from the crystal, which they believed to be fossilized ice. Natural quartz is such a versatile crystal. It is the main crystal of crystal healing and has the ability to take in any low-energy vibrations and transmute and amplify them to a higher level to which you will react favorably. It can also disperse any negativity in the environment, making it a great crystal to use if you travel regularly and stay in different hotel rooms that can still have the energetic "imprints" of all the people who have stayed in them. These can leave an anonymous feel or possibly a sad, lingering unhappiness about the space that needs to be cleared.

CRYSTAL FACTS

CRYSTAL TO USE: natural quartz (clear or milky), pointed, may be striated crystals or clusters

AVAILABILITY: commonly available

QUALITIES OF STONE: disperses negativity in the environment, receives, transmits, and amplifies energy, aids meditation, boosts intuition, protects against electromagnetic stress, stimulates concentration, increases psychic abilities

Polished

HEALTH BENEFITS: powerful general healer, boosts the immune system, can relieve toothache and reduce a temperature, soothes the pain of burns

WHERE TO PLACE THE CRYSTAL: on your nightstand or bedside cabinet

Crystal healing

When you check into a hotel room, open all the windows to let the air do a basic cleansing. Hold your natural quartz crystal in your hands and ask it to use its powers to "spring clean" the room, removing any traces of the previous occupant and lifting its energies. Place the stone by your bed, or if the weather is sunny, leave it briefly on a windowsill and let it amplify the glorious rays of the sun. Leave the room for an hour or so and then come back in, noticing how vibrant and inviting the atmosphere has become. Cleanse the stone after use (see pages 149–153).

ALTERNATIVE ENERGIZING CRYSTALS TO USE

Amethyst: blocks negative environmental energies, energizes with love

Green fluorite: absorbs negative energies, creates harmony

Malachite: takes in negative vibrations, transmutes them to radiate positivity

Boosting vitality when walking with orange calcite

Rough

The word calcite comes from the Latin word *calx* and the Greek word *chalix*, which mean lime. The calcite crystal is commonly found embedded in limestone and marble. Orange calcite is a bright, stimulating crystal that can boost your creativity and bring emotional balance. It is associated with the sun, and its warm, orange color, at the hot end of the color spectrum, is a potent energizer. For walking it is the perfect stone to take with you as it can give an instant energy burst to your muscles when your legs start to ache or feel tired.

CRYSTAL FACTS

Crystal to use: orange calcite, translucent, waxy appearance, occasionally tumbled

Availability: commonly available

Qualities of stone: cleanses and energizes, combats lethargy, encourages action, relieves fear, aids depression

Health benefits: aids the kidneys and bladder, heals reproductive and digestive disorders, alleviates irritable bowel syndrome, aids fatigue, increases energy

Where to place the crystal: in your pocket

Crystal energizing

If your legs are tiring on a long walk, take some time out to have a brief rest and recharge your batteries. Do a few stretches and massage your calves. Take out your orange calcite crystal and hold it in your hands until you feel a slight tingling or pulsating—this is how it starts to energize you. Now hold the crystal to each leg for a few minutes to ease the muscle tension and increase the blood flow, so that you can walk on with renewed vigor. If you regularly suffer muscle tiredness when walking, tape a crystal to each leg as you walk to ease the pain.

ALTERNATIVE REVITALIZING CRYSTALS TO USE

Ruby: restores energy when exhausted, boosts a healthy blood circulation

Kyanite: restores physical energy and activates organs

Reducing cell phone emissions with amazonite

Polished

Amazonite, or Amazon stone, is known to protect against cellphone emissions because of its amazing filtering ability. Cellphones emit electromagnetic radiation to which our brains, in particular, are sensitive. Research has yet to prove whether these emissions can be harmful, but people who use their cellphones for long periods have reported symptoms of fatigue, headaches, and burning sensations in the area where the phone was held.

The energy of amazonite can help dissipate cellphone emissions, along with calming the brain and nervous system; it is also reputed to help repair the body and heal the aura. In magical ritual, amazonite is associated with success—so this crystal may just bring a little more sparkle to all your phone conversations.

CRYSTAL FACTS

Crystal to use: amazonite, has veins, sometimes tumbled

Availability: commonly available

Qualities of stone: powerful filter, absorbs cellphone radiation

Health benefits: aids osteoporosis, helps tooth decay, eases muscular spasms

Where to place the crystal: taped to your cellphone

Crystal cure

Use a cellphone only when really necessary, and try to buy a phone that has one of the lowest recorded emissions of radiation. Use a hands-free device and make shorter calls when possible to minimize potential harm. To reduce health risks further, tape a small amazonite crystal to your phone—the least conspicuous area is on the back of the phone. Amazonite will work hard for you to absorb and neutralize some of the radiation that a cellphone emits when it is held to your ear.

ALTERNATIVE RADIATION-REDUCING CRYSTALS TO USE

Aventurine: defuses negativity, reduces cell phone emissions

Kunzite: provides a protective shield, blocks radiation from cell phones

Black tourmaline: disperses stress, ameliorates cell phone emissions

Polished

Reducing Arian recklessness with purple fluorite

Aries people are very positive and action-orientated, and are known for their ability to get things done. Ruled by the assertive planet Mars, they are often aggressive and can be considered "pushy." They are competitive, dynamic people and are often leaders in their chosen field of business. On the downside, Arians can be prone to bullying people weaker than themselves and can get easily bored and impatient.

♈ Aries

March 21–April 20

Ruling planet: ***Mars***

Element: ***Fire***

Birthstones: ***diamond, ruby***

Related crystals: ***amethyst, aquamarine, aventurine, citrine, garnet, jasper, topaz***

CRYSTAL FACTS

Crystal to use: purple fluorite, transparent, cubic, or octahedral

Availability: commonly available

Qualities of stone: effectively grounds and balances spiritual energies, aids mental concentration and encourages impartiality

Health benefits: relieves painful joints, treats ulcers and wounds, alleviates colds and flu, heals blemishes and wrinkles

Where to place the crystal: on your desk, in your pocket or bag, on your living room table

Crystal healing

One of the major weaknesses of Arians is their tendency to act in a reckless or rebellious manner, and this is where soothing crystal energies can be beneficial. So whenever you feel the inclination to act over-impulsively or make rash decisions, pick up your purple fluorite crystal and turn the stone over and over in your hand for about 5–10 minutes until the crystal's stabilizing vibrations make you feel more able to structure your thoughts constructively and to act in a more restrained and reasonable manner. Repeat as often as is necessary to calm you down.

In medical astrology Aries controls the head. Hold a red jasper crystal to your head to dispel any headaches that you get.

Realizing Arian ambitions with ruby

Cut and polished

Rough

Arians can be very impulsive people who are quick to assimilate facts, but they can find it hard to make big changes in their lives. They can be competitive and may try to get ahead in their career or to be good at a sport. They are born leaders and are often positive and outspoken. Even when they seem to be quite meek and mild, there is always an aggressive streak lurking somewhere in their psyche.

Crystal healing

Arians are generally cheerful and helpful people, and generally do not have a devious or sly side. Their assertive side often needs channeling into positive actions to achieve ambitions. So when you recognize that you are procrastinating about a desired aim, pick up and hold your ruby crystal in your hands for about 5 minutes and let the vibrations of this passionate stone give you the courage and determination to realize your aspiration.

Diamond birthstone

The diamond symbolizes purity and it can help bring Arians' lives together. It can support their strong character by encouraging fearlessness, strength, and fortitude. It can also bring clarity, making them more considerate.

CRYSTAL FACTS

CRYSTAL TO USE: ruby (red), opaque when uncut, transparent when polished

AVAILABILITY: commonly available when uncut

QUALITIES OF STONE: brings courage and integrity, aids strong leadership, helps motivation and realizing attainable ambitions

HEALTH BENEFITS: increases blood circulation, releases toxins, helps functioning of the adrenals, kidneys, and reproductive organs, stimulates brain functions, reduces fever

WHERE TO PLACE THE CRYSTAL: on your desk, in your pocket or bag, on your living room table

ALTERNATIVE ASPIRATIONAL CRYSTALS TO USE

Lepidolite: gives concentrated decision-making and focus

Agate: increases perception, boosts analytical functions (right: brown agate)

Removing Taurean inflexibility with natural quartz cluster

Rough with terminator

Taureans are very stable and dependable people that like consistency and order in their lives. They are patient and steadfast in their work and home life, but can also be very creative and often work in artistic professions. Ruled by Venus, the planet associated with the goddess of love, Taureans are very sensual and tactile people who have a sense of humor and enjoy the good things in life. However, their less attractive characteristics are stubbornness, inflexibility, laziness and a tendency to be opinionated.

CRYSTAL FACTS

Crystal to use: natural quartz cluster (clear), all sizes

Availability: commonly available

Qualities of stone: amplifies energy, dispels resistance to change, and promotes mental adaptability

Health benefits: good for any condition, stimulates immune system, soothes burns

Where to place the crystal: on your desk, in your pocket or bag, on your living room table

Taurus

April 21–May 20

Ruling planet: ***Venus***

Element: ***Earth***

Birthstones: ***emerald, topaz***

Related stones: ***aquamarine, diamond, kunzite, lapis lazuli, malachite, rose quartz, tiger's eye***

Crystal healing

One of worst traits of Taureans is a resistance to change of any sort. So when you feel unable to move on in your life, or make an important change, pick up your natural quartz cluster and hold in your hands for about 5–10 minutes and focus on the change you want to make. If you prefer, meditate on your problem while looking at your stone. As you sense the natural emissions of the crystal, notice how your anxiety about the forthcoming change melts away. Repeat this several times if your resistance is hard to shift.

In medical astrology Taurus controls the throat. Hold an aquamarine crystal to your throat to cure a sore throat.

Polished

Increasing Taurean creativity with bloodstone

Taureans tend to be materialistic and often worry about not having enough money; security and having pleasant objects around is very important to them. They love luxuries and can enjoy eating good food and drinking fine wines. They often like to have reasonable savings behind them to protect them from upsets or changes that they can find so hard to bear. Their artistic side often leads them into architecture, fashion, photography, publishing, or the restaurant trade.

CRYSTAL FACTS

Crystal to use: bloodstone, also known as heliotrope, is a type of green jasper that contains red spots of iron oxide.

Availability: commonly available

Qualities of stone: alleviates stress, encourages inner wisdom and altruism, strengthens intuition, and increases creativity and talent

Health benefits: purifies and strengthens blood circulation and releases toxins from kidneys, liver, and spleen, increases metabolism

Where to place the crystal: on your desk, in pocket or bag, on living room table

Crystal healing

Taureans often have a very lazy side. They can work steadily in their professions but lack the imagination or risk-taking abilities to become very successful. If you recognize these limitations in yourself and often feel the need to stimulate your creative side, work regularly with your bloodstone to bring some motivation. Hold the stone to your Third eye chakra in the middle of your forehead for several minutes daily, sensing how the crystal's stimulating impulses are giving you more vitality, new ideas, and awakening your creative juices.

Emerald birthstone

The emerald is linked to Venus, Taurus' ruler. It is a stone that encourages successful relationships and loyalty, something that most Taureans desire. It encourages unconditional love but also stimulates their hedonistic and pleasure-loving side.

ALTERNATIVE CREATIVITY CRYSTALS TO USE

Lapis lazuli: brings self-awareness, helps express new ideas

Citrine: raises self-confidence, opens creative side

Kunzite: encourages self-expression and creativity

Citrine to give Geminis more patience

Cluster

Geminis are great talkers. They have a versatile intellect and inquiring minds, and their charm can help them through difficult situations. Ruled by Mercury, the planet of communication, they love conversation but their restless personality is always observing what else is going on around them. Their less admirable traits are self-involvement, a lack of attention to detail, obsessiveness, and a tendency to feel the grass is always greener somewhere else.

Crystal healing

A less attractive side of Geminis is their impatience in dealing with life situations, or keeping their attention focused on what is happening, or listening to a person's replies. So when you can feel yourself drifting off into middle distance in an important conversation, take hold of your citrine crystal and clutch it tightly until you feel the crystal working with you, helping your concentration to return, giving you the ability to respond in a reasoned and interested way. Use whenever you feel restless or distracted.

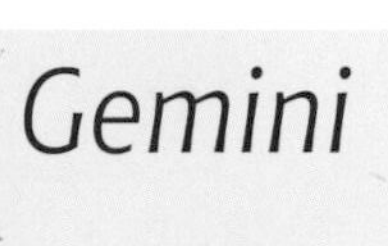

Gemini

May 21–June 20

Ruling planet: ***Mercury***

Element: ***Air***

Birthstones: ***agate, tiger's eye, tourmaline***

Related crystals: ***aquamarine, calcite, chrysocolla, citrine, rutilated quartz, sapphire, topaz***

CRYSTAL FACTS

CRYSTAL TO USE: citrine (yellow, yellow/brown), transparent, often a cluster

AVAILABILITY: natural citrine can be hard to find; citrine produced by heat-treating amethyst is commonly available

QUALITIES OF STONE: strengthens concentration, encourages inner calm and the ability to be more analytical

HEALTH BENEFITS: assists eye problems, detoxifies the blood, relieves digestive upsets, helps menopausal problems such as hot flashes and tiredness

WHERE TO PLACE THE CRYSTAL: on your desk, in your pocket or bag, on your living room table

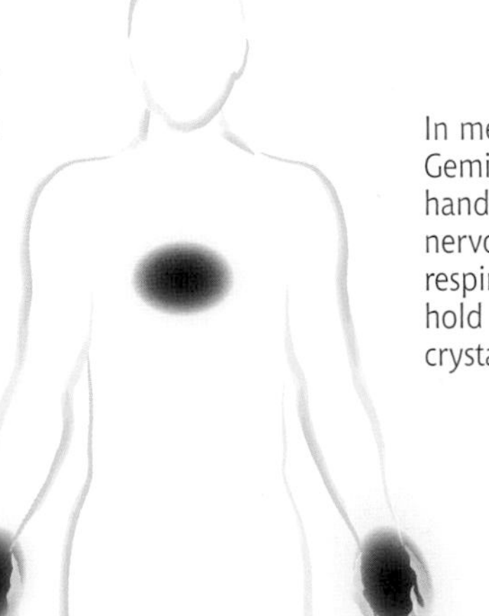

In medical astrology Gemini controls the hands, arms, lungs, and nervous system. For respiratory problems hold a rutilated quartz crystal to your chest.

Soothing Gemini nerves with turquoise

Polished

Geminis love to be on the go. They have a lot of energy and often want to do everything at once. They love a variety of tasks in their work to keep their interest, and they welcome the opportunity to meet new people; stable, routine jobs do not interest them at all. Mentally they are always looking to the next project they can tackle; with their inquisitive mentality the future is always more attractive. They can at times upset friends and family with some emotionless or thoughtless actions to get what they want.

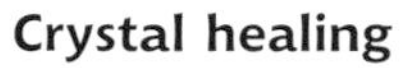

Crystal healing

Trying to achieve so much in their daily lives can create regular nervous tension for Geminis; many live on their nerves. So if you live with this constant tension in your life, work with your turquoise stone to bring some inner peace. When you start to feel agitated and sense your nervous system becoming frayed, pick up your turquoise crystal and place it on your Solar plexus chakra in your upper abdomen. Breathe deeply from your diaphragm and let the healing energies calm your nervous system until you feel nerves in control once again. Use the stone whenever events start to overwhelm you.

CRYSTAL FACTS

Crystal to use: turquoise (green or blue), opaque, often with veins, generally polished

Availability: commonly available

Qualities of stone: helps creative expression, balances emotions, prevents mood swings, calms the nerves

Health benefits: revitalizes blood circulation, regenerates tissue, aids viral infections, soothes cramps and pain

Where to place the crystal: on your desk, in your pocket or bag, on your living room table

Agate birthstone

A grounding stone, agate enhances mental function. It can help to focus Geminis, helping them to study the necessary details to understand the full complexities of a situation.

ALTERNATIVE CALMING CRYSTAL TO USE

Magnesite: reduces emotional stress, intolerance, and nervous tension

Balancing Cancerian moods with rose quartz

Cancerians are very family-orientated. They love security and their homes, and they like to feel they belong. They are protective and caring people. Ruled by the Moon, which is linked to emotions, they are sensitive and intuitive and are often good at jobs that involve helping the public in some way. They are hard-working and can make good politicians. One of the less attractive sides to their characters is their moodiness. They can also be self-pitying and clingy and can have an inferiority complex.

Rough

CRYSTAL FACTS

Crystal to use: rose quartz (pink), normally translucent, can be tumbled

Availability: commonly available

Qualities of stone: emotional healer and balancer, clears resentment, increases love of self, promotes forgiveness

Health benefits: releases toxins from body, increases fertility, soothes burns, aids the complexion, relieves respiratory problems

Where to place the crystal: on your desk, in your pocket or bag, on your living room table

Crystal healing

People who have Cancerians as friends often complain of their regular emotional upsets, and how moody and secretive they can be. So when you start to feel a bit emotionally unbalanced or can feel a sulk coming on, take out your rose quartz crystal and hold it to your heart for about 5 minutes. Let its pure loving vibrations soothe and regulate your mood, filling you with joy and a positive attitude. Use your stone again whenever you start to feel upset or want to withdraw.

Cancer

June 21–July 22

Ruling planet: ***Moon***

Element: ***Water***

Birthstones: ***moonstone, pearl, ruby***

Related crystals: ***amber, aventurine, chrysoprase emerald, moss agate, rhodochrosite***

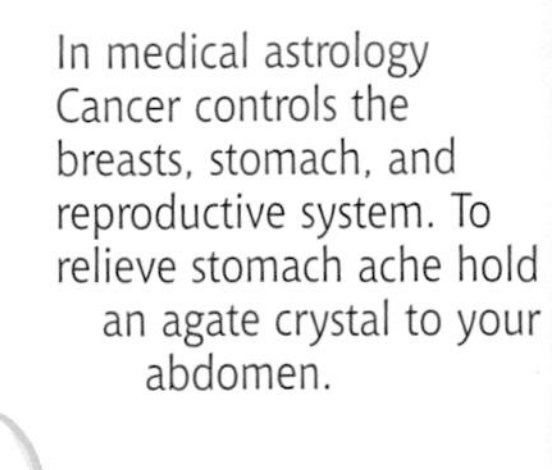

In medical astrology Cancer controls the breasts, stomach, and reproductive system. To relieve stomach ache hold an agate crystal to your abdomen.

Promoting Cancerian security with moonstone

Cancerians live on their emotions. They are great worriers, often concerning themselves about events that never happen. They are great nurturers and homemakers and can excel at cooking. Their heightened sensitivity to people's moods can sometimes make them feel resentful or a victim.

Pearl birthstone

In ancient legends pearls were the tears of the gods. This stone helps to balance a Cancerian's erratic emotions and soothes the Heart chakra. It attracts love and can give courage, attributes that this sign can lack.

Crystal healing

As they worry so much, Cancerians can feel concerned about the future or cling to the past. Often acting in an unsettled, rather helpless manner, they can need a lot of reassurance from the people close to them. If you are aware you can turn these emotions into something positive even as you fight against them. Use moonstone to smooth out your moods, encourage more stability, and heal your stress. When you start to feel insecure and upset, pick up your moonstone and hold it to your Solar plexus chakra in your upper abdomen for several minutes and feel how this caring stone starts to balance your emotions, making you feel safe and protected once more. Use the crystal whenever you start to feel tearful or upset. Avoid working with the stone during a full moon as the effects can be too strong.

CRYSTAL FACTS

Crystal to use: moonstone (white, cream, yellow, blue, green), cloudy and translucent

Availability: commonly available

Qualities of stone: calms overemotional or sharp reactions, soothes and stabilizes and helps to dissolve old, unhelpful patterns

Health benefits: encourages release of waste products, balances PMS symptoms, helps reduce swellings, aids digestion and reproductive organs

Where to place the crystal: on your desk, in your pocket or bag, on your living room table

Polished

ALTERNATIVE SECURITY CRYSTALS TO USE

Agate: a grounding stone that brings emotional balance (right: green moss agate)

Chrysoprase: brings emotional security and trust

Amazonite: soothes any emotional worries and fears

Rough

Calming Leo's over exuberance with watermelon tourmaline

Leo

July 23–August 22

Ruling planet: ***Sun***

Element: ***Fire***

Birthstones: ***garnet, ruby, tiger's eye***

Related crystals: ***amber, carnelian, fire agate, golden beryl (heliodor), onyx, peridot***

Leos love to bask in people's admiration and to be the center of attention. They like to be noticed and often wear dramatic clothing or jewelry to stand out. Ruled by the Sun, which is linked to the ego, they tend to be successful in business and are often figures of authority. They are generous, good-hearted people who look after their families. The less likable characteristics of Leos are their tendencies to be domineering, arrogant, self-centered, and overbearing.

CRYSTAL FACTS

Crystal to use: watermelon tourmaline (green and pink), opaque or transparent, often long and a hexagonal shape

Availability: commonly available

Qualities of stone: instills patience, encourages more tact and diplomacy, dispels old emotional pain and fears

Health benefits: regulates nervous system, reduces stress, treats lymphatic disease

Where to place the crystal: on your desk, in your pocket or handbag, on your living room table

Crystal healing

Leos generally have happy, sunny personalities and will brighten any room they enter. But they can be have tendency to bask in their own glory and to be hedonistic, demanding, and self-righteous. If you recognize that you can be overexuberant or overwhelming in certain situations, calm yourself down by privately taking out your watermelon tourmaline crystal. Hold it tightly in your hands until you feel the stone's balancing energies encouraging you to listen and be more diplomatic and sensitive in what you are saying. Use your crystal whenever you feel yourself becoming unrealistic or too demanding.

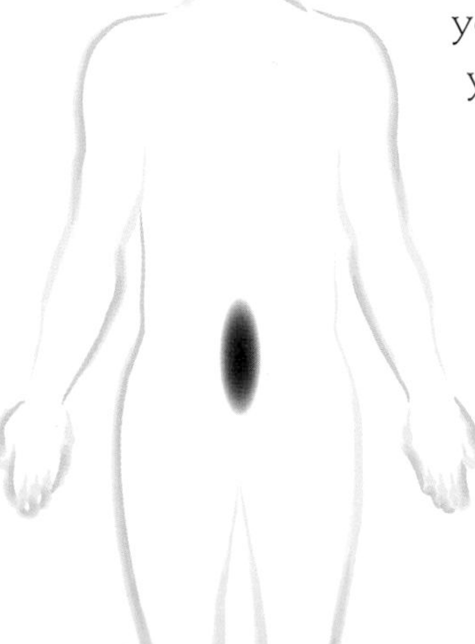
In medical astrology Leo controls the heart and spine. Hold a carnelian crystal to your lower back to relieve backache.

Increasing Leo's self-worth with tiger's eye

Polished red tiger's eye

Leos are life's realists and their optimistic personalities help them to recover from problems and look forward to the future. Their natural ability to project light and warmth wherever they go needs to be controlled, however, as their egos can take over and they can fail to see their own shortcomings. People can also be confused by the supposed self-assurance of Leos—deep down they need to be needed, and they want, above all, to be loved and appreciated.

Crystal healing

Beneath their outgoing and self-possessed exteriors many Leos lack self-confidence and can be very vulnerable to criticism. There is a need to feel that they "count" in the world. If you regularly suffer from a lack of self-worth or want to recover from an upsetting verbal attack, pick up your tiger's eye crystal and hold it on your Sacral chakra in the lower abdomen for several minutes, feeling how the stone's supportive emanations help to resolve any dilemmas and inner conflicts, and rebuild your feelings of self-worth. Regularly use the stone to release any bitterness and frustration.

CRYSTAL FACTS

CRYSTAL TO USE: tiger's eye (browny yellow, blue, red), banded appearance, often tumbled

AVAILABILITY: commonly available

QUALITIES OF STONE: gives insight into your own shortcomings, increases personal power, heals any self-criticism

HEALTH BENEFITS: aids asthma, helps digestive system, heals throat infections

WHERE TO PLACE THE CRYSTAL: on your desk, in your pocket or bag, on your living room table

Ruby birthstone

Ruby is a passionate stone that can increase the generous spirit and overall enthusiasm of the Leo personality. Its dynamic qualities work positively to encourage the best of a Leo's natural leadership abilities.

ALTERNATIVE CONFIDENCE-BUILDING CRYSTALS TO USE

Hematite: boosts self-esteem and gives confidence

Sodalite: releases fears and enhances self-acceptance

Alleviating Virgo's obsessive tendencies with ocean jasper

Polished heart

Virgoans are very practical people. They love to be well organized and are efficient in their work and all the tasks they undertake. They are seekers of information, both in the world around them and also in their own lives, and excel in jobs such as accountancy, the media, IT, or marketing. Ruled by Mercury, the planet of communication and logical behavior, Virgoans are very analytical in their approach to life and love, establishing well-run systems. Their unappealing characteristics include being stubborn, sarcastic, pedantic, and testy and feeling undervalued.

Virgo

August 23–September 22

Ruling planet: ***Mercury***

Element: ***Earth***

Birthstones: ***carnelian, peridot, sapphire***

Related crystals: ***amazonite, citrine, jade, moss agate, opal, rose quartz***

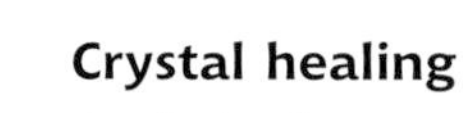

Crystal healing

An irritating aspect of the Virgoan personality is a tendency to be obsessed about their health, worrying about every minor ache and pain. When you sense you are being a hypochondriac, take hold of your ocean jasper crystal and place it on your skin to let its nurturing vibrations work through your body, removing any negative energies, soothing your anxiety, and releasing your obsessive worries. Use your crystal whenever you start to panic about the state of your health.

CRYSTAL FACTS

CRYSTAL TO USE: ocean jasper, opaque, patterned, often tumbled

AVAILABILITY: commonly available

QUALITIES OF STONE: balances and releases obsessive inclinations, nurtures and supports during stress, absorbs negative energy

HEALTH BENEFITS: strengthens liver, gall bladder, circulatory and digestive systems, relieves stomach upsets

WHERE TO PLACE THE CRYSTAL: on your desk, in your pocket or bag, on your living room table

In medical astrology Virgo controls the nervous system and the intestines. To calm your nerves hold a smoky quartz crystal to your abdomen.

Rising above Virgoan irritation with rhodochrosite

Work is important to Virgoans; they like having a good position and being appreciated for their competency. If they have to fight their corner, they can become despondent and lose confidence in themselves. This in turn can make them whine about how no one appreciates them. They get bored easily and need the excitement of taking up many interests, but do not always follow them through.

Peridot birthstone

This visionary stone increases awareness of the hidden detail of different situations, so works well with Virgoans who love to get to the heart of the matter. It also sharpens their minds, bringing increased understanding.

Crystal healing

Virgoans are true perfectionists and when life does not match up to their expectations they can become very irritable. So when your nerves feel frayed, pick up your pink, compassionate rhodochrosite crystal to balance your emotional state. Hold it over your heart and chest for several minutes until you feel your breathing and heartbeat slowing and your frustration and tension releasing. Take hold of your stone whenever you feel you are starting to lose patience.

Polished

CRYSTAL FACTS

CRYSTAL TO USE: rhodochrosite (pinky), banded, can be polished or tumbled

AVAILABILITY: commonly available

QUALITIES OF STONE: emotional balancer, helps confront unreasonable fears, lifts depression, and encourages a positive attitude

HEALTH BENEFITS: aids the kidneys and heart, increases blood circulation, relieves asthma and breathing problems, alleviates migraines, boosts the thryroid

WHERE TO PLACE THE CRYSTAL: on your desk, in your pocket or bag, on your living room table

ALTERNATIVE IRRITATION-RELIEVING CRYSTALS TO USE

Blue apatite: alleviates irritability and emotional exhaustion

Aventurine: calms irritation, promotes feelings of wellbeing

Lavender (purple) jade: encourages emotional release, reduces irritability

Polished

Balancing Libra's critical side with aquamarine

Librans like harmony in their lives, and often seek fairness and balance in everything they attempt. They have pleasant personalities and can mix well at a party, although they can have a tendency to forget the people they have met. Ruled by Venus, the goddess of love and pleasure, Librans like easy going relationships. They have a great love of beauty and need to live in pleasant surroundings. The characteristics that are not so appealing are being indecisive and insincere, lacking self-reliance, and being superficial and vain.

Crystal healing

Another Libran flaw is the habit of being overcritical. They can get very exasperated about other people's faults and their inability to correct them. If you recognize this trait as part of your personality, take out your aquamarine crystal when you feel you are just about to criticize someone, and hold it for a few minutes to your throat. Sense how its supportive vibrations are calming you down, dispersing your judgmental attitudes, and bringing some much-needed tolerance. Use your crystal whenever you feel your sharp tongue is coming into action.

CRYSTAL FACTS

CRYSTAL TO USE: aquamarine (greeny blue), clear/opaque, often tumbled

AVAILABILITY: commonly available

QUALITIES OF STONE: overcomes intolerance of others, helps creative expression, calms nerves and mental confusion, increases sensitivity

HEALTH BENEFITS: alleviates fluid retention, relieves sore throats, swollen glands, acts as a general tonic, reduces hay fever

WHERE TO PLACE THE CRYSTAL: on your desk, in your pocket or handbag, on your living room table

In medical astrology Libra controls the kidneys, bladder, and buttocks. To mitigate a bladder infection, hold a bloodstone crystal to the area.

Libra

September 23–October 22

Ruling planet: ***Venus***

Element: ***Air***

Birthstones: ***chrysoprase, opal, sapphire***

Related crystals: ***aquamarine, aventurine, emerald, opal, peridot, smoky quartz***

Boosting Libran good feelings with chrysoprase

Polished

Librans have a sense of fair play and can make great arbitrators and administrators. They like to be part of a team as they can find decision-making hard work. They like beautiful objects so can be drawn toward design and creative careers. They have a tendency to be in another space mentally, to have "their heads in the clouds," and often need to be grounded or brought back to reality.

Crystal healing

Librans normally have an easygoing personality but can also be prone to moodiness and depression. So if you know that you can feel a bit low at times, hold your chrysoprase to your forehead and allow this serene stone to bring you joy and happiness, letting you enjoy simple things once again. Hold the stone for several minutes and feel its vibrational power lifting your mood and making you feel ready to enjoy a basic pleasure such as a walk by the river or sitting in the sun in your local park. Use the stone whenever you feel yourself becoming depressed.

Sapphire birthstone

Librans love beauty of all kinds so they feel an affinity with this serene stone that promotes harmony and balance. A white sapphire supports their belief in fair play and justice for all.

CRYSTAL FACTS

CRYSTAL TO USE: chrysoprase (green, lemon/yellow), opaque, flecked, often tumbled

AVAILABILITY: commonly available

QUALITIES OF STONE: encourages creativity, stimulates self-acceptance, brings a sense of security and trust, helps when taking on new projects

HEALTH BENEFITS: relieves depression, increases fertility, eases sexual frustration, aids relaxation and good sleep, alleviates skin disease

WHERE TO PLACE THE CRYSTAL: on your desk, in your pocket or bag, on your living room table

ALTERNATIVE MOOD-LIFTING CRYSTALS TO USE

Jet: balances mood swings, dispels depression

Turquoise: brings emotional balance, promotes wellbeing

Lapis lazuli: balances body and spirit, increases creativity and vitality

Bloodstone for banishing Scorpio possessiveness

Polished

Scorpios are intense, magnetic people who are courageous and passionate in everything they undertake. They are also very sensitive, with a well-developed intuition. Ruled by both assertive Mars and secretive Pluto, Scorpios are strong characters who are not always easy to live with or to work for. They love investigative work and are often drawn to professions such as medicine, psychiatry, or journalism. The less appealing side of their personalities is that they can hang on to resentments and be ruthless, suspicious, and have a jealous side.

Crystal healing

One of the least appealing characteristics of Scorpios is their tendency to be possessive with friends and lovers. So when you start to feel jealous because your partner is going out or perhaps resent that a friend is going on vacation without you, close your eyes and hold your bloodstone crystal firmly in your hands for about 5–10 minutes. Feel how its subtle vibrations start to calm your mind, promote selflessness, and release your clinging tendencies. Use the stone whenever you feel possessive.

CRYSTAL FACTS

CRYSTAL TO USE: bloodstone, also known as heliotrope, is a type of green jasper that contains red spots of iron oxide

AVAILABILITY: commonly available

QUALITIES OF STONE: reduces stress and revitalizes body and mind, heals psyche and inner conflict

HEALTH BENEFITS: increases blood circulation, detoxifies liver, kidneys, bladder, and spleen, stimulates the metabolism

WHERE TO PLACE THE CRYSTAL: on your desk, in your pocket or bag, on your living room table

October 23–November 21

Ruling planets: ***Pluto, Mars***

Element: ***Water***

Birthstones: ***aquamarine, malachite, topaz***

Related crystals: ***dark opal, green tourmaline, herkimer diamond, obsidian, turquoise***

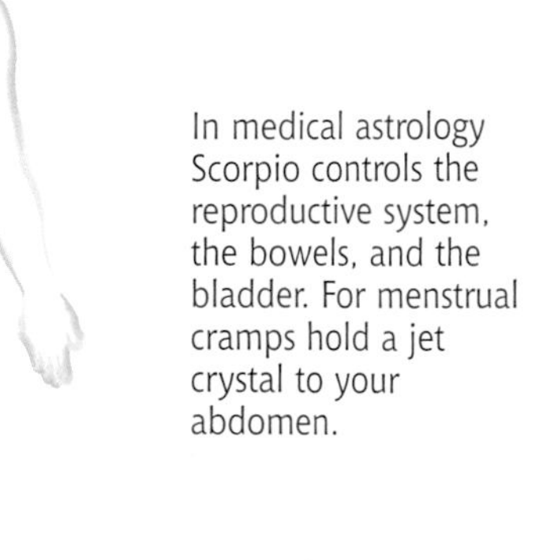

In medical astrology Scorpio controls the reproductive system, the bowels, and the bladder. For menstrual cramps hold a jet crystal to your abdomen.

Scorpios can learn forgiveness with apache tear obsidian

Polished

Scorpios are very emotional signs. They often make decisions emotionally through excitement or anger without always thinking things through. They generally have hot tempers and have a tendency to overreact to situations, often being mortally offended by something someone says, even if no disrespect was intended.

Crystal healing

As their emotions rule their lives, Scorpios can hold a grudge when a friend, colleague, or relative upsets them. They can brood for a long time over the altercation, finding it extremely difficult to get over what has happened, and can make bitter enemies. If you know you have these tendencies and find it hard to forgive and forget, use your apache tear obsidian stone after every upsetting confrontation. Hold the stone to your heart for several minutes daily for a week after the argument, feeling how the crystal is calming you down, encouraging your forgiveness, and working on dispelling the bitterness and distress that you are holding there.

Malachite birthstone

Life is lived more powerfully under the influence of this stone, which suits the adventurous Scorpio perfectly. It promotes risk-taking and change for spiritual growth, and encourages unconditional love.

CRYSTAL FACTS

CRYSTAL TO USE: apache tear obsidian (black), translucent

AVAILABILITY: commonly available

QUALITIES OF STONE: absorbs negative energies, shields the aura, releases deep-rooted grievances, promotes forgiveness

HEALTH BENEFITS: cleanses body of toxins, relieves muscle spasms

WHERE TO PLACE THE CRYSTAL: on your desk, in your pocket or bag, on your living room table

ALTERNATIVE FORGIVENESS CRYSTALS TO USE

Rutilated quartz: soothes black moods, promotes forgiveness

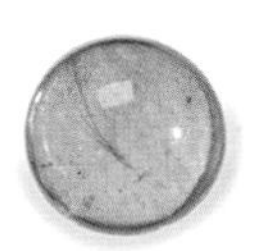

Rhodonite: eases emotional trauma, helps reconciliation and forgiveness

Topaz: healing stone that releases tension, encourages generosity, and aids forgiveness

Rough

Avoiding Sagittarian excessive behavior with lapis lazuli

CRYSTAL FACTS

CRYSTAL TO USE: Blue with gold flecks; may be blue and white (white is calcite); may have black spots of lazulite

AVAILABILITY: commonly available but expensive

QUALITIES OF STONE: gives mental clarity, promotes self-awareness and inner wisdom, increases psychic abilities, releases stress and tension

HEALTH BENEFITS: strengthens thyroid gland, relieves painful headaches, aids depression, cleanses organs and purifies blood, stabilizes blood pressure

WHERE TO PLACE THE CRYSTAL: on your desk, in your pocket or bag, on your living room table

Sagittarians can be very adventurous people as they love to travel, but they also have a conservative side and need a safe, secure haven to which they can return. They are normally cheerful people with an optimistic outlook on life. They are often drawn to publishing or the travel industry. Their wit or sense of humor works well in these professions. The downside of their personalities is the tendency to lose their temper or be tactless. They can also be too confident, boastful, or fixed in their views.

Crystal healing

One of the problems with Sagittarians is their tendency to act excessively, going all out to achieve a goal. If you feel yourself running out of steam trying to excel at a work project or trying to do too many things at once, pick up your lapis lazuli crystal and hold it firmly for about 5 minutes, or hold it to your forehead, feeling how this serene stone is calming your stress, increasing your inner wisdom, slowing you down, and bringing inner peace. Use the stone whenever you go into hyper-drive.

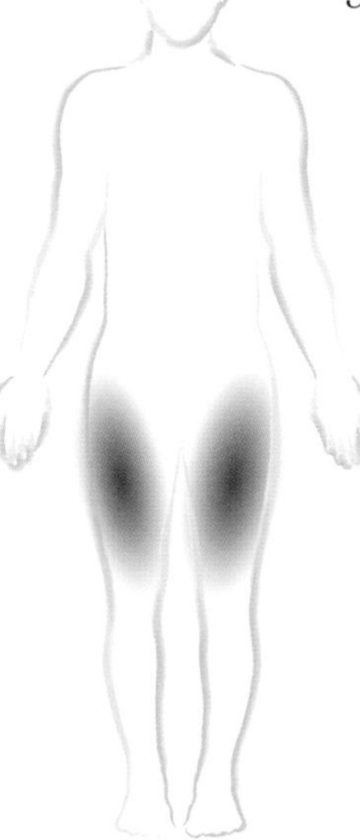
In medical astrology Sagittarius controls the hips and thighs. For a hip problem, treat it with jade.

Sagittarius

November 22–December 21

Ruling planet: ***Jupiter***

Element: ***Fire***

Birthstones: ***sapphire, topaz, turquoise,***

Related crystals: ***amethyst, blue lace agate, garnet, malachite, ruby, smoky quartz, sodalite***

Widening Sagittarians' vision with topaz

Polished

CRYSTAL FACTS

RYSTAL TO USE: blue topaz, transparent, pointed, can be faceted

VAILABILITY: readily available from specialist stores

QUALITIES OF STONE: aids self-expression and creativity, gives clarity, promotes forgiveness, supports positive thoughts and affirmations, helps to achieve own desires

HEALTH BENEFITS: strengthens thyroid gland, regenerates tissue, relieves throat disorders, helps good digestion

WHERE TO PLACE THE CRYSTAL: on your desk, in your pocket or handbag, on your living room table

Sagittarians can be quite altruistic and can burden themselves with society's problems. They like helping others and can end up helping out down-at-luck friends or relatives. The philosophizing "putting the world to rights" side of some Sagittarians can be at odds with their more earthly desires to socialize and to party. Their adventurous personality seeks a merging of their spiritual and physical desires.

Turquoise birthstone

The stabilizing quality of turquoise can bring some calm to this fiery sign when they are going all out for a goal. Mentally it can help with problem-solving and can relieve exhaustion caused by the Sagittarian tendency to overwork.

Crystal healing

Sagittarians are often uninterested in money and can spend a large proportion of their lives on a spiritual quest. Sometimes their aspirations are unrealistic or impractical and they need to be brought back down to earth. If you know that you regularly pursue causes or projects that have little foundation, spend some time working with your blue topaz crystal and let its inspiring rays give a new perspective to what you are trying to do and show a way forward. Hold the stone to your Third eye chakra in the middle of your forehead whenever you have lost your way, and let its vibrant energy move you in a new direction, giving you the light to find the right and true path.

ALTERNATIVE VISION-SEEKING CRYSTALS TO USE

Diamond: stimulates imagination, aids spiritual aspirations

Pietersite: encourages inner guidance and removes spiritual fantasies

Polished

CRYSTAL FACTS

Crystal to use: chalcedony

Availability: commonly available, but can be expensive

Qualities of stone: encourages optimism and goodwill, lifts mood and brings joy, dispels self-doubt, brings a benevolent attitude

Health benefits: improves blood circulation and the functioning of the spleen, bone marrow, and gall bladder, increases physical energy

Where to place the crystal: on your desk, in your pocket or bag, on your living room table

Dispelling Capricorn depression with chalcedony

Capricorns are very sensible and capable people. They are hard-working and ambitious and like a structured lifestyle. Ruled by Saturn, the teacher of the zodiac, they can be affected by the restrictions, struggles, and attention to detail that this serious planet demands. They can be addicted to work and are often found working in industries such as banking and accounting, but may also be self-employed. The less attractive side of Capricorns is their meanness or pettiness, inflexibility, and tendencies to be aloof and to use other people to further their own gains.

December 22–January 19

Ruling planet: ***Saturn***

Element: ***Earth***

Birthstones: ***garnet, jet, onyx***

Related crystals: ***amethyst, moonstone, moss agate, obsidian, peridot, ruby, sugilite***

Crystal healing

One of the unappealing characteristics of Capricorns is their predisposition to be depressed: they can be melancholic or wallow in their own misery. So if you recognize that you regularly feel sorry for yourself, take hold of your chalcedony crystal when your mood deteriorates and hold it in your hands or to your Third eye chakra in the middle of your forehead. Let its nurturing vibrations lift your melancholy and give you back your optimism and enjoyment of life. Use your crystal whenever your emotions take a downturn.

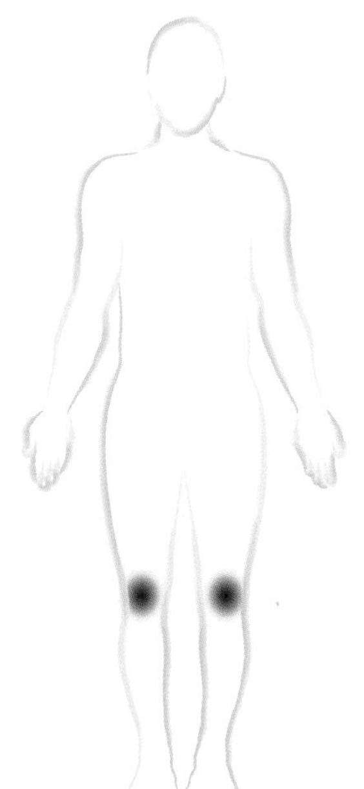

In medical astrology Capricorn controls the body's skeleton, knees, and skin. For knee problems use an azurite crystal.

Capricorns can learn to cope under presssure with yellow jasper

Capricorns can suffer from insecurity, and even when they have savings and a good job they can worry about becoming impoverished. They can be reasonable and caring people but can also possess a hot temper. Many Capricorns suffer from a lack of self-esteem and need to feel valued and have their efforts appreciated, particularly at work. They can seem old at a young age, only becoming more comfortable with themselves and their families as they establish themselves at work and grow older.

Polished

CRYSTAL FACTS

CRYSTAL TO USE: yellow jasper

AVAILABILITY: commonly available

QUALITIES OF STONE: quietens the nerves, encourages balance, supports when under stress, protects you from, and dispels negative energies, aids quick thinking and organizational skills

HEALTH BENEFITS: relieves nausea, bladder, and stomach problems, supports the circulatory system, promotes the release of toxins

WHERE TO PLACE THE CRYSTAL: on your desk, in your pocket or bag, on your living room table

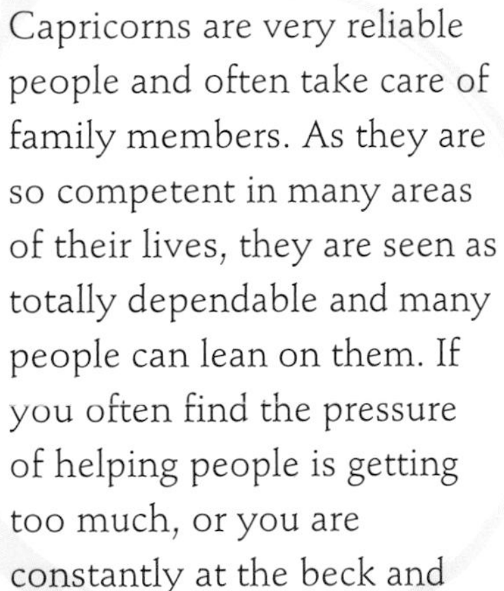

Crystal healing

Capricorns are very reliable people and often take care of family members. As they are so competent in many areas of their lives, they are seen as totally dependable and many people can lean on them. If you often find the pressure of helping people is getting too much, or you are constantly at the beck and call of your family, pick up your yellow jasper crystal and clasp it in your hands or place it on your Solar plexus chakra in your upper abdomen. Focus on what you want to balance in your life and let the stone's nurturing qualities give you the energy and stamina you need to cope.

Onyx birthstone

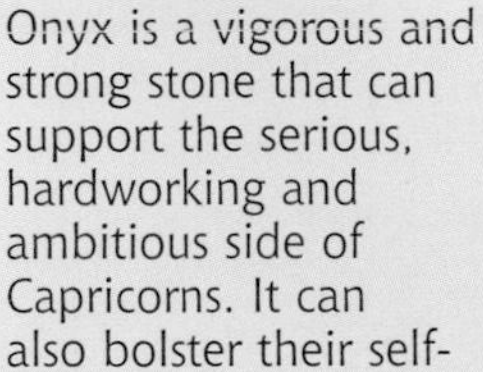

Onyx is a vigorous and strong stone that can support the serious, hardworking and ambitious side of Capricorns. It can also bolster their self-confidence, which is often lacking, despite their abilities.

ALTERNATIVE COPING CRYSTALS TO USE

Amethyst: balances emotional highs and lows, dispels anxiety

Chrysoprase: brings solutions to situations, encourages positive thinking

Celestite: alleviates worries, promotes mental clarity

Reducing Aquarians' impulsive action with aventurine

CRYSTAL FACTS

CRYSTAL TO USE: aventurine (green, blue, red, brown, pale orange)

AVAILABILITY: commonly available

QUALITIES OF STONE: dispels anxiety and fear, encourages calmness and tranquillity, increases perception and creativity, brings empathy and compassion

HEALTH BENEFITS: improves blood flow, balances blood pressure, lowers cholesterol, improves skin complaints, eases migraines, relieves eye problems

WHERE TO PLACE THE CRYSTAL: on your desk, in your pocket or handbag, on your living room table

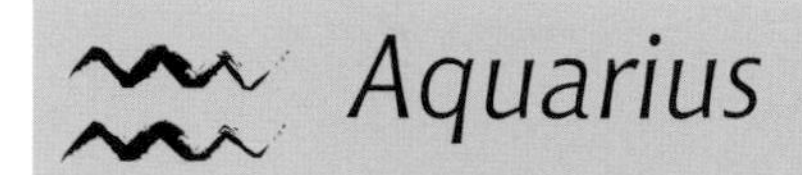

Aquarius

January 20–February 17

Ruling planet: ***Saturn, Uranus***

Element: ***Air***

Birthstones: ***amethyst, aquamarine, kunzite***

Related crystals: ***agate, blue celestite, chrysoprase, garnet, moonstone, natural quartz, turquoise***

Aquarians are logical, intelligent people who like to work out problems analytically. They can have a big circle of friends but may find it hard to maintain a one-to-one, intimate relationship, as they are often more emotionally detached and like their own independence. Ruled by Uranus, the planet of ideals, and Saturn, planet of restriction and limitations, they can be humanitarian but often hang onto fixed ideas. Negatively, Aquarians can be self-centered, pedantic, reluctant to compromise, and inflexible in their attitudes.

Crystal healing

Another unfavorable side of Aquarians is their lack of sympathy or empathy for people. They find it hard to be supportive when someone is ill. If you start to get irritated by a person's negativity or you cannot cope when they are complaining about their problems, pick up your aventurine crystal. Hold it to your Heart chakra in the middle of your chest and feel its compassionate pulsations opening up your caring and loving side. Use the stone whenever you lack a positive emotional response.

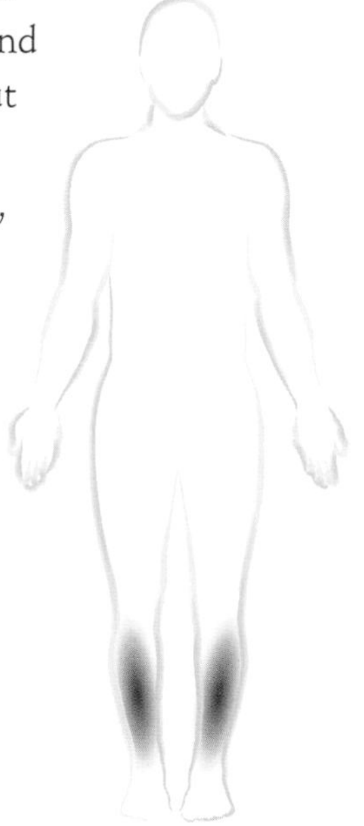

In medical astrology Aquarius controls the calves and ankles. For leg cramps use a hematite crystal.

Aquarians take on new ideas with amethyst

Cluster

CRYSTAL FACTS

CRYSTAL TO USE: amethyst (violet/purple), transparent, geode, cluster or polished

AVAILABILITY: very commonly available

QUALITIES OF STONE: heals mind and emotions, relieves depression, calms or stimulates mind when needed, helps practical decision-making, alleviates stress and tension

HEALTH BENEFITS: cleanses the blood, strengthens the immune and endocrine systems, relieves headaches and tension, soothes bruises and swellings

WHERE TO PLACE THE CRYSTAL: on your desk, in your pocket or bag, on your living room table

Aquarians can be quite eccentric, individualistic people, who are often interested in New Age subjects. They can be competitive in their field of work, but can also be drawn to the caring professions, teaching, or IT, which particularly suits their logical minds. Although Aquarians crave their own space and despise clingy relationships, they are a fixed sign and stay for a long time in a job or relationship, when they have committed to someone. However, if they decide to leave, their decision can be quite cold and clinical.

Crystal healing

The logical Aquarian brain is very versatile, and being with an Aquarian is never boring. However, they do have a tendency to hang onto their fixed views and be reluctant to change their way of life. If you have problems embracing new ideas or projects and feel frustrated that you find it hard to make changes, take your amethyst crystal in your hand or place it on the crown of your head. Close your eyes, and let its soothing energies bring insight and increase your perceptiveness into how you can make changes in your life.

Aquamarine birthstone

Aquarians have very sharp brains and working with aquamarine can help them filter information and gain extra perceptive skills. It also increases feelings of sensitivity, which can aid Aquarians as they can be rather unemotional.

ALTERNATIVE CHANGE CRYSTALS TO USE

Bloodstone: assists adjustment to change

Blue chalcedony: opens the mind to new ideas

Chrysocolla: allows acceptance of change

Overcoming Piscean mood swings with aragonite

Pisceans are sensitive people with a well-developed intuition. They are often spiritually enlightened and may seem to live with their heads in the clouds. Ruled by Neptune, the planet of dreams and illusions, and by Jupiter, the planet of good luck and opportunity, Pisceans can be very altruistic, dreamy, and kind people. At their worst they can be indecisive, and can sink into chaos, become very depressed, and be emotionally unpredictable.

Pisces

February 18–March 20

Ruling planets: ***Neptune, Jupiter***

Element: ***Water***

Birthstones: ***amethyst, black opal, moonstone***

Related crystals: ***beryl, bloodstone, blue lace agate, chrysoprase, tourmaline, turquoise***

CRYSTAL FACTS

Crystal to use: aragonite (white, yellow, gold, green, blue, brown) often translucent with spiky protusions

Availability: commonly available

Qualities of stone: encourages mental discipline, gives insight to problems, grounds and centers the emotions, helps concentration, bring tolerance

Health benefits: strengthens bone structure, pain reliever, aids muscles spasms, boosts immune system

Where to place the crystal: on your desk, in your pocket or handbag, on your living room table

Cluster

Crystal healing

One of the less endearing sides of Pisceans is their moodiness. Because of their sensitivity to what is going on around them, they can soak up a person's unhappiness and become easily upset. So if you sense your mood deteriorating, pick up your grounding aragonite crystal and hold it in your hands or over your Third eye chakra in the middle of your forehead. Let this healing stone soothe and release your emotional stress and balance your sensitivity. Use your crystal whenever your mood takes a downward turn.

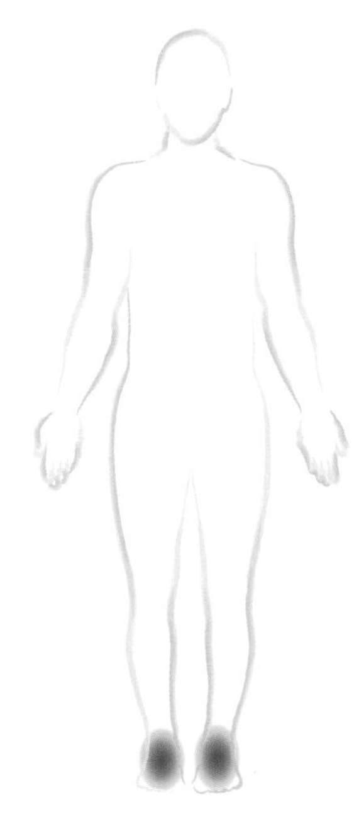

In medical astrology Pisces controls the feet. If you have foot problems use an onyx crystal.

Pisces can foster realistic dreams with smoky quartz

Pisceans love the arts and are often into music, painting, dance, and work in creative industries such as photography and publishing. However, they can often be impractical at home. There can be an innocence about Pisceans, and many never truly grow up, sometimes feeling more at home with children or animals.

Rough

Crystal healing

Pisceans can suffer from self-doubt and worry about the future. They can find it hard to come back down to earth enough to put some of their dreams into practice. If you know that you have a tendency to be on another plane and are often unrealistic about some of your aims, use smoky quartz regularly to focus on what is possible. Hold it to your Root chakra in your lower abdomen for several minutes and feel its grounding emissions clearing your mind, giving you the guidance to follow an attainable dream.

CRYSTAL FACTS

RYSTAL TO USE: smoky quartz (brown/black), translucent and pointed, can be irradiated

AVAILABILITY: commonly available, but check that it is smoky quartz

QUALITIES OF STONE: lifts depression, balances emotions, very grounding, lessens fear, promotes positive thoughts. Clears subconscious blocks, helps realize your dreams

HEALTH BENEFITS: strengthens adrenal glands and kidneys, boosts energy, increases fertility, alleviates pain and headaches, supports the back and nervous system

WHERE TO PLACE THE CRYSTAL: on your desk, in your pocket or bag, on your living room table

Polished

Moonstone birthstone

A moonstone links to the moon's cycles and intuition, so it can increase a Piscean's intuitive side and increase their awareness of inner feelings or messages. It can also soothe emotional instability,

ALTERNATIVE MANIFESTATION CRYSTALS TO USE

Rhodochrosite: gives a positive attitude, helps you choose the right aim

Golden beryl (heliodor): encourages initiative and aids helps turn an idea into reality

How to choose your crystals

Cluster

Crystal facts

Where to buy: ideally in a crystal shop, alternatively by mail order or the internet

Crystal vibrations: crystals transmit energy fields and will communicate with you; their energy will feel good or not right for you

Quality of crystal: check for a crystal with a strong color—e.g., if amethyst is not bright purple, its energy has faded; avoid any stones with chips or indentations

Moving on: crystals sometimes do their work and move on; you may lose one or want to give it to someone else. Let it go freely, knowing that another one will replace it

Watch out for: dyed crystals. Many agates are dyed blue, green, and purple, which alters their energy; turquoise may be dyed howlite (blue howlite) with no flecks of gold; amber may be plastic (rub it against your thumb: it should feel waxy)

Make going out to buy your first crystals a special time. Ideally take half a day or at least a few hours and visit a recommended crystal shop that stocks a wide range of crystals. Ask the owner questions about the crystals: a good shop will sell few dyed crystals. Lose yourself in the beauty and power of this vast array of delightful, colored stones, and remember that a crystal normally chooses you.

Finding your crystals

Make a list before your visit of the stones you need to work on the tips you want to do in the book. Wander around the store, stopping to pick up any crystals that appeal. When you are used to the energetics of the place, go to choose your first crystal. Check whether you want a rough or polished stone, a cluster or one with a terminated point.

- Now stand in front of the first tray of crystals, close your eyes, then open them and see which crystal catches your eye and says "pick me up."
- Hold the crystal in your hands and see if your hands get warm or start to tingle.
- Tune into your senses and see if you feel a surge of energy, a vibration, a humming, or can see light coming from the stone.
- If nothing occurs or it does not feel right, try another one—the best stone for you is the one that produces the strongest sensation.

Polished agate hearts

Work through your whole crystal list using this technique, but remember always follow your intuition: it is invariably right.

Green moss agate

Cleansing crystals in water

Crystals take in energy from their surroundings and people, so when you buy one from a shop it will still contain the energetic imprint of everyone who has handled it. So before you can use it for its chosen purpose, you need to cleanse it so that it will work at its highest vibration. Once crystals are in place at home or in the workplace, or if you wear crystal jewelry, they need cleansing weekly or monthly. If you are using a crystal for a healing purpose, cleanse it after each session or daily, as the stone will absorb the negative vibrations of the illness or emotional upset.

The water method

One of the simplest cleansing methods when you first buy a crystal and do not know its history is to soak it in a glass bowl of still spring water for 24 hours to remove any deeply embedded negativity. To cleanse normally, hold the crystal or piece of jewelry under running water in your kitchen sink for a few minutes, holding the intention to remove negativity and to bring it back to a neutral state. Dry thoroughly after both methods.

CRYSTAL FACTS

WHAT CLEANSER TO USE: spring water

QUALITIES OF CLEANSER: water: a ritual purifier that removes negativity

CRYSTALS NOT TO CLEANSE IN WATER: selenite, lapis lazuli, malachite, turquoise. These stones are either water-soluble or the physical properties are affected by the water

Aqua aura

Polished snowflake obsidian

Cleansing crystals in saltwater

There are many different views and crystal traditions when it comes to saltwater cleansing. Some crystal healers do not recommend it as they feel it is too harsh a technique for crystals; others take the scientific approach—when an electrical charge is introduced to saltwater by the addition of a crystal, a battery effect is set up which will effectively "run down" the crystal's energy.

Polished pietersite

The saltwater method

Salt, however, has been used for thousands of years as a wonderful, natural purifier, for physical healing and in sacred cleansing ceremonies. If you want to try this method, place a handful of sea salt in a glass bowl filled with spring water. Let the salt dissolve completely before immersing the crystal, as the salt can scratch a soft stone. Hold the intention to remove all negativity. Leave for an hour, then rinse the crystal in pure spring water before drying. If you feel your crystals aren't working well using this method, then choose one of the other methods suggested.

CRYSTAL FACTS

WHAT CLEANSER TO USE: spring water with sea salt added

QUALITIES OF CLEANSER: water: a ritual purifier that removes negativity; salt: ancient purifying ingredient with antiseptic qualities

CRYSTALS NOT TO CLEANSE IN WATER OR SALTWATER: selenite, lapis lazuli, malachite, turquoise. These stones are either water-soluble or the physical properties are affected by the water

CRYSTALS NOT TO CLEANSE IN SALTWATER: calcite, carnelian, labradorite, opal, as it changes their physical properties

Rough blue tourmaline

Polished danburite

Cleansing crystals by smudging

Smudging is an ancient Native American tradition that clears a space of any unpleasant sensations or negative energies. Smudge sticks are made from rolled-up dried herbs and when lit produce a cleansing smoke. Sage is one of the most powerful purifiers, and its healing smoke can effectively cleanse your crystals of negative vibrations. It is particularly good for crystal jewelry.

Smudge sticks

The smudging method

To cleanse a new crystal or jewelry, or several, place them in a bowl. Light your smudge stick, holding it over a fireproof bowl, blow out the flame, and then waft the smoke over your crystal several times to remove negativity and bring its vibrancy back to normal. This purifying method can also cleanse you and the room. Rinse under the faucet to extinguish.
Incense is less powerful than smudging but can purify one crystal at a time. Light your incense stick, and when it is smoldering, gently waft the smoke over the crystal a few times, then leave to burn out on the holder.

CRYSTAL FACTS

WHAT CLEANSER TO USE: a sage smudge stick or, if unavailable, a frankincense incense stick

QUALITIES OF CLEANSER: sage smudge stick: a powerful cleanser that removes psychic debris, negative influences or energies; frankincense incense stick: purifies crystals and is spiritually uplifting

Cleansing with a singing bowl

Metal singing bowls have been used in the East for centuries for healing and to aid meditation. Made from seven metals, they are commonly used today in the West by therapists to raise energy levels. They are effective cleansers, and the humming sound they make when stroked can purify and lift the vibrancy of crystals.

The singing bowl method

Place the crystal, or several together, in the singing bowl and start to stroke the bowl's mallet around the inner or outer edge of the bowl and feel the sound building up. As you move the mallet in faster circles, negative energy from the crystals whirls away and brighter, positive energy is pulled in. Slowly stop playing the bowl and remove the crystals.

CRYSTAL FACTS

WHAT CLEANSER TO USE: metal Nepalese or Tibetan singing bowl

QUALITIES OF CLEANSER: a singing bowl creates a sound vibration that dispels negativity

CRYSTALS NOT TO CLEANSE BY SINGING BOWL: terminated crystals (with a point) as they can chip when moving around the bowl

Polished quartz, smoky quartz, and rose quartz with singing bowl

Cleansing by breath

When you have used a crystal for a quick healing treatment and are not able to use one of the more powerful cleansing methods detailed (see pages 149–150), perhaps if you are away from home and cannot easily use water, smudging, or the other cleansing methods, you can simply purify it with the power of your own breath.

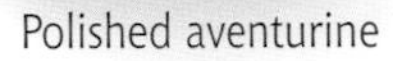
Polished aventurine

Polished kunzite

Polished larimar

CRYSTAL FACTS

What cleanser to use: your own breath

Qualities of cleanser: sending an intention with your breath can remove negativity

Rough snow quartz

Rough azurite

The breath method

Take a few deep breaths and clear your mind. Pick up your crystal and focus on removing any negativity it holds, saying to yourself: "I cleanse this crystal with love." Breathe in deeply and exhale forcefully on it. Visualize any bad energy that comes off it being absorbed by the ground and changed by Mother Earth into vibrant energy once more. For a large crystal, breathe into every facet or side of the crystal.

Re-energizing crystals with sunlight

Although this is not an essential process, it can be good to do when you first buy your crystals. The natural, fiery energy of the sun can boost the crystal's own subtle vibrations so that they work at their highest power.

The sun method

To re-energize your crystals they need to be in full sunlight for about 24 hours. On a sunny day, place your crystals on the outside of a sunny windowsill (glass reduces the sun's strength) in the early morning and take them in at dusk; repeat on the next sunny day. Alternatively leave them out in your garden covered by a linen cloth. However, do not place crystal balls in the sunlight, as this poses a fire risk.

Alternative methods

You can also energize crystals in moonlight, putting them out at night and retrieving them in the morning; try to choose a particular phase such as a new or full moon. The more emotional moon energizes in a gentle, subtle way, suiting the opaque stones such as agates, moonstones, and obsidians.

Polished sunstone

CRYSTAL FACTS

WHAT ENERGIZER TO USE: sunlight

QUALITIES OF ENERGIZER: sunlight is a natural energizer

CRYSTALS NOT TO BE ENERGIZED IN FULL SUNLIGHT: amethyst, aquamarine, aventurine, beryl, celestite, heat-treated citrine, fluorite, kunzite, lapis lazuli, malachite, opal, rose quartz, tourmaline, turquoise, as they can fade or be adversely affected by the heat

Polished red garnet

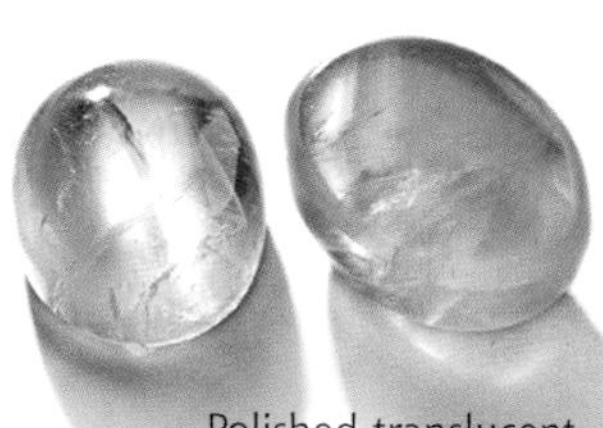

Polished translucent moonstone

Polished labradorite egg

Dedicating your crystal

Rough gold calcite

Rough purple fluorite

Rough blue apatite

Polished turquoise

Before you start working with your newly cleansed crystal it is a good idea to dedicate it. This simple empowerment can make a big difference to how well your crystal will work for you; it literally "turns on" its special vibrational frequency, making sure it works on the right wavelength. Making a special dedication ensures that the crystal works for the highest good of all the people concerned.

The dedication method

Hold each crystal individually in your hands, visualize it surrounded with white light, and say out loud: "I am going to use this crystal for the best and highest intentions." Now move on to the attuning process on page 156.

Rough pink tourmaline

CRYSTAL FACTS

What crystals to use: all the new crystals that you have cleansed

Polished red tiger's eye

Polished carnelian

Polished amethyst

Attuning (or programming) your crystals

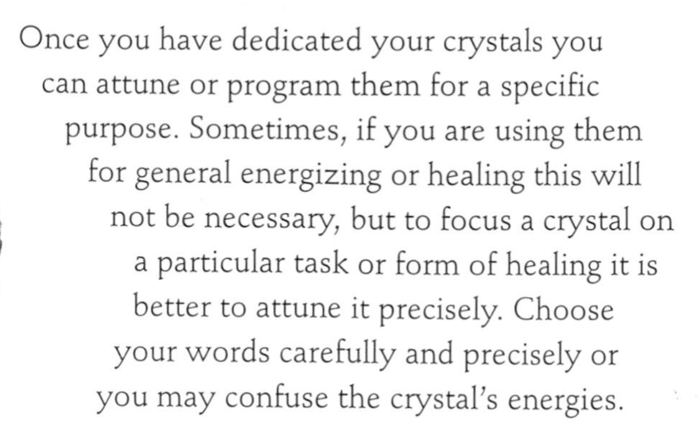

Rough sodalite

Once you have dedicated your crystals you can attune or program them for a specific purpose. Sometimes, if you are using them for general energizing or healing this will not be necessary, but to focus a crystal on a particular task or form of healing it is better to attune it precisely. Choose your words carefully and precisely or you may confuse the crystal's energies.

Polished hematite

Rough blue tourmaline

The attuning method

Pick up your first crystal to attune for the tip you have chosen to do in the book. Think carefully about your intention, about the area you want to change, or how the crystal can cure or have a stimulating influence. Formulate the exact words in your head, such as: "I intend this crystal to protect my entrance" or "I intend this crystal to help cure my headaches." When you are sure of your intention, take your crystal in your hands and sense its energy. When you feel spiritually connected, speak your intention in a clear voice. Say it two or three times to fix it firmly in the crystal. Let yourself be open to your higher wisdom and any guidance it gives you. When you intuitively feel the intention is locked in your crystal, put it down and move away from it. To use an attuned crystal for another purpose, you will need to cleanse it and reprogram it.

Polished chiastolite

Polished opaque moonstone

CRYSTAL FACTS

WHAT CRYSTALS TO USE: all your new crystals that you have dedicated (see page 155)

Choosing and dedicating a crystal as a gift

If you are buying a crystal as a gift for someone, hold an image of them in your mind or mentally say their name as your walk around the crystal shop. Handle different crystals, feeling their shape and energy, until one seems to resonate well with your friend's image or name. Turn it over a few times in your hand to make sure its vibrations are right, and you are happy with the stone.

Attuning the crystal

At home, cleanse your chosen crystal (see pages 149–153), then pick up and hold it firmly in your hands until you feel its subtle pulsations. Ask it to keep your friend safe and secure and to work for his or her highest good. Do not try to impose any of your views about how any of their characteristics could be improved. Give the stone to this person with your highest regard and with love.

Polished rhodochrosite

CRYSTAL FACTS

What crystal to use: your gift crystal that you have cleansed (see pages 149–153)

Glossary/Index

CRYSTAL	QUALITIES	PAGE
Agate	grounding, brings security, heals broken heart, stimulates spiritual growth, calms, clears negativity	9, 41, 58, 68, 81, 101, 108, 113, 125, 128, 129, 131, 144
Blue lace agate	cools and calms, helps expression, dissolves mental stress	117, 119, 140, 146
Dendritic agate	aids perseverance	55
Fire agate	grounds and protects, ignites sex drive	47, 67, 118, 132
Green agate	boosts self-esteem	50
Moss agate	absorbs negative energies, treats infection, boosts immune system, improves self-esteem	42, 90, 93, 97, 102, 112, 130, 134, 142
Pink agate	promotes love	46
Amazonite	reduces worries, filters electro-magnetic pollution, calms brain, aids cramps	34, 48, 56, 99, 115, 123, 131, 134
Amber	absorbs negative forces, encourages wisdom, promotes joy, eases stomach ache, absorbs pain	10, 41, 47, 54, 59, 85, 92, 94, 108, 118, 130, 132
Amethyst	balances emotions, promotes love, protects, promotes spirituality, aids headaches, enhances visualization	10, 18, 19, 22, 26, 33, 41, 53, 64, 65, 76, 84, 100, 114, 116, 118, 121, 124, 140, 142, 143, 144, 146
Apophyllite	aids decision making, dissolves worries	56, 102
Aquamarine	brings peace, love and inspiration, aids creative communication, relieves pain and hay fever shields aura	10, 22, 31, 35, 41, 62, 63, 77, 93, 94, 96, 100, 107, 119, 124, 126, 128. 136, 138, 143
Aragonite	gives insight to problems	146
Aventurine	enhances prosperity and creativity, positive attitudes, heals heart, reduces cell phone emissions	10, 17, 20, 23, 41, 69, 74, 78. 123, 124, 130, 135, 136, 143
Green Aventurine	settles nausea	27, 39, 98
Azurite	clears worries, cleanses Third eye	29, 76
Beryl	relieves throat infections	96, 146
Golden beryl (heliodor)	encourages initiative, promotes will to succeed	10, 60, 132, 147
Bloodstone	strengthens intuition, revitalizes atmosphere, gives vitality, protects	39, 41, 43, 58, 120, 127, 138, 146
Blue apatite	alleviates irritability	135
Blue kyanite	lessens fears	40, 41, 56
Calcite	stimulates memory	38, 128
Blue calcite	dissolves pain, helps eczema	89, 91
Gold calcite	boosts memory	30
Green calcite	removes rigid beliefs	105
Orange calcite	stimulates energy, alleviates stress	10, 59, 115, 122
Pink calcite	releases sadness	104
Red calcite	increases energy and vitality	11, 22
Carnelian	restores vitality, aids business success, alleviates apathy, soothes pain	10, 17, 28, 35, 41, 50, 55, 59, 89, 132, 134
Celestite	promotes good communication, helps meditation, brings in love, heals ears, calms	10, 40, 52, 64, 66, 92, 104, 117, 143
Blue celestite	promotes purity of heart	144
Chalcedony	encourages optimism and good will	142
Blue chalcedony	stimulates learning skills	30
Red chalcedony	helps reach goals	147
Chiastolite	calms fears, clears hidden guilt	102, 111
Chrysocolla	removes destructive emotions, treats PMS, muscle cramps, heals heartache	31, 68, 69, 86, 99, 103, 109, 111, 113, 128
Chrysoprase	encourages positive solutions, unlocks blocked emotions	8, 10, 27, 50, 104 130, 131, 136, 137, 143, 144, 146
Citrine	brings wealth, success and joy, lifts atmosphere, revitalizes mind, eases menopause, brings inner calm	14, 22, 23,26, 35, 39, 60, 79, 87, 103, 112, 124, 127, 128, 134
Diamond	encourages strength and fortitude	124, 125, 126, 141
Herkimer diamond	brings love and clarity	138
Emerald	increases love	75, 78, 126, 130, 136
Fluorite	dispels electromagnetic stress, helps assimilate information, balances aura, stabilizes relationships, aids infection	24, 30, 38, 48, 65, 75, 90, 94, 95, 108, 124
Blue fluorite	relieves pain	92
Green fluorite	dissolves negativity, relieves travel sickness	35, 98, 121
Purple fluorite	purifies negative energies, expands mental capabilities	33, 39
Garnet	reduces emotional upset, encourages true love, reduces anger, energizes, protects	10, 41, 46, 67, 70, 79, 101, 106, 113, 120, 124, 132, 140, 142, 144
Hematite	protects, dispels negativity, helps muscle cramps, protects aura	9, 12, 27, 99, 107, 133
Howlite	increases memory, teaches patience	30, 41, 119
Jade	reduces stress, increases self-love, reduces irritability	17, 42, 68, 134, 135
Green jade	brings good luck, protects and cleanses, balances emotions	12, 34, 42, 75
Lavender (purple) jade	calms nervous system, regulates heartbeat	10, 100
Jasper	supports in conflicts, protects	41, 52, 118
Brown jasper	brings stability, reduces inflammation, grounds energy	14, 17, 91, 97, 117, 124
Ocean jasper	supports under stress	134
Red jasper	stimulates energy	22, 35
Yellow jasper	releases toxins, aids travel sickness, quietens nerves	85, 98, 143

ACKNOWLEDGMENTS

I would like to thank Liz Dean for her support and creative input on this book. Also my thanks go to Jerry Goldie for his inspired design and Trina Dalziel for her attractive illustrations. As always a big thanks to my sister Gill for her love and positive encouragement and to all my friends, particularly Anna, Paul, Claire, Matt, and Janet, for their support as I wrote this book.

Mary Lambert is based in London and can be contacted for reiki treatments and feng shui and clutter-clearing consultations for homes and businesses via her website: www.marylambertfengshui.com

PUBLISHER'S ACKNOWLEDGMENTS

Many thanks to Philip Permutt of iSiS who provided invaluable information and to Charlie's Rock Shop, London, for supplying many of the crystals shown within these pages.

iSiS Crystals
1 Market Place
St Albans
Hertfordshire
AL3 5DR
+44 (0)1727 866720
www.thecrystalhealer.co.uk

Charlie's Rock Shop
Unit 1 The 1929 Shop
Merton Abbey Mills
18 Watermill Way
London SW19 2RD
+44 (0)20 8544 1207
www.charliesrockshop.com

Jewelry featured on pages 77 and 78 made by Linda Jones; photographs by Jacqui Hurst.

FURTHER READING

The Book of Crystal Healing, Liz Simpson, Gaia, 1997
Crystals and Crystal Healing, Simon Lilly, Select Editions, 1998
Crystals for Health, Home and Personal Power, Ken and Joules Taylor, Collins & Brown, 1999
The Illustrated Guide to Crystals, Judy Hall, Godsfield, 2000
Crystal Healing, Cassandra Eason, Foulsham, 2002
Crystal Healing, Roger Croxson, Hodder Arnold, 2003
Cunningham's Encyclopedia of Crystal, Gem and Metal Magic, Llewellyn, 2003
The Crystal Bible, Judy Hall, Godsfield, 2003
The Power of Gems and Crystals, Soozi Holbeche, Piatkus, 2003

A TABLE IN TUSCANY

• ABOUT THE AUTHOR •

Born and educated in Canada, Leslie Forbes first studied English, Philosophy & Political Sciences, but in 1973 turned to graphic design, graduating from Vancouver School of Art in 1977 as best design student. She then came to England to study at the Royal College of Art, came second in the annual VOGUE talent contest & worked as a designer & illustrator until 1980. A six~week trip to Tuscany started what is proving a long love~affair with the region. Since 1981 she has worked as a designer and illustrator at BBC television.

To my friend ANDREW THOMAS
for putting up with me,
To LORRAINE, PENNY & KATI
for keeping me to the (fairly) straight & narrow,
To everyone at the LOCANDA dell'AMOROSA
for showing me what the joys of a
table in Tuscany really are,
To GUISEPPE, MAURIZIO, PAULA de FERRARI CORRADI,
GIOVANELLA STIANTI & the PANERAIS for
teaching me about Tuscan wine,
and to CARLO,
EMILIANA & everyone at PONTI di SASSO, ANGELA,
LETIZIA, MARIELLA, EBE & RENZO & FIAMETTA,
LEONARDO, JILL & everyone at IL FEDINO, FRANCA &
BEPPE near Fiesole, CLAUDI & ELIZABETHA & Signora PIRAS
on Elba, MARY at Tiglio, ANNA at the Castello di Spaltenna,
CESARE at Vipore, and my Mum, whose years of very
inspired cooking were the inspiration
for this book.

A TABLE IN TUSCANY
CLASSIC RECIPES
· from the ·
HEART of ITALY
COLLECTED and
ILLUSTRATED by
LESLIE FORBES
Penguin Books

PENGUIN BOOKS

Published by the Penguin Group
27 Wrights Lane, London W8 5TZ, England
Viking Penguin Inc., 40 West 23rd Street, New York, New York 10010, USA
Penguin Books Australia Ltd, Ringwood, Victoria, Australia
Penguin Books Canada Ltd, 2801 John Street, Markham, Ontario, Canada L3R 1B4
Penguin Books (NZ) Ltd, 182–190 Wairu Road, Auckland 10, New Zealand

Penguin Books Ltd, Registered Offices: Harmondsworth, Middlesex, England

First published in Great Britain by Webb & Bower (Publishers) Ltd
5 Cathedral Close, Exeter, Devon, England EX1 1EZ, 1985

Published in Penguin Books 1989
10 9 8 7 6 5 4 3 2 1

Produced by Johnson Editions Ltd, 15 Grafton Square, London SW4 0DQ

Art editor: Lorraine Johnson   Editor: Penny Clarke

Printed and bound by Arnoldo Mondadori Editore, Verona

CONTENTS

· INTRODUCTION ·

A kitchen table on a farm near Mont Amiata, strewn with wild asparagus and giant porcini mushrooms, freshly gathered. A cafe table in Siena with slices of rich panforte and frothy cappucini for two. A table in a crowded Florentine trattoria, its checked cloth covered in plates of steaming spinach pasta. A pine table laden with pens, pencils and sketchpads in an olive grove north of Lucca. These are some of the many tables at which I ate, talked, drank and learned about Tuscany's culture and people as well her food and wine, and finally at which I distilled what I had learned into this book, more a sketchbook that grew than a traditional cookbook.

It started as a series of drawings and cooking notes on a trip to Tuscany five years ago. From that first trip my interest in the region developed over subsequent visits into a passion. I was hooked. For me Tuscany was, and still is, an irresistable combination of practical little family run restaurants casually serving up Italian sausages and beans next to grand Renaissance churches, of colourful food markets sprawling uninhibitedly across cobbled medieval piazzas and especially of people, some raucous and crafty, some gentle and reserved, all of them passionately and understandably proud of their region and its food & wine.

Tuscany was relatively poor until the recent onslaught of mass tourism, and as a result most of its cooking traditions are firmly rooted in what Italians call 'la cucina povera', the poor kitchen. A good Tuscan restaurant conforms to the principles of economical home cooking, using fresh local products rather than expensive imports. Chestnuts gathered from giant trees are used for sweet chestnut flour, the basis for many desserts. Pigs living outside for most of the year graze on

ASPARAGO

FUSILLI

BORAGINE

PENNE

FAGIOLI

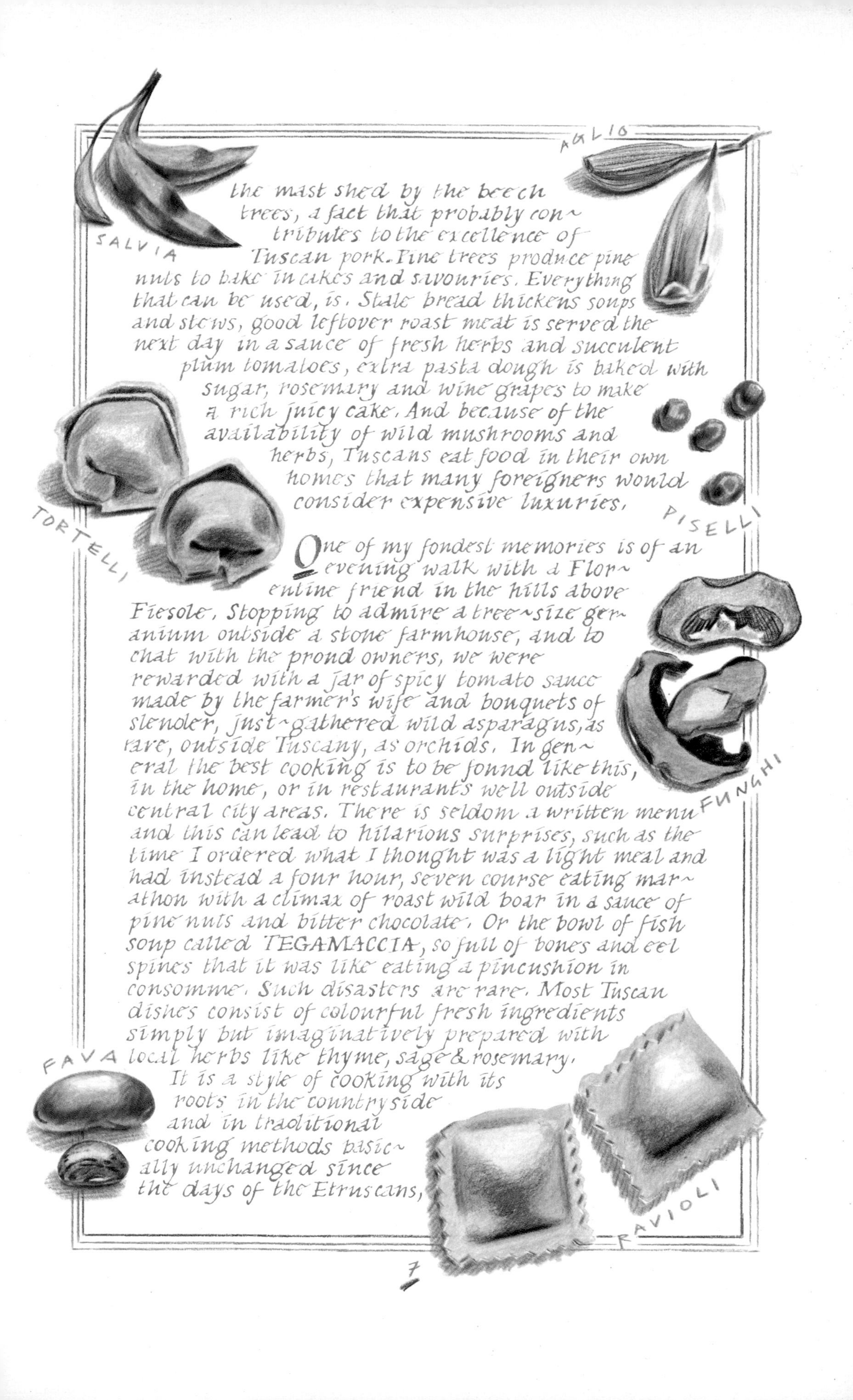

the mast shed by the beech trees, a fact that probably contributes to the excellence of Tuscan pork. Pine trees produce pine nuts to bake in cakes and savouries. Everything that can be used, is. Stale bread thickens soups and stews, good leftover roast meat is served the next day in a sauce of fresh herbs and succulent plum tomatoes, extra pasta dough is baked with sugar, rosemary and wine grapes to make a rich juicy cake. And because of the availability of wild mushrooms and herbs, Tuscans eat food in their own homes that many foreigners would consider expensive luxuries.

One of my fondest memories is of an evening walk with a Florentine friend in the hills above Fiesole. Stopping to admire a tree-size geranium outside a stone farmhouse, and to chat with the proud owners, we were rewarded with a jar of spicy tomato sauce made by the farmer's wife and bouquets of slender, just-gathered wild asparagus, as rare, outside Tuscany, as orchids. In general the best cooking is to be found like this, in the home, or in restaurants well outside central city areas. There is seldom a written menu and this can lead to hilarious surprises, such as the time I ordered what I thought was a light meal and had instead a four hour, seven course eating marathon with a climax of roast wild boar in a sauce of pine nuts and bitter chocolate. Or the bowl of fish soup called TEGAMACCIA, so full of bones and eel spines that it was like eating a pincushion in consommé. Such disasters are rare. Most Tuscan dishes consist of colourful fresh ingredients simply but imaginatively prepared with local herbs like thyme, sage & rosemary. It is a style of cooking with its roots in the countryside and in traditional cooking methods basically unchanged since the days of the Etruscans, the ancient Italian tribe that first brought civilisation to Tuscany over 2000 years.

During the Renaissance, Tuscan cooking, like its art, underwent a drastic change. This was the era when one enthusiastic gourmet recommended stuffing a wild boar with a goose, the goose with a pheasant, the pheasant with a partridge, etc. on down the line to finish with an olive. Florentine chefs took their skills to barbaric France (where that very Italian device, the fork, was still a rarity) and changed history. Recently some of the dishes from those more exotic times have been reintroduced by chefs anxious to bring more sophistication to Tuscan restaurants. But for me the best moments are still the simple & unsophisticated ones ~ those spent learning from a cook the exact moment when eggs have absorbed enough flour to give a firm but not tough pasta dough. Or listening, in a tiny cramped Florentine trattoria, while a chef describes how to make the perfect artichoke omelette. Or sniffing the aroma of the chestnut cake 'castagnaccia' baking in a friend's kitchen, & burning my fingers & tongue on deep-fried, sugary cenci, hot from a pan.

Each recipe in this book evokes a strong memory for me. They were collected in extremely pleasant circumstances from both professional & amateur cooks all over Tuscany. Some are the inventions of individuals I met casually ~ like the dandelion soup made by a Montalcino grandmother or the recipe for hunter's sauce given by a travelling porchetta vendor in San Gimignano.

Not all the recipes come word for word from the restaurants mentioned. Some I have had to adapt from notes scribbled while a harassed chef continued to cook the daily speciality. Most of the recipes can be adapted to suit personal taste & some are just quick ideas for giving a particularly Tuscan flavour to a standard recipe, such as the rosemary ~ flavoured oil that, added to basic bread dough, instantly conjures up a steamy Florence bakeshop at Easter.

I hope that, when cooked in some distant kitchen, these recipes will bring at least a few of the pleasures of a table in Tuscany. And that everyone who shares my nostalgia for such pleasures will find something in this book to stir fond memories.

THE VALE OF FLORENCE
PASTELLI
A COLORI
FILA
PRATO
The MUGELLO
VIA BOLOGNESE
FIESOLE
Villa I Tatti
POGGIO a CAIANO
CARMIGNANO
ARNO
FLORENCE
AUTOSTRADA DEL SOLE
S. ANDREA in PERCUSSINA
SAN CASCIANO VAL di PESA
·RESTAURANTS·
·FLORENCE·Borgo Antico · Coco Lezzone · La Carabaccia · Ganino's · Sostanza · FIESOLE · Le Cave di Maiano · Il Lordo · S. ANDREA PERCUSSINA · Taverna Macchiavelli ·
·SIGHTS·
·CARMIGNANO · wine · Villa Artimino · FIESOLE · Roman ruins · villas · caves · POGGIO A CAIANO · Villa Medicea · PRATO · Duomo · frescoes · THE MUGELLO · villas of Cafaggiolo & Trebbio ·

· INTRODUCTION ·

'Fiorentin mangia fagioli
Lecca piatti e tova glioli.'
The Florentine who eats beans
Licks the plates and tablecloths
(OLD TUSCAN SAYING)

Aldous Huxley called Florence a 'third rate provincial town' which is unfair. But certainly in spite of its wealth of art and culture the city sometimes seems designed to annoy the uninformed visitor. From six in the morning when the huge covered central market rings with the shouts of what sounds like the entire Florentine population, the noise of traffic and people fills the streets. VIVOLI, the best and most famous ice cream shop in Florence is busier at midnight than any other time. Museums are open only in the mornings, shop hours alter with a bewildering frequency and just when you think you have cracked the system, everything shuts at one o'clock for lunch. Grey steel shutters clang down abruptly to cover all the tempting displays of goodies, leaving formerly lively shopping streets bare and bleak. For four hours nothing moves except the occasional fly and in the summer heat of Florence (one of the hottest and most humid cities in Italy) even the flies can be a little sluggish.

The only solution is to follow the Florentine example. Rise early to shop and see the staggering variety of museums and churches and save the afternoon for a long, lazy lunch in a cool restaurant. Or picnic and siesta in the huge formal Boboli gardens behind the Pitti Palace. If you can cope with the heat explore the narrow streets lined with medieval and Renaissance palaces in the precious quiet hours between one and five o'clock. During the rest of the day whining mopeds are a constant hazard, whizzing merrily down so-called 'pedestrian only' thoroughfares and missing tourists and Florentines alike only by centimetres.

The city is not now and never has been a restful place to visit. Exhilarating, yes. Restful, no. Its centuries-long participation in a conflict between the Guelfs, who supported the Pope, and the Ghibellines, who supported the Emperor, divided the whole of Tuscany. And although by 1266 the Guelfs were the main faction in

Florence, the internal politics were still so unstable that Dante (1265–1321) compared his hometown to a sick woman, twisting and turning on her bed to ease her pain. It took Cosimo de' Medici in 1434 to initiate a period of relative stability, and it was during the rule of the Medici family, the height of the Renaissance, that Tuscan artists, sculptors and architects shaped Florence into the tightly-packed urban treasure house that it is today.

E.M. Forster called the Renaissance '...all fighting and beauty' and the fighting was not limited to politics. Pietro Torrigiano broke Michelangelo's nose in a fistfight on the steps of the Carmine church. They were arguing about the stunning frescoes by Masaccio in the Brancacci chapel. And Brunelleschi, after losing the commission to Ghiberti to sculpt the doors of Florence's Baptistry, left the city in a huff, returning only to design the famous cupola of the Duomo. His advanced ideas caused an uproar in the city but were finally realized in 1436. The raising of the massive red dome was the outstanding engineering feat of the Renaissance period. Visible for miles in all directions, its size was unmatched even by Michelangelo's dome of St. Peter's in Rome, a generation later.

To Florentine food lovers the 'bistecca fiorentina' is as much a masterpiece as Brunelleschi's dome is to architects. Sit in a crowded trattoria near Florence's huge central market and you will hear arguments as passionate about grilling the perfect steak as those about politics or art. Whether the 'fiorentina' (a steak of truly monumental proportions) should be first brushed with oil and then grilled, or never see oil at all, is an argument that can last as long as the parties involved are willing to continue. But Tuscans, and especially Florentines, will argue about anything. Preferably with the benefit of a meal and some good wine for stimulation.

The best arguments and the best food are to be found not in hyperelegant hotel restaurants with elaborately served international food but in local Florentine trattorias. Eat perhaps just a plate of the white beans of which the Florentines are notoriously so fond, simmered to a creamy smoothness in sage & garlic and then drenched in fine fruity olive oil. Or ask for a slice of roast pork off the spit, its skin crackling with rosemary and black pepper. These simple dishes served in unpretentious surroundings are the real flavour of Florence, nowhere better than in one of the little neighbourhood restaurants like LA CARABACCIA, GANINO'S or SOSTANZA, sitting elbow to elbow with your fellow diners at long communal tables.

It is hard to decide the best way to enter Florence for the first time. Arriving in the main railway station of Santa Maria Novella one senses only the presence of the modern city with all its attendant modern problems - noise, traffic, smell and heat. The city of Dante & Michelangelo is as distant as the blue Appennine mountains. But drive in from the north, down the old Via Bolognese (the SS65 from Bologna) and the Florence & Tuscany of the Renaissance come to life. From the dramatic Futa Pass the road runs through the gentle Mugello valley, birthplace of Ghiotto & Fra Angelico, past some of the grandest of the Renaissance villas. First there is Michelozzi's Cafaggiolo, then Trebbio and the medieval castle of Salviati where, in the 17th century, Jacopo Salviati received the severed head of his mistress as a New Year's gift from his wife. The road then leads past Sir Harold Acton's Villa La Pietra, with one of the most beautiful formal Italian gardens in Tuscany. And along the Via Bolognese for the last stretch Roman Fiesole rises on its villa & cypress covered hill to the east. Finally Brunelleschi's famous red dome comes into view, dwarfing every building for miles around, and you are in Florence.

S is for soup, or in Tuscany Z is for zuppa ~ any soup served over bread, as most are. They can vary widely from the simplest clear broth with fresh herbs used to boil a chicken, to zuppa di agnello in which there is only enough 'zuppa' left to soak the bread under a rich stew of lamb and tomatoes. The key to ordering or cooking a good Tuscan soup is the season ~ check the market for best buys and choose your recipe accordingly. In Tuscany it is stale bread that thickens soups, not flour or pasta and usually a jug of olive oil is served as dressing.

· LA · CARABACCIA ·

Each day at La Carabaccia in Florence, Luciano Ghimassi serves different, carefully researched Florentine dishes, largely based on ingredients produced by himself and his family. His intimate little restaurant is always packed with locals and booking is essential unless you are the friend of a regular customer.

· LA CARABACCIA ·

Onion soup (4)

This dish is just one of many Tuscan dishes that form part of a centuries-old debate. In 1533 Catherine de' Medici went to France to marry the future Henry II, taking with her a retinue of chefs and so starting the debate about the origin of certain dishes. Some are internationally identified with French cuisine but the Tuscans claim them for their own. Who now knows whether Catherine and her chefs changed the course of French cooking with dishes such as anitra all'arancia (canard à l'orange) or whether the inspiration came from the French and filtered back to Italy with lonely Tuscan chefs returning home? Perhaps Catherine's chefs, homesick for their Tuscan cypresses, cooked dishes like carabaccia, which later evolved into the ubiquitous soup à l'oignon of every French bistro. This first recipe is certainly of Renaissance origin, with the characteristic thickening of crushed almonds.

· RENAISSANCE VERSION ·

2 LB 2 OZ / 1 KG ONIONS, FINELY SLICED
4 OZ / 100 G ALMONDS, SKINNED & POUNDED TO A PASTE IN A MORTAR
1 TBSP CASTER SUGAR
4 TBSP OLIVE OIL
WHITE WINE VINEGAR
CINNAMON STICK
1 3/4 PT / 1 LTR STOCK
PINCH WHITE PEPPER
PINCH SALT
POWDERED CINNAMON (OPTIONAL)
4 SLICES BREAD

Put the crushed almonds and the cinnamon stick in enough vinegar to cover, leave about 1 hour, heat the oil in a medium-sized pan, saute the onions in it until soft, using more oil if necessary. Rinse the almond paste in a sieve and add to the onions a tablespoon at a time until they are well blended. When the mixture is smooth add the sugar, powdered cinnamon if liked, white pepper, salt and stock. Cook for a further 30 minutes. Put a slice of bread that has been grilled crisp and brown into each bowl, pour the soup over.

LA CARABACCIA
190
la Carabaccia

• LA CARABACCIA

MODERN VERSION

The second version of Carabaccia makes a much less extravagant soup, more acceptable to modern palates.

2 LB 2 OZ / 1 KG ONIONS, FINELY SLICED
SEVERAL LEAVES BASIL, TORN IN SMALL PIECES
2 3/4 PT / 1½ LTR CHICKEN STOCK
4 OZ / 100 G GARDEN VEGETABLES (PEAS, BROAD BEANS ETC)
WHITE WINE
PECORINO OR PARMESAN CHEESE, GRATED
SALT & PEPPER
4 SLICES BREAD

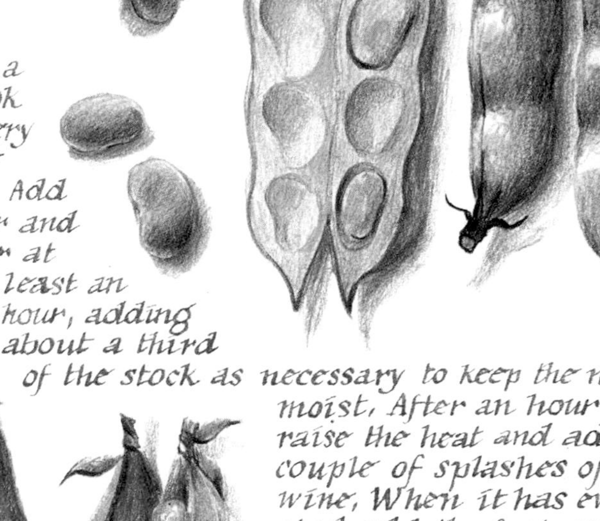

Heat the oil in a large pan. Cook the carrots, celery and basil in it for 5 minutes. Add the onions, cover and cook gently for at least an hour, adding about a third of the stock as necessary to keep the mixture moist. After an hour raise the heat and add a couple of splashes of white wine. When it has evaporated add the fresh vegetables. After about a minute pour in the remaining stock, reduce the heat and cook until the vegetables are just soft. Before serving sprinkle a few tablespoons of cheese into the soup, stir well, put a slice of bread in each bowl and pour the soup over.

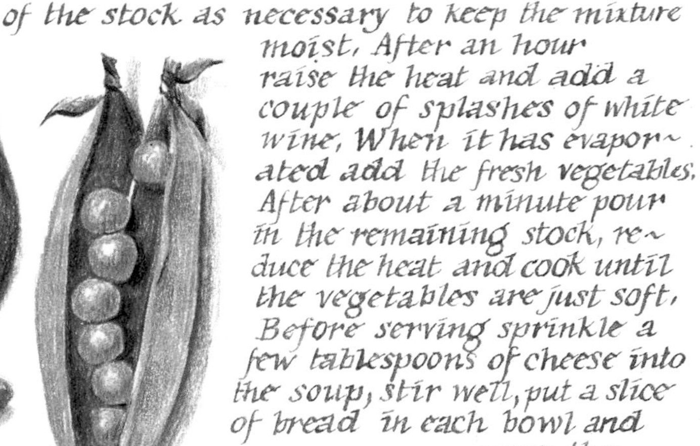

• TRATTORIA • SOSTANZA •

The Trattoria Sostanza opened in 1869 and is still one of the best-known working-men's cafes in Florence. Go there to eat the huge bistecca fiorintina & sit at long communal tables where it is impossible not to share your conversation with half the restaurant. According to one customer who had been eating there regularly for 40 years, the two owners who had the cafe previously once had a terrible row & for years never spoke to each other. One worked in the front of the restaurant, the other at the back. Communication was only through waiters like Mario, who has himself been there for 50 years. But the food never reflected the conflict, unless perhaps it had an extra zest.

• TRIPPA alla FIORENTINA •

— Florentine Tripe (4) —

You, too, may be wary of tripe, but the Florentines have an undeniable way with it. Try it, you might be converted.

- 1 3/4 LB/800 G TRIPE, READY COOKED
- 1 LB 2 OZ/500 G TOMATOES, PEELED & ROUGHLY CHOPPED
- 1 1/2 TSP MARJORAM
- 1 1/4 OZ/30 G PANCETTA (OR FATTY HAM)
- 3~4 TBSP OLIVE OIL
- 2 CELERY STICKS
- 1 CARROT
- SALT & PEPPER
- 1 ONION

Put the tripe in a big saucepan with half the onion and a celery stick. Cover with water and boil for 10~15 minutes. Meanwhile finely chop the remaining onion and celery & the carrot and pancetta and cook gently in the oil in a flame-proof casserole. Drain and slice the tripe into small, fine strips about 2 in/2.5 cm long. When the onion is slightly coloured, add the tomatoes, tripe and seasoning. Cover & continue to cook over a low heat. After 30 minutes remove the lid, turn up the heat and cook until the sauce thickens (about 10 minutes), stirring occasionally to ensure that the tripe does not stick & burn. Serve with plenty of grated parmesan.

• TORTINO di CARCIOFI •

Artichoke omelette

'Carciofi' is Italian for artichokes, and if there is one way to eat them that is better than just boiling them and dipping them in good oil, this is it. The artichokes should be young, preferably Italian, the leaves closely packed at the end of long thin stems.

2 EGGS PER PERSON
2~3 ARTICHOKES PER PERSON, DEPENDING ON SIZE
¼ PT/150 ML GOOD OLIVE OIL
CLOVE GARLIC
2~3 TBSP. FRESH PARSLEY, FINELY CHOPPED
SALT & PEPPER
JUICE OF 1 LEMON

Peel off any tough outer leaves on the artichokes and, if using non~Italian ones, trim away the chokes. Slice the 'flowers' thinly from the top down through the stem, and soak for 15 minutes in water and lemon juice. Heat the oil in a frying pan with the garlic. Drain the artichoke slices and pat dry. Put them in the pan with the oil, cover and leave the artichokes to simmer over a low heat, turning once or twice. When they are golden brown add the eggs, beaten with the salt, pepper and parsley. Continue cooking over a medium heat until the eggs are set, stirring all the time to prevent burning. At the Trattoria Sostanza they serve their tortinos with a squeeze of fresh lemon juice and plenty of crusty bread to mop up the delicious juice.

When using non~Italian artichokes be sure they are very young and small and use only the most tender inner leaves.

· GANINO'S ·

Ganino's is the place where poets rub shoulders with film stars, and are served by the entire Bernadoni family (most of whom could pass for film stars themselves). In spring the tagliatelle with wild asparagus is worth dieting for, and all year round the crostini di fegatini are the best in Tuscany.

CROSTINI di FEGATINI
Chicken livers on toast (6)

Crostini probably appear on every antipasto menu in every Tuscan trattoria, but all too often they arrive as gritty grey paste on soggy bread. At Ganino's the bread is first grilled over an open wood fire, then brushed with good green olive oil and at the last minute annointed with this hot creamy mixture of chicken livers, sharpened with capers and anchovy.

- 6 CHICKEN LIVERS, CLEANED
- 1 ANCHOVY, FINELY CHOPPED
- 1 TSP TOMATO PUREE
- WINEGLASS WHITE WINE
- BUTTER
- 2 TBSP CAPERS, CRUSHED IN A MORTAR
- 10 OR MORE SLICES FRENCH BAGUETTE BREAD
- 1 MEDIUM ONION, FINELY CHOPPED
- CHICKEN STOCK
- GRATED PARMESAN

Melt some butter in a small saucepan and saute the onion in it until transparent. Add the chicken livers and break them up with a fork as they begin to colour. After a few minutes pour in the wine and allow to evaporate slowly. When evaporated add the anchovy and capers, and the tomato puree mixed in a little hot stock. Continue to cook for about 15 minutes, adding more stock when necessary to keep the mixture very creamy. Just before serving beat the livers well (or whisk in a food processor) and serve very hot on toasted bread with a generous sprinkling of freshly grated parmesan or pecorino cheese over the top.

· COCO · LEZZONE ·

In their minute kitchen off an equally tiny white-tiled restaurant, the Paoli family manage to produce some of the best traditional Tuscan cooking in Florence.

· FARFALLINE con PISELLI ·
Pasta butterflies with fresh peas (4)

Theoretically, this is not a difficult dish to make. Stand next to a field of fresh peas with a frying pan in your hand in which is simmering gently a generous handful of pale pink prosciutto and perhaps a few finely chopped green spring onions. Wait until the peas are barely ripe ~ still tiny and bright green in their pods. At that precise moment start shelling them straight into the pan, toss them quickly in the sauce, pour onto a bowl of freshly cooked farfalline (butterfly-shaped pasta) and run with them to the nearest table. If you do this and they were good peas to start with, they might, perhaps, taste as good as the peas and pasta served at Coco Lezzone. Failing a field of peas, take:

20 PASTA 'BUTTERFLIES' PER PERSON
2 LB/900 G FRESHLY SHELLED PEAS ~ TRY ONE RAW, IF IT IS NOT SWEET, ADD A GENEROUS PINCH OF SUGAR WHEN COOKING
4 OZ/100 G PROSCIUTTO OR GOOD COOKED HAM SLICED IN THIN STRIPS
2 SPRING ONIONS, FINELY CHOPPED
1 TBSP OLIVE OIL
SALT & PEPPER

Put the pasta to cook in a large pan of boiling salted water. Heat the oil in a frying pan. Saute the onions gently in the oil until soft but not brown. Add the peas (and sugar if necessary) and a tablespoon or two of water. Cook them as quickly as possible, about 10~15 minutes (less if they are small & very tender). About 5 minutes before they are ready add the ham and allow to heat through. Pour over the pasta which should be cooked and drained ready for serving. Serve immediately

• FAGIOLI al FIASCO •

Beans in a Chianti bottle (6)

This must be one of the oldest and simplest of Tuscan dishes. It is excellent barbecue food but first drink your Chianti...

12 OZ/350 G FRESH WHITE TUSCAN, HARICOT OR CANNELLINI BEANS
4 TBSP GOOD OLIVE OIL
5~6 SAGE LEAVES
2 CLOVES GARLIC, CRUSHED

Having drunk the Chianti, cut the straw wrapping off the bottle (capacity should be about 3 pints/1½ ltr) but keep it to use as a stopper. Rinse out the bottle and fill it about ½ to ⅔ full with beans (the beans need room to swell). Add the oil, sage leaves, garlic and about 1½ cups of water. Stuff the straw loosely in the top of the flask so that the water can evaporate ~ to achieve their characteristic creamy taste, the beans must absorb oil, not water. Put the bottle beside or above the embers of the fire for 3~5 hours. Failing a campfire put the bottle in a warm place, such as an airing cupboard, the warm place on a stove, or beside the boiler or a solid fuel cooker. Leave until the water has evaporated and the beans have absorbed the oil. Serve hot or cold with plenty of salt & freshly ground black pepper and a jug of good fruity olive oil to pour over.

·LETIZIA·

Letizia Volpi is an artist living and working in Florence, and a passionate collector of old recipes for Tuscan sweets. Perhaps one day she will write her own book on the subject. In the meantime she is content to delight all her friends and family by cooking six times the usual quantity for recipes such as this one. And there is an added bonus. One evening of cooking crunchy CENCI is enough to fill the house for days with the delicious smell of vanilla and icing sugar.

CENCI

Fried pastry twists

'Cenci' means 'stuff' or scraps of fabric used for dusting and cleaning. Like its fabric counter-

part, the pastry comes in all shapes and sizes, from huge pastry handkerchiefs and long strips tied in bows and lover's knots, to the heart-shaped dolce d'amore made by Letizia Volpi. They are generally popular at carnival time, just after Christmas.

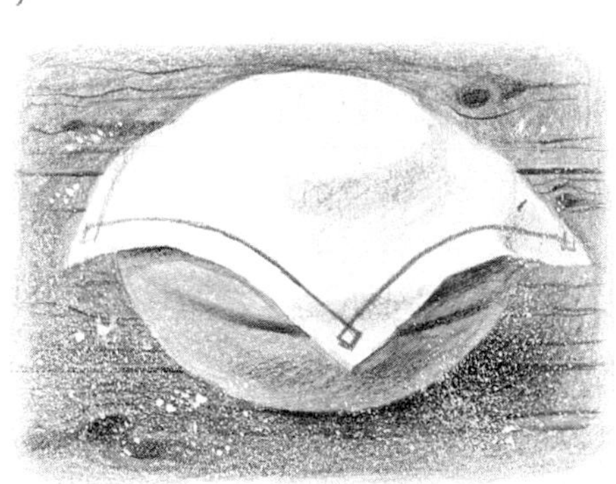

9 oz/250 G PLAIN WHITE FLOUR
1 oz/25 G BUTTER, JUST MELTED
1 oz/25 G GRANULATED SUGAR
1 EGG
3 TBSP VIN SANTO ~ VIN SANTO IS AN ITALIAN SHERRY~LIKE WINE BUT YOU CAN USE SHERRY OR RUM
1 TSP VANILLA POWDER
PINCH SALT
OIL FOR DEEP FRYING

Make a little volcano of sifted flour with a crater in the middle. Into this put the egg, salt, sugar, vanilla and butter. Gently work this into a dough with your hands. When the dough begins to get stiff, moisten with a little vin santo, as the dough should always be quite pliable. Knead well, cover with a cloth and leave in a cool place to rest. After about an hour, roll the dough out very thinly and cut into whatever shapes you like. Probably the most traditional is a strip about 8 in/20.5 cm long and ½ in/3 cm wide tied in a bow or knot.

Deep fry these pieces, 2 or 3 at a time, in hot oil until they puff up & turn golden brown. Drain on paper towels and sift icing sugar over the tops. They can be eaten hot or cold and keep well in an airtight container.

LE • CAVE • DI • MAIANO

· LE · CAVE · DI · MAIANO ·

The famous grey stone 'PIETRA SERENA' from which half the buildings in Florence are constructed, comes from the quarries near Fiesole, le Cave di Maiano. The trattoria of the same name is no longer the haven for workers from the nearby quarries that it once was. A more international crowd comes now for the stunning views of cypresses and villas in the Fiesolan hills, rather than for their essential evening meal. But there are still some very good traditional dishes to be found on the menu if you know your traditions and are willing (and able) to ask about them.

· PAPPA al POMODORO ·

Tomato and bread soup (8)

This thick, richly tomato-tasting soup that was once almost the porridge of Tuscany is one such traditional dish. If you make sure the tomatoes and basil are fresh, the bread stale and the garlic lavish, you cannot go far wrong. It can be, and is, served hot or cold, tepid or, less authentically, with ice cubes and topped with a generous handful of fresh chopped basil. (Failing basil, other fresh herbs can be almost as good ~ try thyme, rosemary or parsley.)

- 8 FL OZ / 225 ML VERY GOOD OLIVE OIL
- 3~4 CLOVES GARLIC, CRUSHED
- 8 LEAVES BASIL, OR MORE IF YOU LIKE
- 1 LB 2 OZ / 500 G TOMATOES, PEELED & CHOPPED
- 1 LB 2 OZ / 500 G WHOLE WHEAT BREAD
- 1 MEDIUM LEEK, FINELY CHOPPED
- 2¼ PT / 1.4 LTR STOCK
- SALT & PEPPER
- (½ TSP CRUSHED CHILI PEPPER ~ OPTIONAL)

Heat the oil in a deep pan & saute the leek, garlic (& chili if using). When they are soft, add the tomatoes & basil & boil for 5~10 minutes. Then add the stock, salt & pepper. When the soup is boiling add the stale bread torn into small pieces. Cook for 2 minutes, cover & let stand for an hour. Then mix well, pour on some fresh oil and serve with parmesan.

MASHA INNOCENTI

Masha Innocenti runs a cookery school in Florence for foreigners pining to learn the secrets of Italian cooking. She comes from a whole family of Tuscan cooks and her culinary inspiration is as much from a Lucchesan mother as from a cordon bleu chef's course.

CONIGLIO con OLIVE NERE

Tuscan rabbit with black olives (6)

This recipe for rabbit with black olives is especially typical of the region around Lucca where both rabbits & excellent olives are plentiful.

3 LB/1.4 KG RABBIT WASHED & CUT INTO PIECES
2 CLOVES GARLIC
8 FL OZ/225 ML OLIVE OIL
2 OZ/60 G BUTTER
4 FL OZ/110 ML WHITE WINE
1 TBSP TOMATO PASTE
6 TBSP BLACK OLIVES
8 FL OZ/225 ML STOCK
SALT & BLACK PEPPER

Remove skin from the garlic cloves and slash each clove halfway through. Heat the oil and butter or margarine in a large saucepan or fireproof casserole. Add the garlic and rabbit & brown on all sides over a medium heat. When brown add the wine, turn up the heat & let it evaporate. Then lower the heat, add the tomato paste and stock, cover and cook over a medium heat for 15 minutes. Season to taste, add the black olives & cook for another 25~30 minutes until the meat is tender & has turned a light pink. Add more stock if the stew appears to be in danger of drying out.

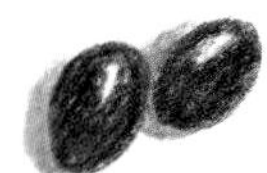

POLLO in FRICASSEA

Chicken in lemon sauce (6)

This classic method of cooking chicken in lemon sauce is equally good with loin of veal cut into pieces.

3 LB / 1.4 KG CHICKEN, CLEANED, DRIED AND CUT IN PIECES
2 OZ / 60 G BUTTER
4 FL OZ / 110 ML OLIVE OIL
SMALL WHITE ONION, CHOPPED
JUICE OF 1 LEMON
2 TBSP FLOUR
3 EGG YOLKS
SALT & WHITE PEPPER
2 TBSP CHOPPED PARSLEY
6 FL OZ / 165 ML ~ 8 FL OZ / 220 ML STOCK

Heat the oil and butter in a shallow heat-proof casserole, add the onion and saute gently until transparent. Add the chicken pieces and brown well all over. Pour in about 4 fl oz / 110 ml of stock, cover and cook gently for 15~20 minutes, adding more stock if necessary to prevent drying out or burning. Mix the flour to a paste in 2 fl oz / 50 ml of stock & stir slowly into the liquid in the casserole to thicken it. Season to taste. Beat the yolks & lemon juice together. When the chicken is cooked, in approximately 40 minutes, remove casserole from the heat & add the yolks & lemon juice mixture, blending in well. Add parsley & serve.

TORTA della NONNA
Grandmother's cake (8)

Grandmothers all over Tuscany make this cake, and so do many restaurants, cafes and pastry-shops. Basically it is a deliciously rich and creamy flan filled with confectioner's custard and covered with a mixture of pastry, toasted almonds, pine nuts and icing sugar, but there are dozens of variations on the same theme.

FOR THE CREAM:

2 EGG YOLKS
1¼ OZ / 35G PLAIN WHITE FLOUR
1 PT / 575ML MILK
2¼ OZ / 75G CASTER SUGAR
SLIVERED ALMONDS & PINE NUTS FOR TOPPING

FOR PASTRY:

12½ OZ / 350G PLAIN WHITE FLOUR
1 EGG & 1 EGG YOLK
2¾ OZ / 75G CASTER SUGAR
4 OZ / 100G BUTTER
1½ TSP BAKING POWDER

First make the cream. Heat the milk until it starts to boil, remove from the heat. Beat the yolks and sugar together until they form a ribbon. Stir in the flour, blending well. Add one tbsp of the hot milk to the yolk-sugar mixture and blend in well with a wooden spoon. Add the mixture to the milk and return to the heat, stirring until the cream thickens. When thickened, pour into a clean bowl and brush the surface with some melted butter to stop a skin forming. Allow to cool.

In the meantime toast a generous handful of almonds and pine nuts on a baking sheet until they are sligtly browned.

To make the pastry sift the flour and baking powder into a mound on a pastry-board or work surface, make a well in the middle and put all the other ingredients into it. Work everything into a dough with your hands. Form into a ball and chill in the refrigerator for 30 minutes. When ready to use, cut the dough in half, roll out one half into a circle 1/8 in / 3 mm thick and place on an 8 in / 20.5 cm greased pie plate, making sure that there is about ½ in / 1 cm hanging over the plate's edge. Pour the cream onto the pastry base, making sure that the middle is somewhat higher than the edges. Fold the pastry rim inwards and brush with some water. Roll the remaining piece of dough out to fit and place gently on top of the cream. Press well onto the pastry border & trim off any excess. Top with the almonds and pine nuts and bake in a preheated oven at 350°F / 180°C / Gas 4 for 25~30 minutes until golden brown. Cool and sift with plenty of icing sugar before serving.

*They serve a very good version of this sweet at the little, crowded trattoria 'Il Lordo' off the main square in Fiesole.

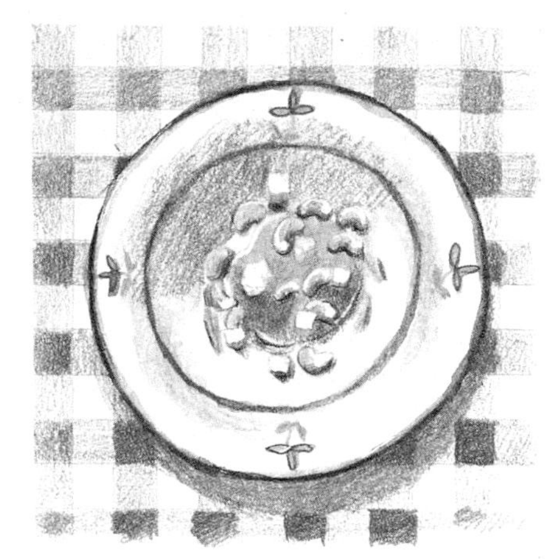

~4~
Simple Dishes
Some of the best food in Tuscany is also the easiest to prepare.

At the Borgo Antico in Florence they serve a delicious salad of freshly shelled 'baccelli' (broad beans) and equal parts pecorino cheese & slivers of prosciutto. Everything is then tossed in lots of good olive oil and served with fresh ground pepper.

The traditional ending to a Tuscan country meal is a bowl of pears, peeled & served with pecorino cheese. Eaten young pecorino can be rubbery, but ask for piccante & you will get a cheese a bit like parmesan that goes well with ripe pears.

At Il Cibreo in Florence, a trattoria near the Santa Ambrogio market behind Santa Croce, they mix fresh ricotta cheese with marjoram, grate pecorino cheese on top & grill until golden brown.

Fettunta is toast (usually grilled over an open fire) that is rubbed with garlic & dranched in olive oil & sea salt. It is called Bruschetta when topped with a mixture of raw tomatoes & fresh basil.

· LEONARDO · MACCHIAVELLI ·

Niccolo Macchiavelli is one of the least liked and most misunderstood personalities in Tuscan history, probably because he made the mistake of telling the truth in his book, The Prince. His name is synonymous with treachery & deviousness. The Albergaccio Macchiavelli just outside Florence is doing much to rectify that. Directly opposite the villa (open to the public) where the original Machiavelli spent his 15-year exile from Florence, this little trattoria serves good wine, good garlic bread and good Fagioli all'uccelletto.

· FAGIOLI all'UCCELLETTO ·

Beans cooked like small birds (4)

This famous Tuscan dish is perhaps called 'all'uccelletto' because an uccelletto is a small bird and these beans are cooked in the same way that small birds are cooked during the hunting season. The recipe comes from another Machiavelli. Leonardo claims to be one of the last surviving members of the family and is himself a political thinker, although more usually the maker of vin santo and fine CARMIGNANO wines. The excellent Carmignano wines are made in a small area near the Medici villa of Poggio a Caiano north of Florence. They are not widely available outside Italy, but there is a wide selection at the little enoteca (wine store) in the centre of Poggio a Caiano, among them Leonardo's gold-medal winning Vino Carmignano from the Fattoria Ambra that he manages.

- 2 LB 2 OZ / 1 KG FRESH WHITE TOSCANELLI BEANS OR
- 14 OZ / 400 G DRIED WHITE BEANS
- 14 OZ / 400 G PEELED TOMATOES
- 2~3 CLOVES GARLIC
- OLIVE OIL
- 5 OR MORE FRESH SAGE LEAVES
- SALT & FRESHLY GROUND BLACK PEPPER

Soak the dried beans overnight & then rinse, or if using fresh beans shell & wash. Boil in slightly salted water for 30~40 minutes. Heat several tablespoons of olive oil in a medium-sized heat-proof casserole. Brown the garlic, sage & pepper in the oil and then add the beans, stirring for a few minutes to allow the flavours to blend. Add the tomatoes, chopped roughly, salt to taste & continue cooking covered for about 15 minutes.

NB. These beans can be turned into a Tuscan version of wieners or bangers & beans if you saute 2 spicy sausages per person over a low heat until browned, remove from pan and continue recipe as above, using the sausage fat instead of olive oil. About 15 minutes before the end of cooking, return the sausages to the pan and add four tablespoons of red wine.

ABOVE: Grapes for VIN SANTO drying on straw mats in the attic of Leonardo's farmhouse near Poggio a Caiano.

· ANITRA con VIN SANTO ·
Duck with vin santo (4)

Each Tuscan winemaker makes his own version of vin santo or 'holy wine', but because of the painstaking and lengthy production it is extremely difficult to buy outside Tuscany. Made from semi-dried grapes, it must be aged for a minimum of 3 years before emerging into the sunlight as vin santo. At its best it has a wonderfully smoky aromatic flavour rather like fine old sherry or Madeira and is traditionally served as a dessert wine with Biscotti di Prato (page 36).

- 1 4 lb/1.8 KG DUCK WITH GIBLETS
- 2 WINE GLASSES VIN SANTO (OR GOOD MEDIUM DRY SHERRY)
- 1 ONION
- 1 STICK CELERY
- 5 oz/150 G CHOPPED PROSCIUTTO OR FATTY HAM
- 1 CARROT
- 4 SAGE LEAVES
- OLIVE OIL
- SALT
- WHITE PEPPER
- 14 oz/400 ML CHICKEN OR BEEF STOCK

Chop the onion, celery, carrot, sage and prosciutto and put in a heatproof casserole with the oil

over a medium heat. When transparent and soft add the duck, cut in pieces, and brown on all sides. Season with salt and white pepper and pour in the vin santo. Cover and cook for several minutes over a low heat. Then add ½ the stock and the finely chopped duck liver. Cover again and continue to cook for about an hour, adding a few tablespoons of stock from time to time. The resulting sauce should not be too liquid. It is best to let the dish cool and then skim off the fat, as duck tends to give off a lot of fat. Reheat after skimming and serve the sauce over plain flat maccheroni, the pieces of duck to follow as a separate course perhaps with fagioli all'uccelletto or, for a less heavy meal, this dish of spinach and swiss chard.

One of the most outstanding vin santos in Tuscany is from the AVIGNONESI estate. They sell only 1000 bottles a year but also serve it in their splendid restaurant 'LA CASANUOVA' near Chianciano.

BIETOLE & SPINACI • con PINOLI •

Spinach & swiss chard with pine nuts (4)

- 1 LB 4 OZ / ½ KG SPINACH, TRIMMED OR EQUIVALENT BEETTOPS
- 1 LB 4 OZ / ½ KG SWISS CHARD, TRIMMED
- 1 GARLIC CLOVE
- SMALL HANDFUL PINE NUTS
- SMALL HANDFUL RAISINS
- SALT & PEPPER
- OLIVE OIL

Boil the spinach and swiss chard in separate pans of salted water until just tender (about 15 minutes). Drain both vegetables well and squeeze into a ball. Chop them coarsely and put them in a frying pan in which the oil, garlic, pine nuts and raisins have been gently simmering. Saute for several minutes to blend the flavours, and serve hot with freshly ground black pepper.

· VILLA · I · TATTI ·

At the end of the last century, when the art historian Bernard Berenson was a young man, he rode out on his bicycle every morning from his Florence pensione, his pockets filled with candles to light the obscure corners of unknown churches all over Tuscany, returning in the dusk to write up discoveries that would one day make him famous. In later, more prosperous years, his charming villa, I TATTI, just outside Florence, became the focal point for all the visiting members of the literary and artistic set. Now it is a Renaissance study centre (visits for ordinary tourists can be arranged through the Italian Tourist Board in Florence) and lucky Harvard University students can freely prowl the formal gardens. And equally freely supply a Renaissance recipe like this one. It is good served with a selection of other Tuscan antipasti such as crostini, prosciutto and olives, or a salad of beans & cheese.

• INVOLTINI di SALVIA •
Sage Leaf Rolls

It is difficult to gauge quantities for these little hors d'oeuvres as it depends on the greed of the people eating them. Essentially the recipe is this: for each sage roll take two large sage leaves & one anchovy (the anchovy should be soaked in milk for 30 minutes to remove salt). Make these into a 'sandwich' with the anchovy in the middle, roll them up & secure with a toothpick. Each of these is then dipped first in beaten egg, then in flour, & finally deep fried in hot oil until crisp & puffed up.

• BISCOTTI di PRATO •

Prato biscuits (1 lb)

1 LB 2 OZ / 500 G CASTER SUGAR
1 LB 2 OZ / 500 G WHITE FLOUR
7 OZ / 200 G PEELED ALMONDS
5 OZ / 150 G PINENUTS
4 EGGS, BEATEN
1 TSP GRATED ORANGE PEEL
½ TSP VANILLA EXTRACT
½ TSP BAKING POWDER
SALT
BUTTER

Probably the most common conclusion to a dinner in Tuscany is the arrival of a plate of these curiously hard, oval biscuits. Dunked liberally in a glass of vin santo, they are magically transformed into a surprisingly moreish dessert. They should be hard and dry to start with (and will keep for months in a tightly closed container) and in fact the bakers in Prato put ammonium bicarbonate, an old-fashioned leavening agent, into their biscuits to ensure an extra long hard life. In Italy Prato biscuits are seldom served without vin santo to accompany them. However if vin santo is unavailable you can use a good sweet sherry instead.

* Biscotti di Prato are also available commercially in packages, but lack the flavour & consistency of these home-made biscuits.

Preheat oven to 375°F/190°C/Gas 5. Toast the almonds in the oven for a couple of minutes and chop roughly with the pinenuts. Sift the flour onto a pastry board or work surface. Make a well in the middle and pour in eggs, baking powder, sugar and a pinch of salt. Work to a smooth consistency with your hands and then mix in nuts. Roll pieces of the dough into long 'fingers'. Place on a greased, floured baking sheet & bake in the oven for about 15 minutes. Remove & slice dough fingers on the diagonal, about ½ in/1cm thick, and bake for another 25 minutes until brown.

• BORGO • ANTICO •

The little birreria, Borgo Antico, in Florence's Piazza Santa Spirito serves a modern version of an authentic Renaissance Tuscan dish & definitely without the original's near disastrous consequences.

CIBREO

Cibreo was one of Catherine de'Medici's favourite dishes. There is a story that one day after eating too many heaped platefuls she nearly died of indigestion. Considering that Cibreo was once made with the livers, kidneys, testicles & crests of cockerels, this seems hardly surprising!

1 LB 2 OZ/500 G CHICKEN LIVER, ROUGHLY CHOPPED
1 SMALL ONION OR LEEK VERY FINELY CHOPPED
2 OZ/50 G BUTTER
2 EGG YOLKS
JUICE OF ½ LEMON
FLOUR
SALT & PEPPER
A LITTLE CHICKEN STOCK

Melt the butter in a medium-sized pan, saute the onion in it until soft but not brown. Roll the liver in flour, add to the pan with salt & pepper and cook over a low heat, adding a few tablespoons of stock as necessary to keep the mixture moist and creamy. Meanwhile lightly beat the yolks & lemon juice together. When the liver is just cooked through, take from the heat and stir in the egg mixture. Leave for two minutes and serve with toast as a light first course or luncheon dish.

• PAN di RAMERINO •

Rosemary buns

The fragrant and sticky 'pan di ramerino' is a famous sweet bun popular with Florentine children during the Easter holidays. To make these buns add 3 oz/75 g of sugar to the bread ingredients on page 67. Work into a dough and leave to rise in a warm place until doubled in size. Then put the dough on a table and mix into it 1½ wine glasses of olive oil in which 2 sprigs of fresh rosemary have been slowly heated for 10~15 minutes. Add 4 oz/100 g of raisins and 2 tbsp of finely chopped rosemary leaves to the dough and form into buns of 3 in/7.5 cm in diameter. Make a cross on the top with a pair of scissors, brush with beaten egg and bake until golden (20~30 mins) in an oven preheated to 400°F/200°C/Gas 6.

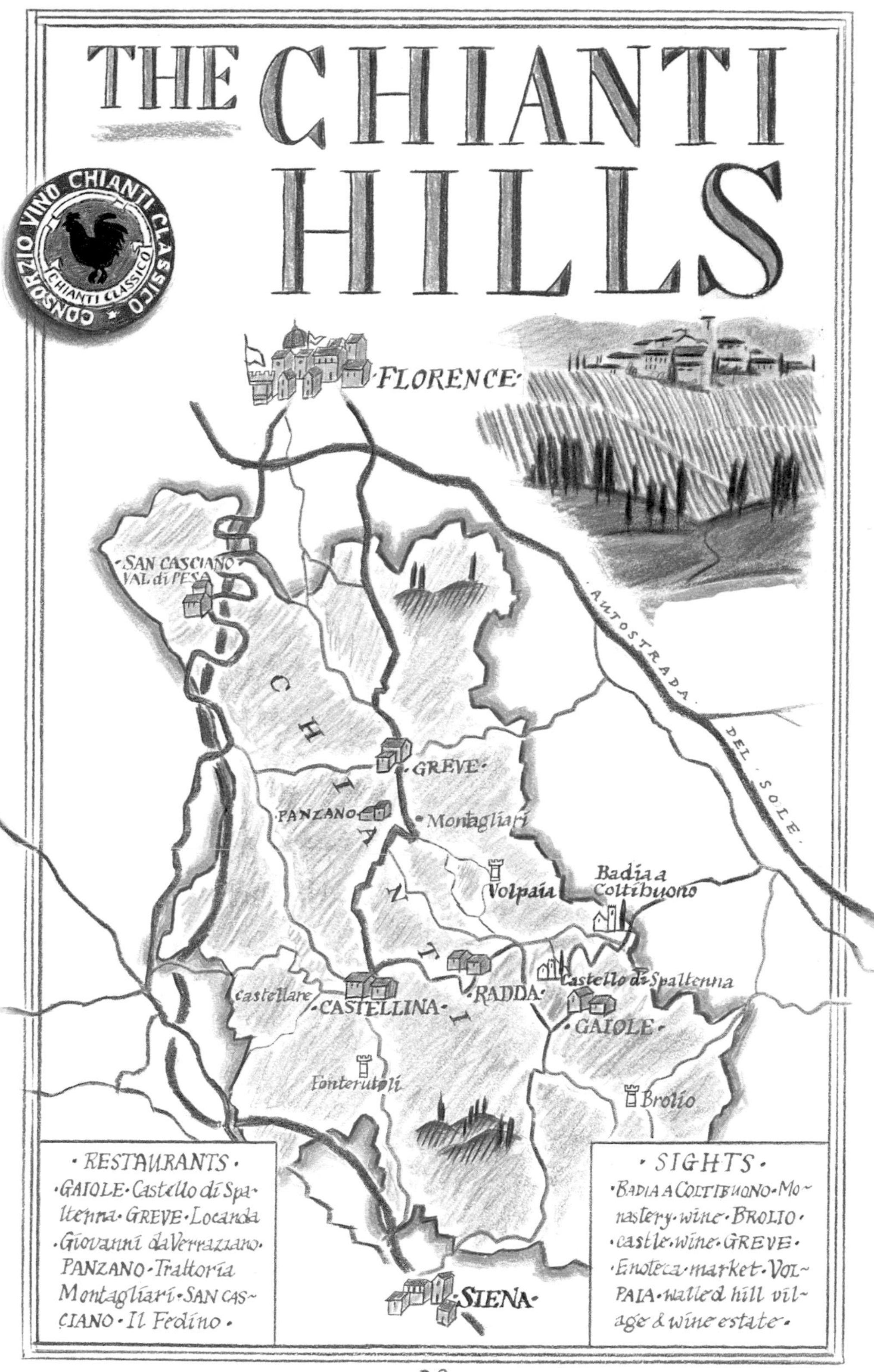
THE CHIANTI HILLS
CONSORZIO VINO CHIANTI CLASSICO
CHIANTI CLASSICO
FLORENCE
SAN CASCIANO VAL di PESA
AUTOSTRADA DEL SOLE
CHIANTI
GREVE
PANZANO
Montagliari
Volpaia
Badia a Coltibuono
castellare
CASTELLINA
RADDA
Castello di Spaltenna
GAIOLE
Fonterutoli
Brolio
SIENA
RESTAURANTS
GAIOLE · Castello di Spaltenna · GREVE · Locanda Giovanni da Verrazzano · PANZANO · Trattoria Montagliari · SAN CASCIANO · Il Fedino ·
SIGHTS
BADIA A COLTIBUONO · Monastery · wine · BROLIO · castle · wine · GREVE · Enoteca · market · VOLPAIA · walled hill village & wine estate ·

· INTRODUCTION ·

The Chianti wine district of Tuscany stretches from north of Florence, west to Pisa, south as far as Chiusi and east to Arezzo. But the soul of Chianti is the area of pine-clad hills rambling for 30-40 miles between Florence and Siena. This is the domain of the Chianti 'League' founded by feudal barons in the thirteenth century to protect their interests, one of the earliest regions to put controls on wine and an area almost constantly at war during the middle ages.

There is little evidence now of Chianti's turbulent past. The splendid views of vineyards and castles made famous in Renaissance paintings are more likely to be disturbed by the buzz of mopeds and Fiats than battles. Even the Castello di Volpaia, a medieval hill castle that was the scene of many violent clashes between Florence and Siena is now better known for its excellent Chianti and for the art exhibitions put on in the twelfth-century church.

The Castello di Volpaia is one of the prettiest of the walled hill villages, with a reputation for good wine dating back to the fifteenth century, but throughout the region there are castles and villages unchanged since medieval times, most selling their own wines, delicate olive oils and local products like the soaps and colognes made from olive oil and local lavender (called 'spigo' in the Chianti region), at the hill town of Fonterutoli. Tiny dusty roads link vineyards to yellow-ochre farmhouses, farms to walled villages and villages eventually to bigger wine towns. Originally the only real 'Chianti'

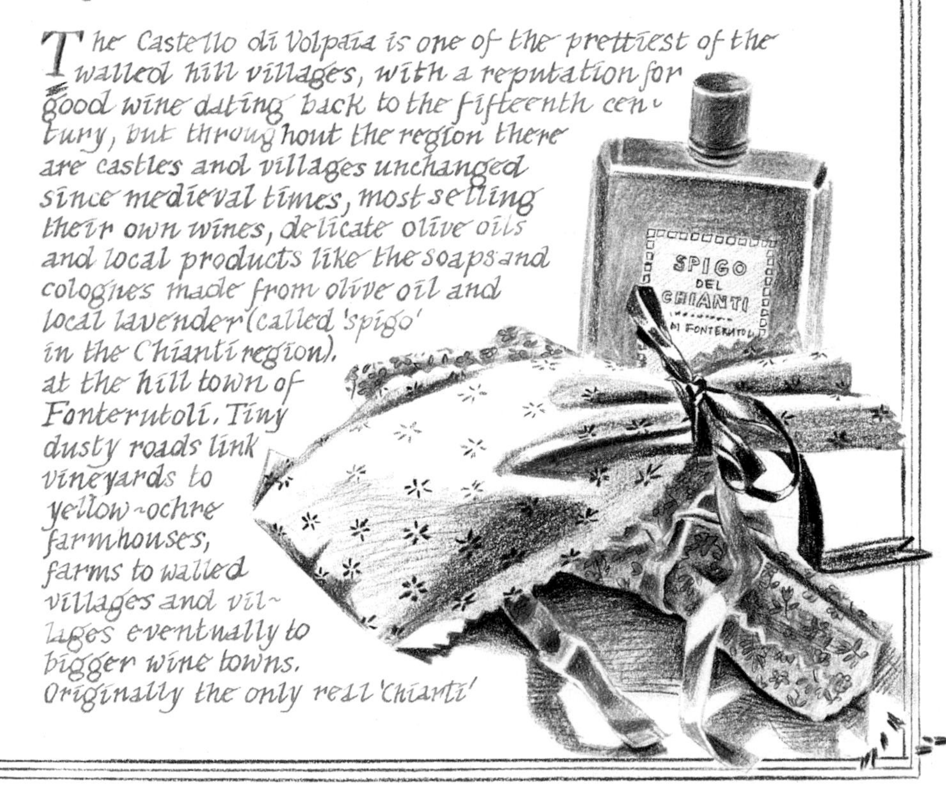

towns were Radda, Castellina and Gaiole. Now the main market town of Greve, on the stunning Via Chiantigiana (the SS222), is also included. A lively wine festival is held every September in Greve's charming seventeenth-century Piazza Matteoti and the town's Enoteca di Gallo Nero sells a complete selection of Chianti Classico, the DOC-registered wine identified by a black cockerel on the label. The Gallo Nero 'Classico' wines are not the only good Chiantis however. The black cockerel guarantees only that the wine has met the standards set by the DOC, Denominazione di Origine Controllata, originally set up by a group of Chianti producers, the Italian equivalent of the French Appellation Contrôlé system.

The history of Chianti wine is almost as long as that of the district itself. By the time the straw-covered flask became famous (around 1860) it had been made for at least six centuries. It is possible that monks were the first Chianti producers. Certainly the monks at the beautiful abbey of Badia a Coltibuono (now a wine estate) were making wine at least as early as the twelfth century and continued to do so for hundreds of years. At the Castellare estate of Castellina grapes were grown for wine long before Lorenzo de' Medici ruled Florence in the fifteenth century. Monks from the nearby San Niccolò monastery worked the hard, stoney terrain with hoes in vineyards that are still producing good wine.

Chianti has evolved and changed considerably over the centuries. In the nineteenth century Baron Ricasoli of the Castello di Brolio established a basic 'recipe' for the blend of white and red grapes that would give modern Chianti its characteristic taste. Today it is one of the most famous wines in the world but not without certain problems. Disagreements on quality control amongst its producers and in some cases a lack of interest in modern techniques and an overuse of easy-to-grow white grapes have made a few Chiantis pale and insipid. This has damaged the wine's overall reputation. Fortunately Chianti is still popular thanks to the constant efforts of young wine-makers to improve and refine the taste of their wine while still maintaining its original rich quality.

There is the same diversity in the food and cooking of the Chianti region. A good meal can be as simple as a slice of creamy fresh ricotta and a handful of tiny jewel-

FOUR · CHIANTI · TOWNS

GAIOLE

RADDA

CASTELLINA

GREVE

red wild strawberries picked and eaten still warm on a steep hillside. A village trattoria may serve its own salty pecorino cheese and rough young Chianti with a dish of fresh olives from local trees, or a plate of home-made pasta with just a chunk of crusty bread to mop up the plain sauce of oil and sage leaves. Or elaborate Renaissance dishes fit for a Medici banquet may be elegantly served with a mellow, aged Chianti 'riserva' in a castle's cool vaulted dining hall. This is the country where a whole roast wild boar is not an uncommon feast during the autumn hunting season. In fact the name 'Chianti' is popularly believed to stem from the Latin 'clangor,' a word for the loud blast a trumpet makes on a baronial hunting party.

More than any other part of Tuscany, wine in the Chianti region is an inescapable part of life. The people there eat, drink, talk and sleep it. They serve food to complement wine rather than the reverse. Despite this enthusiasm and such a good end product, there is little formal wine tourism in the district. However most wine estates welcome visitors and more frequently now have a trattoria or even more rustic osteria on the premises where both local wine and good simple food are served beside views of vineyards, cypresses and medieval castles.

· CASTELLO · DI · SPALTENNA ·

Next to an eleventh-century village church on one of the vine-covered hills above Gaiole in Chianti is the Castello di Spaltenna, a beautiful and serene hotel cum restaurant. If you are lucky and go on the right day, Anna, the local cook might be there. She comes up regularly from Gaiole and in season cooks local dishes at the Castello that are seldom found outside Tuscany. She also has the Italian knack of making gnocchi & fresh pasta seem easy ~ make a pile of flour, put 5 eggs in the middle, work it a bit with enough water and there's your pasta...

· PANZANELLA ·

Bread & tomato salad (6)

This is the kind of recipe, if you can call it a recipe, that sounds awful and tastes delicious. Like many of Tuscany's deceptively simple dishes, it relies on perfectly fresh ingredients (apart, of course, from the stale bread!) and the idiosyncracies of individual cooks. Some less generous cooks use mostly onions and bread for panzanella, but it is best made with masses of very red and juicy tomatoes when they are at their ripest from June until the end of August. Don't be put off by the idea of stale bread in a salad, but do wring it out very well

8 ~ 10 PIECES HARD STALE BREAD
6 VERY RIPE TOMATOES, ROUGHLY CHOPPED
2 LARGE ONIONS, PREFERABLY RED ONIONS, SLICED THINLY
2 STICKS CELERY AND LEAVES, DICED
1 CUCUMBER CUT IN CHUNKS
8 OR MORE FRESH BASIL LEAVES, BRUISED IN A MORTAR
GOOD OLIVE OIL
SALT & PEPPER
RED WINE VINEGAR

Soak the bread in cold water for 15~20 minutes. Squeeze it out very well and crumble into a salad bowl. Add the vegetables, oil, basil, salt and pepper. Chill in the refrigerator for 2 ~3 hours. Just before serving toss with wine vinegar and some more basil if you have it.

SCHIACCIATA con L'UVA
Traditional flat cake with grapes

Schiacciata means 'squashed flat' and this is a very ancient flat cake that has been made at the time of the vendemmia (grape harvest) in Tuscany since Etruscan times over 2000 years ago. It was devised, like so many dishes, as a method for using existing materials; left-over bread dough for the base and quantities of black wine grapes for the topping. If you are bothered by the seeds in Schiacciata you can make it with seedless grapes, or de-pip the grapes you are using, but it will not be as authentic, or as much fun - there won't be any pips to spit out, although a polite crunching sound is more usual in restaurants.

FOR THE BASE

1 LB 2 OZ/500 G PLAIN WHITE FLOUR, SIFTED
1 OZ/25 G FRESH YEAST
PINCH SALT
2½ OZ/60 G GRANULATED SUGAR
½ OZ/15 G ANISE SEED (SWEET CUMIN)
3/4 CUP WATER

FOR THE TOPPING

2 LB 2 OZ/1 KG LARGE JUICY BLACK GRAPES, WASHED
4 OZ/100 G CASTER SUGAR
SEVERAL SPRIGS FRESH ROSEMARY
6 ~ 8 TBSP OLIVE OIL

Warm the water and add the yeast, blend until smooth. On a pastry board or work-surface make a mound of the flour, salt and

granulated sugar. Make a well in the middle and slowly pour in the yeast mixture, blending with a wooden spoon or spatula until smooth. When the yeast has been incorporated, knead the dough for 5–10 minutes as you would for bread. When it is smooth and elastic, cover and put in a warm room. When it has doubled in size, grease a rectangular baking tray (about 20" × 12"/51 × 30.5cm) with oil. Roll out the dough so that it is no more than ½"/1cm thick and 2"/5cm bigger all around than the tray. Place the dough on the tray and cover completely with the grapes. Sprinkle with the sugar and pour oil (in which you have heated the rosemary for several minutes) over the top. Fold up the sides of the dough and pinch at the corners to make a rectangular shape. Bake for 30 minutes in an oven preheated to 350° F/175°C/Gas 4. It is best to put another pan underneath the Schiacciata as the juice from the grapes may overflow. Use these juices to baste the top of the cake. Chill in the refrigerator and just before serving drizzle it with honey.

There is another method for making Schiacciata con l'uva. At Spaltenna Anna makes the dough as above and then mixes into it the grapes and oil in which she has heated the rosemary and a cup of walnuts. She then rolls it out to no more than 1"/2.5cm and bakes it like a crusty flat bread or scone (at the same temperature). When the grapes are really lush, their juice stains the cake a deep crimson.

·FATTORIA·DI·MONTAGLIARI·

Giovanni Cappelli, the owner of the Fattoria di Montagliari, an excellent trattoria & vineyard near Panzano, is a faithful patron of the Antica Macelleria in Greve (pages 50~51). His cook specialises in local Chiantigiana cuisine and Signor Cappelli himself is quite a culinary expert. These recipes are from his own handwritten collection. The Fattoria di Montagliari also has one of the largest vin santeries in Tuscany and produces one of the best vin santos. The Riserva 1968 is particularly fine.

· CROSTINI ROSSI ·

Piquant tomato crostini (4)

1 PIECE WHOLEWHEAT BREAD
1 CLOVE GARLIC
1 TBSP CAPERS
3 TBSP OLIVE OIL
COARSE SALT
FRESHLY GROUND BLACK PEPPER
WINE VINEGAR
3 TBSP FRESH PARSLEY
2 TBSP FRESH THYME
2 LARGE RIPE TOMATOES, PEELED
8 PIECES FRENCH BREAD OR DEEP FRIED POLENTA

Soak the wholewheat bread in vinegar and wring out well. Put in a mortar with the rest of the ingredients (except for the French bread) and pound to a rough paste. Chill and serve on toasted French bread or deep fried polenta (see recipe opposite)

· CECINA ·

Chickpea savoury bread (4)

9 OZ/250 G CHICKPEA FLOUR
1 3/4 PT/1 LITRE WATER
1/2 GLASS OLIVE OIL
SALT

Sift the flour into a bowl, make a well in the middle and slowly add the water, beating well to avoid lumps forming. Add the oil and salt and blend in. Pour into a greased shallow baking tin to a depth of not more than 1/2 in/1cm. Bake in an oven pre-heated to 450°F/230°C/Gas 8 until golden brown. Serve cut in wedges with plenty of freshly ground black pepper.

· SALSA di NOCI ·

Walnut sauce for pasta (6)

A recipe for pasta sauce that Giovanni Cappelli believes dates from at least the 1400s in Siena. He serves it in his restaurant with tortelli but it is also very good with a flat pasta like tagliatelle

7 OZ/200 G WALNUTS
2 OZ/50 G PINE NUTS
2 CLOVES GARLIC
3 BASIL LEAVES OR MORE ACCORDING TO TASTE
2 TBSP BREADCRUMBS
½ PT/300 ML MILK OR MORE ~ ENOUGH TO MAKE A SAUCE THE CONSISTENCY OF THICK CREAM
3 TBSP OLIVE OIL
SALT
PEPPER

If you want to feel authentically quattrocentoish, you could pound all the above ingredients together in a mortar to make the sauce. A food processor is faster, if less romantic. Serve the sauce over the pasta and then sprinkle with whole walnuts and more basil to make the dish especially good.

· POLENTA FRITTA ·

Deep fried polenta (4~6)

Polenta is a corn meal porridge more popular in the north than in Tuscany. Tuscan cooks tend to prefer it first chilled and then crisply deep-fried in small golden wedges under rich game sauces, or to replace toast in antipasti.

7 OZ/200 G COARSE~GRAINED CORN MEAL
SALT
OIL FOR DEEP FRYING

Boil 2 pints of water in a large saucepan, add salt and lower heat. When water is just simmering begin to add cornmeal, pouring in a thin stream, stirring constantly with a wooden spoon to prevent lumps forming. Continue stirring for about 15~20 minutes after all the cornmeal has been added. The polenta is cooked as soon as it begins to stand away from the side of the pan. Pour immediately into a shallow baking tray to a thickness of not more than ½ in/1 cm. Smooth out any lumps and chill. When cool enough to slice, cut into diamond shapes that are approximately 2½ in/5 cm long by 2 in/4 cm wide and deep fry in hot oil a few at a time. They are cooked when transparent yellow and crusty on both sides.

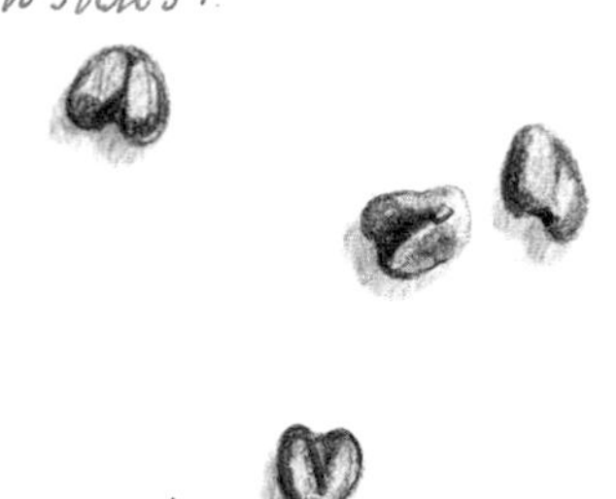

· ANTICA · MACELLERIA · FALORNI ·

Just off the main square in Greve is the Antica Macelleria Falorni, a butcher's shop that every harassed dinner-party giver would like to live next to. This business, established in the 1840s, has become justifiably famous all over Italy for the quality of its meat. The proprietors, Lorenzo and Stefano Bencistà, proudly claim that every morning on opening there are at least 60 different cuts of meat for sale, as well as roasts, meatballs and Tuscan shishkebabs prepared to their mother's recipes with fresh herbs, juniper berries, tomatoes & red peppers. Their acclaimed FINOCCHIONA sausage is made not with the usual cultivated fennel, but with feathery wild fennel gathered locally in the Chianti hills. And most astonishing of all, they still make, to an antique and ridiculously non-commercial recipe, prosciutto casalingo sotto cenere, now completely unavaible anywhere else. The ham is first stamped with the date, and then buried under wood ashes for up to two years. Originally the Tuscan peasants preserved their pork in this way throughout the summer months to have it, pink and tender, to eat during the long cold winter. Lorenzo does it now, he says, not to make money, because its impossible to do on a large scale, but 'purely for the satisfaction of it, to keep the old traditions alive'. The Antica Macelleria Falorni also exports wild boar sausages and prosciutto all over Europe.

ARISTA di MAIALE • ARROSTO •

Roast loin of Pork (5~6)

If bistecca fiorentina is Tuscany's most famous meat dish, this recipe comes a close second. 'ARISTA' is the Tuscan word for loin of pork, and at the Falorni Macelleria they cut the loin to keep long bones on the chops. These are then used as a kind of natural grilling rack. In some restaurants Arista is made with boned pork with not such a tasty result as this one.

NORCINERIA

- 4 ½ LB / 2 KG LOIN OF PORK
- 2 CLOVES OF GARLIC
- OLIVE OIL
- 2 SPRIGS FRESH ROSEMARY
- 1 WINEGLASS WHITE WINE
- SEA SALT
- BLACK PEPPER, COARSELY GROUND

Finely chop the garlic and rosemary together. With a sharp knife make several cuts in the pork near the bone and stuff with the herbs. Lightly score the outside of the meat and rub plenty of salt, oil and pepper into it to give a crispy skin. Put the wine in a roasting pan and then place the meat resting on its bones in the roasting pan (see drawing). Cook in a moderate oven preheated to 350°F/180°C/Gas 4 for 1½ ~2 hours, basting occasionally with the juices. Serve with plain boiled cannellini beans and a jug of olive oil to pour over according to taste. Or skim the fat off the pan juices, simmer for a few minutes with some more wine and herbs and pour the resulting sauce over the beans instead of using olive oil.

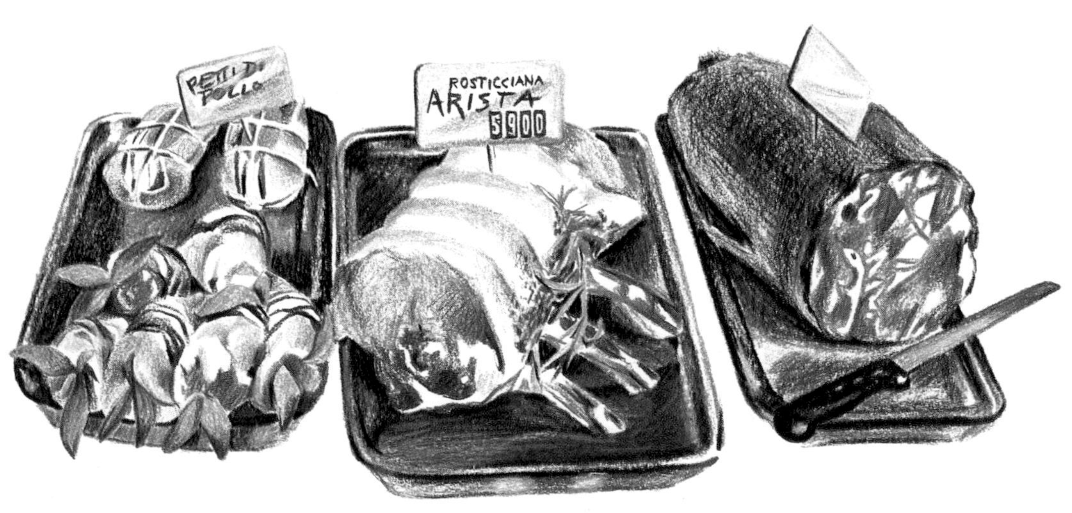

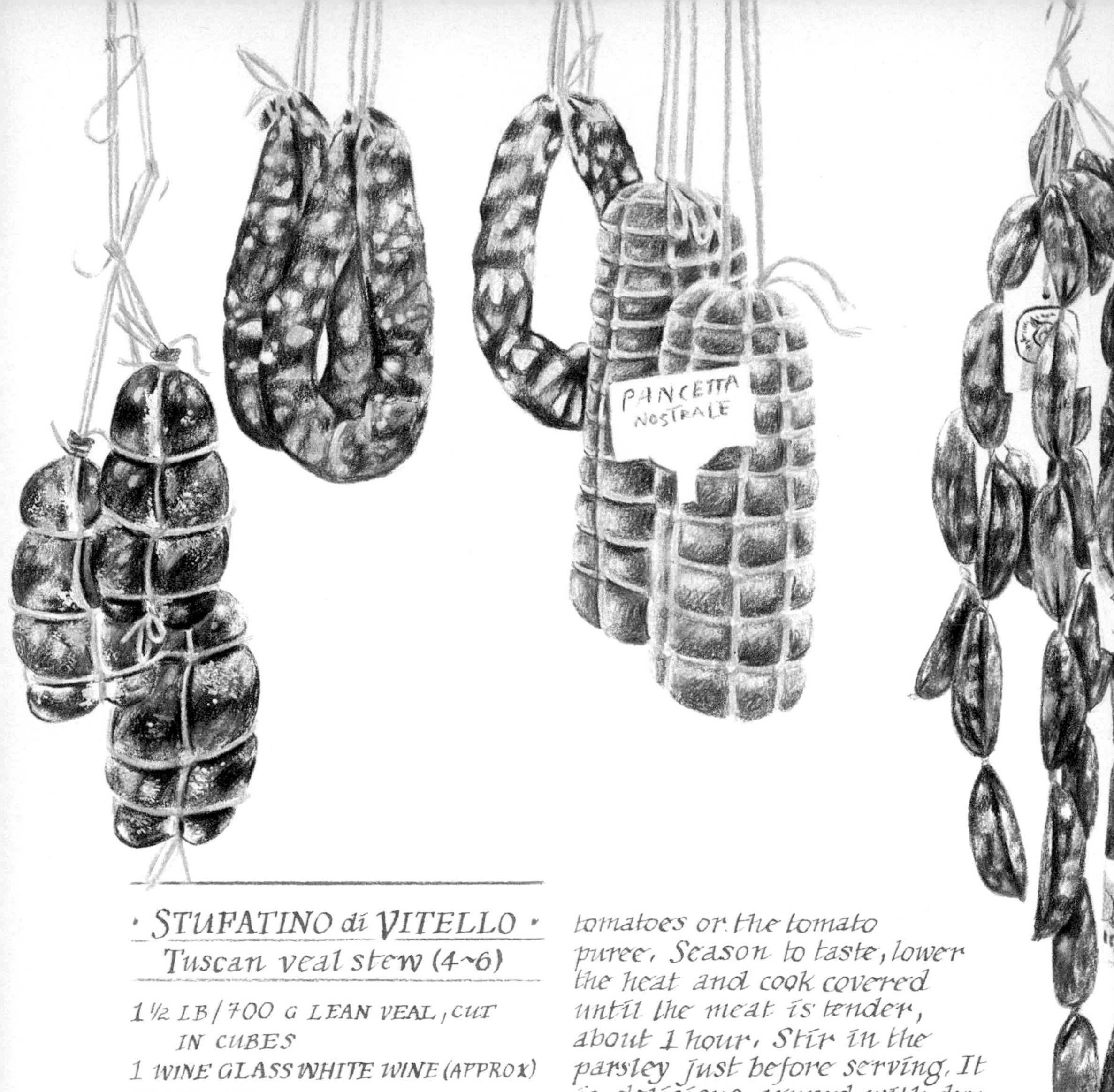

· STUFATINO di VITELLO ·

Tuscan veal stew (4~6)

1 ½ LB / 700 G LEAN VEAL, CUT IN CUBES
1 WINE GLASS WHITE WINE (APPROX)
OLIVE OIL
SALT
PEPPER
¼ CHILI PEPPER, FINELY CHOPPED
1~2 LARGE RIPE TOMATOES, PEELED, SEEDED & CHOPPED OR 3 TBSP TOMATO PUREE IF TOMATOES ARE NOT TASTY
2 CLOVES GARLIC, CRUSHED
3 TBSP CHOPPED PARSLEY
FLOUR

Brown the garlic and chili pepper in oil in a heavy casserole. Add the veal, well dusted with flour, and let it brown. Pour in the wine and when nearly evaporated, add the tomatoes or the tomato puree. Season to taste, lower the heat and cook covered until the meat is tender, about 1 hour. Stir in the parsley just before serving. It is delicious served with deep-fried polenta and fagioli all'ucceletto. A thinly sliced fennel bulb added 10 minutes before the end of cooking makes an excellent addition to the classic version of the dish.

· POLPETTINI ·

Tuscan meatballs (6)

Every country has its version of the meatball. In Tuscany they're called POLPETTINI if they're small. When, as often happens, they are almost the size of a meat loaf, they are

called POLPETTONE. At the Locanda dell'Amorosa near Siena they serve tiny spicy polpettini, crunchily deep-fried, as a hot appetizer in the winter months.

- 1 LB 2 OZ / 500 G COOKED PORK OR BEEF, CUT IN CUBES
- 3 OZ / 75 G GRATED PARMESAN OR PECORINO
- 4 OZ / 100 G PROSCIUTTO (OR HAM)
- 2 POTATOES, PEELED AND COOKED
- 2 EGGS, BEATEN
- 2 CLOVES GARLIC, CRUSHED
- HANDFUL PARSLEY, CHOPPED
- 4 SAGE LEAVES, CHOPPED
- JUICE OF 1 LEMON
- SALT
- PEPPER
- ½ TSP NUTMEG
- (OPTIONAL ¼ TSP CINNAMON)
- OIL FOR DEEP FRYING

Put the meat and potatoes through a fine grinder, mincer or food processor and then mix well with other ingredients. Form tiny round meatballs of a maximum 1 in / 2.5 cm diameter and roll in cornmeal or, better still, breadcrumbs. Deep fry a few at a time in oil until crunchy and golden brown. Drain well and serve hot with a selection of other antipasti.

· LOCANDA · GIOVANNI ·

Go into the Antica Macelleria first thing in the morning and you are likely to run into half the cooks and restaurant-owners in the area. Rossella Rossi, proprietress of the Locanda Giovanni da Verrazzano in Greve does her shopping there and, with the Bencistà brothers' excellent lean veal, makes this unusual version of a classic Tuscan dish. This recipe for Stracotto, meaning overcooked, comes from an old Florentine cookbook and supposedly dates from the sixteenth century.

STRACOTTO al CHIANTI CLASSICO

• Beef with red wine (6) •

4 ½ LB / 2 KG BONED FILLET OF VEAL OR BONED TOP RUMP OF BEEF.
3 OZ / 75 G PINE NUTS
3 OZ / 75 G RAISINS
3 OZ / 75 G PEELED TOASTED ALMONDS
½ HOT CHILI PEPPER, CHOPPED
1 ONION, FINELY CHOPPED
1 CARROT, FINELY CHOPPED
1 BOTTLE CHIANTI CLASSICO
2 CLOVES GARLIC
HANDFUL FRESH PARSLEY
1 PINT GOOD BEEF STOCK
SALT & PEPPER

DA · VERRAZZANO ·

Soften the onion, chili pepper & carrot in oil in a deep casserole, Meanwhile chop the nuts, raisins, garlic and parsley roughly. With a small sharp knife make cuts in several places all over the meat and stuff with half the nut mixture, Tie into a neat shape with string and brown on all sides in the casserole. Pour in the wine, add remaining nut mixture and top up with stock so the meat is just covered, Simmer covered for at least 2¼ hours, or untill meat is tender, adding more stock to keep the meat covered. Remove the string, slice meat thinly and keep warm. Reduce the sauce and serve over meat, making sure some of the nuts and raisins are included. This is a wonderfully rich tasting dish that is best served with something simple such as plain buttered pasta or crisp greens.

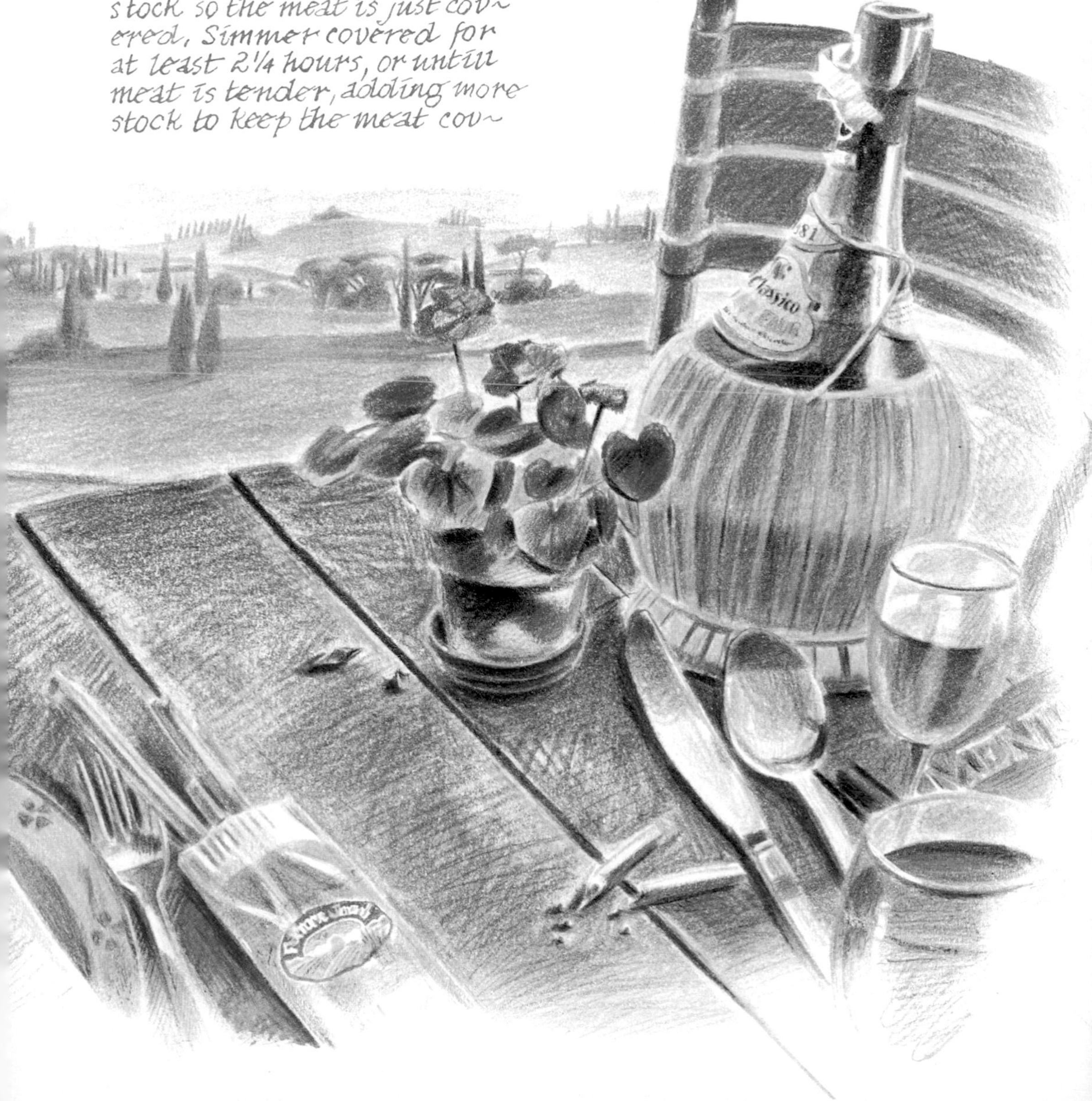

• RISTORANTE • IL • FEDINO •

In the busy town of San Casciano in Val di Pesa, the locals have their own special gathering place ~ the Ristorante Il Fedino, a 15th-century villa on the road to Florence. The proprietor serves essentially rustic dishes in the cool wine cellars below the family home.

CONIGLIO RIPIENO

• Stuffed Rabbit (6) •

This way of cooking rabbit is the speciality at Il Fedino. You can use frozen rabbit from the supermarket, but the flavour will not be as good as when wild rabbit is used.

- 1 LARGE RABBIT, CLEANED, BONED AND FLATTENED
- 2 EGGS
- 6 TBSP GRATED PECORINO OR PARMESAN CHEESE
- 1/2 TSP GRATED NUTMEG
- SEVERAL SPRIGS FRESH THYME
- 8 FL OZ/225 ML BEEF STOCK
- OLIVE OIL
- BUTTER
- COARSE SEA SALT
- PEPPER

Get your butcher or game dealer to clean and bone the rabbit ~ it is not an easy task for the unskilled. Beat the eggs with the salt and pepper and cook in butter to make a thin omelette. Lay the rabbit out flat and put the omelette on it. Dot with butter and sprinkle on the pecorino, nutmeg & thyme. Roll the rabbit up and tie it carefully, having tucked the ends in. Rub plenty of pepper and coarse sea salt into the rabbit. Heat a few tablespoons of olive oil in a shallow flame-proof casserole and brown the rabbit on all sides in it. Reduce the heat & add the stock, cover. Continue cooking for 1½ hours, adding more stock if necessary. When tender, remove the string and serve sliced very thinly in the pan juices with more fresh thyme snipped over the top.

FEGATELLI di MAIALE

Tuscan pork liver • bruschettes (4) •

A classic Tuscan dish cooked either in a frying pan or grilled, as in these two recipes, over charcoal. At Fedino's they vary the recipe slightly by chop~~ping & pre-cooking the liver before gril~ling, which guar~antees its tenderness ~ this is given as the second version of the recipe.

- 4 AROMATIC TWIGS (IE: BAY, ROSEMARY ETC.) FROM WHICH THE LEAVES HAVE BEEN STRIPPED
- 1 LB 2 OZ / 500 G PORK LIVER
- 1 TBSP FENNEL SEEDS
- 4 TBSP BREADCRUMBS OR 4 PIECES BREAD, CUT IN CHUNKS
- OLIVE OIL
- ABOUT 1 LB / 450 G CAUL FAT* OR BACON
- HANDFUL FRESH SAGE OR BAY LEAVES
- SALT & PEPPER

• METHOD I •

Crush the fennel seeds in a mortar with the salt & pepper. Soak the caul fat in water to soften. Cut into squares approx~imately 4 x 4 in / 10 x 10 cm. Cut the liver into bite size chunks and roll in the fennel. Then wrap each piece in caul and skewer on a twig, alternating the liver with a sage or bay leaf and a chunk of bread dipped in olive oil. Cook over fire for 15 ~ 20 minutes or until caul fat is crisp.

• METHOD II •

Crush the fennel seeds with the salt and pepper, breadcrumbs and 3 sage leaves. Chop liver into small pieces and cook until slight~ly browned. Mix with other ingre~dients, wrap in fat and then in a sage or bay leaf. (If using dried bay leaves soak them well first.) Skewer & grill for 10 minutes or until caul fat is crisp.

* CAUL FAT or PORK NET (obtainable from butchers in ethnic neighbourhoods) is a lacy fat from the pig's intestines. If you cannot get it or are squeam~ish, wrap the liver in bacon instead. The fat, however, does add a remarkably flavourful juice to the liver and keeps it very moist.

• PINZIMINIO •

Olive-oil dip

At the CASTELLARE estate near Castellina in Chianti, the olive oil is sold in lovely square glass decanters and the wines and olive oils are distinguished by painted labels of local Chiantigiana birds.

The best way to test the flavour of a good olive oil is to make Pinziminio, nothing more than oil into which generous amounts of coarse sea salt and black pepper have been ground. Tuscans use it as a dip for fresh or briefly scalded vegetables such as fennel root, artichokes, red peppers and asparagus.

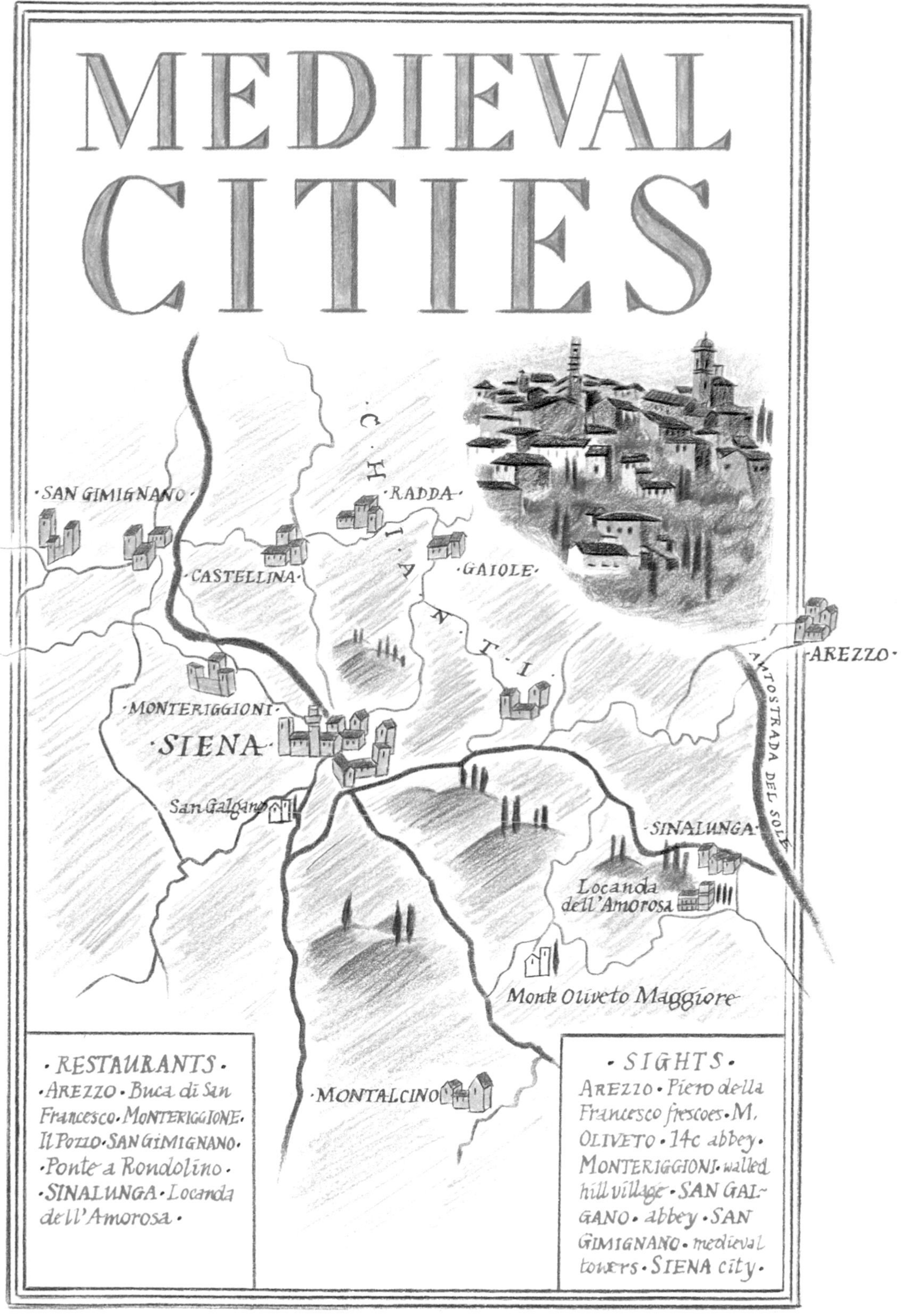
MEDIEVAL CITIES
CHIANTI
SAN GIMIGNANO
RADDA
CASTELLINA
GAIOLE
AREZZO
AUTOSTRADA DEL SOLE
MONTERIGGIONI
SIENA
San Galgano
SINALUNGA
Locanda dell'Amorosa
Monte Oliveto Maggiore
MONTALCINO
RESTAURANTS
AREZZO · Buca di San Francesco · MONTERIGGIONE · Il Pozzo · SAN GIMIGNANO · Ponte a Rondolino · SINALUNGA · Locanda dell'Amorosa ·
SIGHTS
AREZZO · Piero della Francesco frescoes · M. OLIVETO · 14c abbey · MONTERIGGIONI · walled hill village · SAN GALGANO · abbey · SAN GIMIGNANO · medieval towers · SIENA city ·

· INTRODUCTION ·

The story goes that Senius and Aschio, sons of Remus, fled Rome in search of peace and founded a castle in Tuscany that became Siena. There is little remaining Roman influence today apart from the wolf symbol that is prominent in the city's emblems. Siena is a city of Gothic art and architecture, built of red~gold 'burnt Siena' bricks and surrounded by what Virginia Woolf called 'the loveliest of all land~scapes'. It is famous for the beauty and clarity of its language, for its rich oriental~tasting sweets like panforte and ricciarelli and for the Palio, a bare~backed horse race of medieval origins that provides a year~long undercurrent of tension to an other~wise gentle, dreamy city.

The city's past is not a peaceful one. For hundreds of years Ghibelline Siena was the sworn and violent enemy of Guelf Florence. In nearby medieval and Renaissance towns like San Gimignano, Monteriggioni, Montepulciano and Montalcino constant battles were fought between the two city~states. Siena's greatest victory came in 1260 with the defeat of Florence at the battle of Montaperti. Still celebrated today as a glorious event, the battle is less significant than the overwhelming Florentine victory nine years later. This victory, although galling for the Sienese, and in the long run destroying their prosperity, was initially the start of a 'Golden Age' for Siena.

In 1287 'Nine Good Men' chosen from the mid~dle classes to rule the city were responsible for a seventy~year period of great prosperity and art~istic achievement. Most of the work on Siena's magnificent Duomo, begun in the late twelfth century, was completed during this time, including the astonishing black and white striped mosque~like interior. Even more successful was the development of Siena's central square, the Campo, into one of the most magical city centres in Italy. Entered through narrow, covered archways, the square slopes inwards like the hub of a giant wheel. The mellow brick paving is divided into nine spokes symbolizing the Nine Good Men responsible and at the centre is the elegant and much-copied Palazzo Pubblico. Its graceful bell-tower of 503 steps soars into the air over the Campo's fourteenth-century palaces. During the build-up to the Palio, the bell rings methodically and rythmically like the city's heart-beat until minutes before the race begins.

It could be said that the Palio itself is the city's heartbeat, and to understand the Palio is to understand Siena. Briefly it is this: a race three times around the Campo in which ten jockeys ride bareback horses representing the ten contrade (city wards) competing in the race. There are seventeen wards in all, each one a sworn enemy of the other, but for safety's sake not all compete. The only official prize is a silk banner called the 'Palio', and the race for it lasts roughly a minute. But this minute is the culmination of a whole year's hopes and preparation, of a final three day's feasting, parades and sometimes violent fights between rival contrade. At the end of this minute the winning contrada will go, quite

AREZZO
CARTA DELLA PROVINCIA
Scala 1:150.000
5.8
2.87
ENTE PROVINCIALE PER IL TURISMO
Monna Lisa
caseificio salcis siena
SPECIALITA' MANDORLATO
Città di S. Gimignano Panorama

simply, mad with joy; laughing, crying, singing and marching the streets of Siena all night carrying the Palio banner. It is entirely medieval, unlike any other spectacle in the world. People faint from heat and excitement. Jockeys are thrown into the barriers and killed. Horses, drugged before the race, roll over, crash into one another, break legs and are shot. It has been criticized for its barbarity and it is barbaric without a doubt. But no one who has seen it, who has stood inside a church before the race and watched a priest bless a horse, listened to his strange cry 'Vai cavallino e torna vincatore!' (Go little horse and return a winner!) and to the haunting accompanying canto of the surrounding people, who has watched the two hour medieval parade through the streets or the river of people that floods the race square up to the last possible minute; who has seen the old and wily horse Panezio, winner of an astonishing eight Palios, thread his nimble way through the pack of careening jockeys and riderless horses, around the virtually right-angled corner of the Campo that is the most dangerous, or who has heard the spine-tingling cry 'Daccelo' (Give it to us!) after the victory, can fail to be moved by the Palio. To say that it is just a horserace is like saying that Everest is just a mountain. The Palio is not an event that occurs twice a year at Siena. It _is_ Siena.

The only place to eat in Siena is in the street the night before the Palio. Each of the city's wards has a traditional dinner, with tables a quarter of a mile long laid for 200 and 300 people. The jockeys are there, feted and kissed by beautiful girls. Siena's nobility sit next to the local barbers. There are speeches and songs, and somehow miraculously in the middle of all this the food arrives, hot and good, for those who are not too excited to eat it. If you cannot beg, borrow or steal a ticket to one of these meals, there are still plenty of restaurants that push their tables into the street and serve up the Palio atmosphere as well as food.

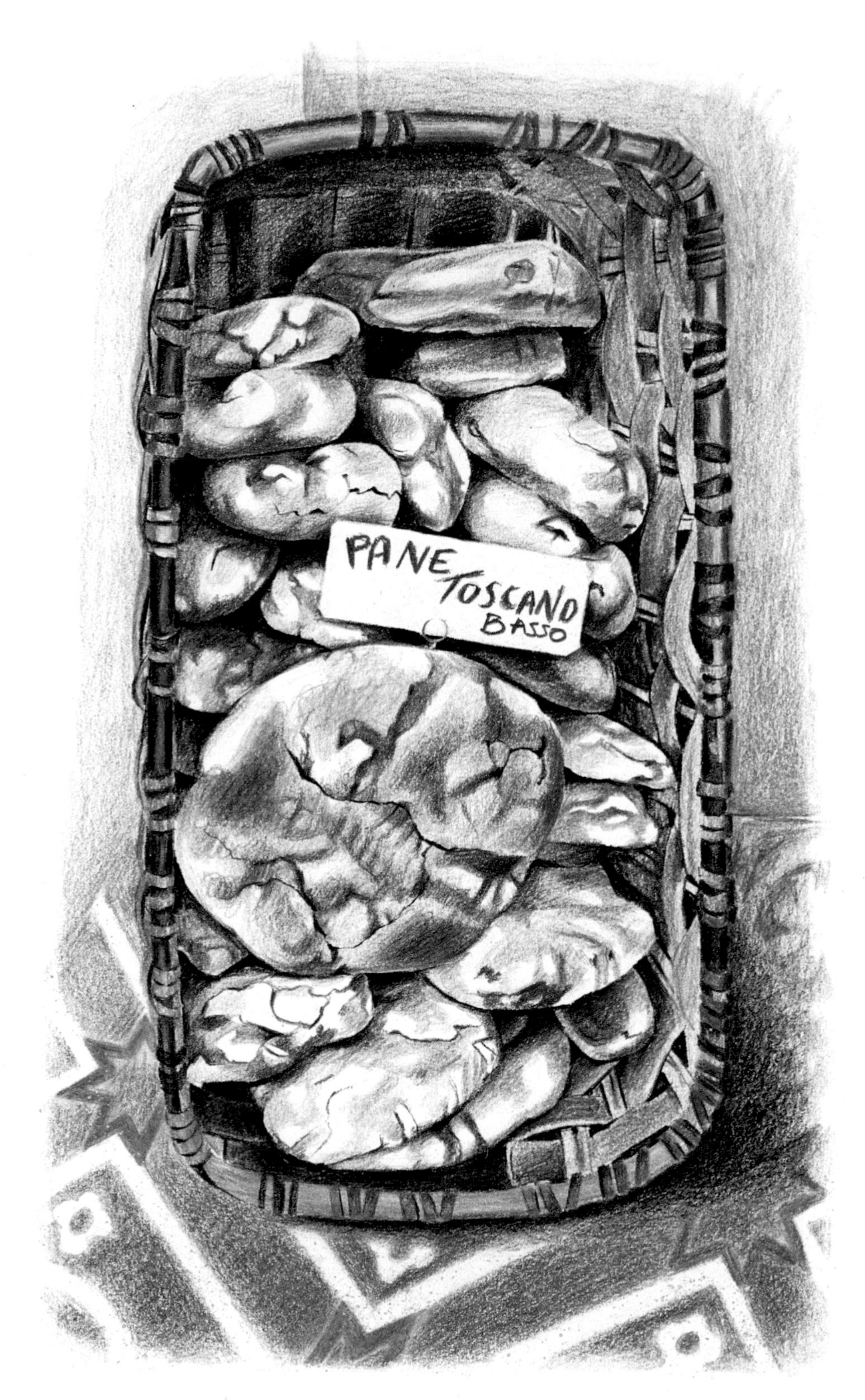
PANE TOSCANO
BASSO

· PANIFICIO · MODERNO ·

Bread is the pasta of Tuscany. It is used far more than flour or pasta to thicken soups & stews & give textures to sauces. A good Tuscan 'pan basso' loaf has almost no salt & when stale it tends to go hard & dry rather than moldy, thus remaining useful for cooking. At A. Sclavi's Panificio Moderno the bread variations are endless, all displayed in old wicker baskets around the shop. And the fresh pasta is so good that the Locanda dell'Amorosa restaurant near Sinalunga used to send a bus to Siena every weekend to collect a fresh batch.

• PANE BASSO •

Tuscan country bread (2 loaves)

At the Panificio Moderno the baker uses brewer's yeast in the bread but this recipe using fresh yeast gives a similar result. You can make Pane integrale, the closest the Tuscans get to wholewheat bread, by substituting 1/4 lb/100g bran for the same quantity of white flour in the following recipe.

2 OZ/50G FRESH YEAST
1 PT/500 ML WARM WATER (LUKEWARM)
2 LB/900G STRONG WHITE FLOUR

Dissolve the yeast in 3 fl oz/175 ml of the warm water in a small bowl. Sift in enough of the flour to make a soft dough, mixing with the hands. Cover & put in a warm place to rise. When the yeast dough has at least doubled in size, begin making the rest of the dough. Sift the remaining flour onto a wood or marble surface. Make a well in the middle, pour a little water into it & begin working the flour towards this with your hands. When the dough has absorbed enough water to bind together, add the yeast dough and work in. Knead for 5~10 minutes, occasionally lifting the dough & smacking it on the table. Continue until it no longer sticks to your hands. Sprinkle a large bowl with water and put the dough in it. Cover with a cloth & let rise in a warm place until doubled in size (about 30 minutes). Knead again 5~10 minutes and form into 2 balls. Let stand another 20 minutes and then bake on a greased, floured baking tin until crusty (about 30 minutes) in an oven preheated to 350°F/180°C Gas 4.

PANFORTE di SIENA

• Traditional Siena •
spice cake

The history of Panforte or 'strong bread' dates back as far as, or further, than Siena itself and there are many recipes for it, some of which seem almost too spicey for modern palates. When panforte was first made this over-spicing probably served to preserve, as well as to cover the unwelcome taste of mold. Today the brightly-wrapped Panforte cakes in Siena are as much a part of the city as the Palio. Made before Christmas and stored in an air-tight container, the cake will keep for about a month. Served in thin slices with strong black coffee it makes an interesting alternative to christmas cake. In Siena it is often topped with melted dark chocolate instead of the icing sugar used in this recipe.

5 OZ/150 G SUGAR (GRANULATED)
7 OZ/200 G ALMONDS, PEELED
7 OZ/200 G WALNUTS, CLEANED
11 OZ/300 G MIXED CANDIED FRUIT, CHOPPED
4 OZ/100 G HONEY
4 OZ/100 G DRIED FIGS
2½ OZ/60 G COCOA POWDER
¼ TSP POWDERED CORIANDER
¼ TSP POWDERED CLOVES
½ TSP POWDERED NUTMEG
¼ TSP WHITE PEPPER
¾ TSP CINNAMON
2 OZ/50 G FLOUR
10 LARGE BAKING WAFERS OR RICE PAPER

Toast the nuts in a hot oven and chop roughly. Put in a bowl with all the dried fruit, spices and cocoa. Sift in the flour and mix well. In a double saucepan or a basin over a pan of boiling water, boil the honey carefully & melt in the sugar. Stir constantly until it will form a soft ball between your fingers (remember to dip your fingers in cold water before testing for this). Immediately pour onto the fruit and blend in well with your hands. Form the dough into a flat round cake about 1in/2.5cm

thick. Lay the wafers on a buttered baking sheet and place the cake on top. Bake for 40 minutes, until dry, in an oven preheated to 350°F/180°C/Gas 4. When cool trim wafers to fit the cake and dust the top of the cake with a mixture of icing sugar and cinnamon.

• RICCIARELLI •

Sweet almond biscuits (2 dozen)

These sweet and wickedly rich macaroons are almost as famous in Siena as panforte. They have the taste of oriental sweetmeats about them and are costly to make and buy, even in Siena. If you buy your ricciarelli at A. Sclavi's they will wrap them, however few, with ribbon and pretty paper, as if they were precious Christmas gifts.

12 1/4 OZ/360 G PEELED ALMONDS
6 OZ/180 G ICING SUGAR, SIFTED
8 3/4 OZ/240 G CASTER SUGAR, SIFTED
1 TBSP GRATED ORANGE PEEL
2 EGG WHITES
2 DOZEN ROUNDS RICE PAPER

Crush the almonds to a powder in a mortar, or put through a nut-grinder, making sure you don't lose any of the oil. Mix well with the caster sugar and rub through a sieve into a large bowl. Whip the egg whites to form soft peaks. Fold into the almond/caster sugar mixture together with the icing sugar and orange peel. It should make a soft, smooth paste. Form into diamond-shaped lozenges, each lozenge about ½ in/1cm thick, 2 in/4.5 cm long and 1½ in/3.5 cm wide. Dust heavily with more icing sugar, place each lozenge on a piece of rice paper and leave for 12 hours. Bake in an oven so low that it is just warm (275°F/140°C/Gas 1) for about 15 minutes. Cool on a wire rack and serve with more icing sugar sifted on top. It is always a good idea to use vanilla sugar for this (sugar stored with a vanilla pod).

CONSORZIO AGRARIO
PROVINCIALE DI SIENA
OLIO EXTRA
VERGINE DI OLIVA
STELLARIN
Rosolio
di
Menta
CASTELLARIN · SIENA
Panforte
Margherita
IDROLITINA

• SAN • GIMIGNANO •

Seen from the valley below, San Gimignano lives up to its reputation as a medieval Manhattan. Fifteen stone towers rise above the ochre~coloured walls, the last reminders of how all towns in Tuscany looked 600 years ago. In 1300, when Dante visited San Gimignano as ambassador, there were 72 towers, all built as keeps during the struggles between two warring families, the Ardinghelli and the Salvucci. Over centuries of feuding the towers were destroyed one by one until today only the fifteen remain, their crevices rootholds for straggling wild capers.

Politics may be less violent and towers may have fallen, but San Gimignano has kept its medieval appearance and apart from the growing collection of tourist shops, is virtually unchanged since the fourteenth century. In the Piazza della Cisterna, water flows from a thirteenth~century cistern and the cobbled square is surrounded by houses built in the golden limestone of that region. One of the towers dominates the Piazza del Poppolo and once a week the timeless bustle of a street market fills the Piazza del Duomo.

• SALSA • per la CACCIAGIONE

Hunter's Sauce

In San Gimignano's market you can find everything from the local hand~painted blue and white china to ravioli rolling pins and homemade pasta. Or buy a hot courgette flower fritter and a fresh bread roll filled with roast wild boar that has been basted in a sauce such as this.

2 CLOVES GARLIC, CRUSHED
OLIVE OIL
1 TBSP CAPERS
7~8 SAGE LEAVES, CHOPPED
LEAVES FROM 1 STALK ROSEMARY, CHOPPED FINELY
2 WINEGLASSES RED WINE
1 ANCHOVY FILLET, MASHED

Fry the garlic in the oil until golden. Add capers, sage and rosemary and cook for a minute or two. Pour in the red wine and bring to the boil. When slightly reduced, stir in the anchovy and use to baste any barbecued game from rabbit, or pigeon to pheasant. It is also excellent with roast pork. When the meat is cooked, spoon any remaining sauce over it and serve hot.

• FIORI FRITTI •

Courgette flower fritters (6)

Freshly picked courgette flowers are a delicacy usually available only to people fortunate enough to have their own vegetable gardens. In Tuscany, however, the huge orange and green blossoms are available throughout the summer in most markets.

(continued on next page)

16 ~ 18 COURGETTE (ZUCCHINI) FLOWERS
SMALL HANDFUL FRESH HERBS (PARSLEY AND/OR THYME) FINELY CHOPPED
3¾ OZ/96 G PLAIN WHITE FLOUR
½ PT/300 ML COLD WATER
SALT & PEPPER
OIL FOR DEEP FRYING

Gently wash & dry the flowers. Trim off stems. In a bowl slowly sift the flour into the water, beating well with a wooden spoon until the mixture is like a smooth pancake batter. Mix in the herbs. Heat the oil in a deep pan and when very hot, dip the blossoms quickly into the batter & then into the oil. When they are golden brown drain on a kitchen towel & sprinkle with salt and pepper. Serve immediately while still hot. In Tuscany this method is used to cook many different flowers and leaves, such as clematis and borage.

· FIORI con RIPIENO ·
Stuffed zucchini flowers (6)

For a more filling version of the fritters the flowers can be filled with a savoury stuffing.

6 OZ/175 G GRATED PARMESAN
2 OZ/60 G HAM OR BACON CHOPPED
1 CLOVE GARLIC, CRUSHED
2 TBSP PARSLEY, FINELY CHOPPED
3 OZ/75 G FINE BREADCRUMBS
SALT & FRESHLY GROUND BLACK PEPPER
1 BEATEN EGG
2 TBSP MILK

Mix all the ingredients together. Spoon the mixture carefully into the flowers, tucking over the petal tops so it won't escape, then follow the previous recipe for simple flower fritters. Serve hot.

· PONTE·A·RONDOLINO ·

For July, in Siena, by the
willow tree,
I give you barrels of white
Tuscan wine...

(SAN GIMIGNANO FOLKLORE)

And that most Tuscan of Tuscan white wines ~ Vernaccia di San Gimignano is as much a part of San Gimignano as its towers. Reputedly favoured by Dante it is now sold in shops & cantinas all over the town. Some vineyards, such as Fattoria di Cusano, Raccianello & Pietrafitta, are open to the public. Enrico Teruzzi's Ponte a Rondolino vineyard serves one of the best vernaccias at its own excellent trattoria just outside town.

RISOTTO alla VERNACCIA

• Risotto with white wine (6) •

Of the several risotto recipes in this book, this is the plainest & most delicate & therefore the most easy to make badly. The rice must be Italian Arborio rice for the proper outer creaminess & inner firmness & both the stock & the wine must be of good quality. For preference use Vernaccia, a vigorous tasting white wine, but if it is not available, use a similarly strong flavoured white wine. Be lavish, the risotto should taste of wine, not water.

1 MEDIUM ONION, FINELY CHOPPED
1½ OZ/40 G BUTTER
12 OZ/350 G ITALIAN ARBORIO RICE
1½ PTS/900 ML CHICKEN STOCK (APPROX)
6 FL OZ/175 ML VERNACCIA (OR MORE)

Melt the butter in a medium~sized pan. Saute the onion until a pale brown and then add the rice, stirring until glistening & semi~transparent. Meanwhile heat the stock in a saucepan. Turn up the heat under the rice and pour in the wine, when it has almost disappeared add about ½ pt/300 ml hot stock and, when absorbed, add a similar amount. Continue to add more stock (or wine for a stronger flavour) a spoonful at a time as it is absorbed by the rice (the rice will become noticeably flat on top when it needs more liquid). It should take about 20~30 minutes to cook. Stir frequently while adding liquid & just before serving stir in some butter & several tablespoons of grated pecorino or parmesan cheese.

· LOCANDA · DELL' AMOROSA ·

The best Sienese food is served not in Siena but half an hour's drive away near the old town of Sinalunga. A long straight line of spiky black cypresses leads up a hill to a brick archway, the entrance to the Locanda dell'Amorosa, the 'lover's' inn. It is less a hotel and restaurant than a small village, the heart of a busy farm estate or 'fattoria' producing its own Chianti colli Senesi (chianti from the Sienese hills) as well as olive oil, homemade marmelades, jams and honeys.

In Siena's Museo Civico there is a fresco showing the farm as it was in 1300, but it could hardly have been a more beautiful or magical place then than it is now. The restaurant, built into the old stables, looks out on a peaceful central courtyard of the 1400s where roses climb over mellow pink bricks. The menu changes to suit each season and is skilfully supervised by the shy and dedicated Guiseppe Vacarini, who is also one of the best sommeliers in Italy. The owner, Carlo Citterio, whose family has lived and worked at

l'Amorosa
for generations,
is completely enam-
oured of his home, as are
all his staff. It shows.
It is possible to arrive at
l'Amorosa, tired and har-
assed, with half of Tuscany's
considerable insect population stuck to your car's
windshield and to leave
there (though unwillingly)
two hours later appetite
satisfied and spirits restored completely.

LOCANDA dell'AMOROSA

The food at the Locanda dell' Amorosa can be as simple as a plate of fresh raw porcini mushrooms sliced paper thin and marinated in local oil and garden herbs, or rabbit simmered slowly in wine with the subtle taste of wild fennel seeds. In season there is the elegance of grilled quail and pheasant from the Sienese hills, or more traditional and substantial recipes like these two, excellent for cold days in late autumn when the first frost is on the ground.

• STRISCE con CECI •

Ribbon noodles & chickpea soup (4)

STRISCE are wide ribbon noodles ideal for this thick soup that is more like noodles with a chickpea sauce.

14 oz/400 g DRIED CHICK PEAS (SOAKED FOR 10 HRS, WATER DISCARDED)
4 oz/100 g CARROTS, FINELY CHOPPED
1 SMALL ONION, FINELY CHOPPED
1 STICK CELERY, FINELY CHOPPED
4 TBSP OLIVE OIL
3 CLOVES GARLIC, PEELED
1 SPRIG ROSEMARY OR 2 TSP CHOPPED DRIED ROSEMARY
5 BLACK PEPPERCORNS
SALT
STRISCE OR MACCHERONI FOR 4~5 (PASTA RECIPE PAGE 76) OR 250 g COMMERCIAL PASTA

Put the chickpeas in a deep saucepan with the garlic and pepper. Add enough water to cover plus one inch. Cover and cook slowly on a low heat for 3 hours. When tender remove the chickpeas, saving the liquid, and put all but 6 tablespoons of the chickpeas through a food processor or vegetable mill with the garlic. Heat the oil in a large saucepan and saute the carrots, onion, celery and rosemary until softened. Put everything, including the remaining chickpea liquid, into a saucepan & cook for another 30 minutes. Add salt to taste & the pasta & cook until just tender. Serve hot with grated parmesan.

• BOLLITO in SALSA di DRAGONCELLO •

Boiled beef & tarragon sauce (4)

Except for the Siena area tarragon is not commonly used in Tuscany. When it does appear it's often raw, rather than cooked in the French method. At the Locanda dell'Amorosa fresh tarragon for this recipe is grown in their old walled herb garden on a hill overlooking the surrounding vineyards.

• SAUCE •

3 oz/80 g FRESH BREADCRUMBS
1 oz/20 g FRESH TARRAGON
1 TBSP WHITE WINE VINEGAR
5 TBSP OLIVE OIL
3 CLOVES GARLIC
SALT

• BOLLITO •

14 oz/400 g FATTY BEEF BRISKET, RUMP OR CHUCK STEAK
14 oz/400 g BONED SHOULDER OF VEAL OR BEEF IN ONE PIECE
1 CARROT
1 SMALL ONION
1 CELERY STICK
1 TBSP CHOPPED PARSLEY
1 TSP SEA SALT

Put 3 litres of water into a deep saucepan with the vegetables, salt & parsley & bring to the boil. Add the meat & simmer slowly for 3 hours. Skim off any scum that rises to the surface. In the meantime make the sauce. Soak the breadcrumbs in vinegar for 15 minutes & squeeze out. Crush the tarragon & garlic to a paste in a mortar & rub through a sieve with the breadcrumbs. Mix well & slowly beat in the olive oil to obtain a thick smooth sauce. Salt to taste. When the beef is cooked slice it thinly, pour several ladles of broth over it & serve it with the tarragon sauce on the side.

· PASTA ·

Commercial pasta bears little resemblance to the homemade variety, apart from a similar shape. Where pasta 'asciutta' (dry pasta available in packets) is only a vehicle for its sauce, homemade pasta is good enough to be an end in itself. The main difference is that the homemade varieties are made with fresh eggs and obviously worked by hand instead of machine. But many things can affect the quality of even an expert cook's pasta. Onelia, the pasta cook at the Locanda dell'Amorosa, cannot achieve the same degree of tenderness when making pasta dough at l'Amorosa as she can using the same technique in the Chianti district. One reason is the difference in water. Another is that many of the eggs in Chianti have very large yolks which absorb more flour. And as every good pasta cook knows, the more flour used, the firmer the dough and the firmer the dough, the better the pasta. Unfortunately for the novice, it is more difficult to work a very stiff dough.

· RAVIOLI con SPINACI ·

Ravioli stuffed with spinach & ricotta (6)

Although pasta is not as much a speciality in Tuscany as it is in Emilia~Romagna, it is still very popular. This recipe is one of the best Tuscan ways of serving fresh pasta, but the same ingredients for the dough may also be used to produce tagliatelle or pappardelle.

PASTA INGREDIENTS:

11 ~ 13 oz / 300 ~ 375 g plain unbleached flour
3 eggs
pinch of salt

STUFFING:

2 ½ lb / 1.2 kg fresh spinach (or nettles) washed well
½ tsp salt
½ tsp nutmeg
2 egg yolks
12 oz / 350 g ricotta cheese

1 First make the stuffing. Wash the spinach and put it into a saucepan with just the water that clings to the leaves. Add the salt. Cover and cook for 15 ~ 20 minutes, until tender. Drain, squeeze out moisture and chop very finely. Mix together with the other ingredients & salt to taste.

2 To make the pasta sift the flour with the salt on to a wooden table. Make a well in the middle of the flour and pour in the yolks, beaten lightly together with a fork. With your hand start stirring in flour from inside the well until the eggs are no longer liquid, and continue to work in until the eggs have absorbed as much flour as possible without losing pliability.

3 Wash your hands, clean the work surface of flour & knead the dough for about 10 minutes until it is a shiny flexible ball. Fold it over and turn it continuously as you knead it. Leave, covered, for about 10 minutes.

4 At this point you can use a pasta machine to do the final rolling out. Otherwise divide dough in two to make it easier to handle. Always keep unused dough covered. Rub some oil into a long thin rolling pin (24~30 in/60~75 cm long and 2 in/5 cm diameter is a good size) & then dust with flour. On a floured surface begin to roll the dough out as quickly as possible into a regular oval shape. Roll it smoothly away from you & turn it after each roll. As it gets thinner, occasionally wrap the sheet of pasta around a rolling pin and stretch towards you. When paper thin, fold loosely, cover & repeat the process with the other half.

5 Lay one sheet on a floured surface, cut into an even rectangular shape & place small teaspoonfuls of spinach filling approximately 1½ in/4 cm apart in straight rows. Between rows brush water, lay the other sheet of dough on top & with the side of the hand press firmly down between rows to seal. Cut into squares with a pastry cutter and place on greaseproof paper. Cover.

(Continued on following page)

(Continued from preceding page)

6 Boil 8 pints/4.5 litres of water with 1 tbsp oil & a tsp of salt. Add the pasta and about 5 minutes after the water has returned to the boil remove the ravioli, which should be cooked al dente. Serve immediately with butter and grated cheese or with butter in which you have fried 6~8 leaves of sage.

RAVIOLI GNUDI
Naked Ravioli (6)

There is another type of so-called 'ravioli' that is particularly popular in Tuscany although almost unavailable in any restaurants there. It is a bit like the stuffing without the pasta and in fact is called 'Ravioli gnudi' in Arezzo to indicate 'naked' ravioli. It is a great delicacy, good enough to eat with just freshly chopped tomatoes and a sprinkling of parmesan on top.

1½ LB/675 G FRESH SPINACH, COOKED AS PREVIOUS RECIPE & FINELY CHOPPED
9 OZ/250 G RICOTTA CHEESE
4½ OZ/130 G PLAIN FLOUR
3 EGG YOLKS
5 OZ/150 G FRESHLY GRATED PECORINO OR PARMESAN
½ TSP NUTMEG
½ SMALL ONION, FINELY CHOPPED
2 OZ/50 G BUTTER
SALT

Melt the butter in a large saucepan. Cook the onion in it until golden. Add the spinach and salt and saute for about 5 minutes. Cool slightly and then in a large bowl mix together thoroughly with the ricotta and flour. Add the yolks, nutmeg and pecorino and work together well. Salt to taste. Chill well for easier handling and then form into oval pellets about 1 in/2.5 cm long by ½ in/1 cm across. Boil 8 pints/4.5 litres salted water and cook the ravioli a few at a time. They should be ready about 3 or 4 minutes after the water has returned to the boil. Remove and keep warm until ready to eat. In the unlikely occurrence of leftovers, roll them in egg yolk and breadcrumbs the next day and deep fry until crunchy and brown.

e repliche
INTERVISTA
Franco
SERA

BUCA DI SAN FRANCESCO

Arezzo is a prosperous, rather austere provincial town, the centre of a rich farming zone. It is internationally famous for the stunning frescoes there by Piero della Francesco but locally more famous for Mario de Filippis' friendly little trattoria, Buca di San Francesco. There you can sit in the frescoed cellar of a sixteenth-century palace and eat specialities such as zuppa di fagioli (bean soup), homemade tagliolini, ricotta with acacia honey, and chicken from the nearby Valdarno cooked 'in porchetta'. Porchetta is a whole roast piglet usually sold from stalls by travelling vendors throughout Tuscany and Umbria. Chicken cooked in the same way is stuffed with quantities of leafy wild fennel, sage leaves and garlic.

SFORMATO di VERDURE con FEGATINI

Spinach souffle with chicken livers (4)

Buca di San Francesco is one of a group of restaurants 'del Buon Ricordo' (good memory), established to keep alive the traditions of regional cooking in Italy. Each one has a dish, like this one, particularly typical of the area, called the 'Piatto del Buon Ricordo', and a regional menu that the restaurant's owner will recommend on request. This recipe uses spinach for the sformato, but is equally good made with nettles or swiss chard.

SFORMATO

- 2 LB 2 OZ / 1 KG SPINACH
- 3 FL OZ / 75 ML THICK BECHAMEL
- 3 EGG WHITES, BEATEN STIFFLY
- 1 EGG YOLK, BEATEN
- 1/4 ~ 1/2 TSP NUTMEG
- 2 1/2 TBSP PARMESAN
- 2 OZ / 50 G BUTTER
- 4 OZ / 100 G FINE, DRY BREADCRUMBS
- SALT & FRESHLY GROUND PEPPER

• SAUCE •

- 1 LB/450 G CHICKEN LIVERS, TRIMMED OF FAT & WASHED
- 1 SMALL ONION, FINELY CHOPPED
- 4 ~ 6 TBSP OLIVE OIL
- 2 WINELASSES WHITE WINE
- 9 ~ 10 SAGE LEAVES, CHOPPED

Wash the spinach in several changes of cold water. Cook in a covered saucepan for 15 minutes. Cool, chop and put through a coarse sieve. Melt the butter in a frying pan & gently saute the spinach for about 10 minutes. Remove from heat & stir in the bechamel, egg yolk, nutmeg, parmesan, salt and pepper. Fold in the egg whites and pour into a deep baking dish, buttered & dusted with breadcrumbs. Place in a bain marie & bake in an oven preheated to 400°F/200°C/ Gas Mark 6 for 20 minutes, or until golden on top.

In the meantime saute the onion in olive oil over a medium heat. When just golden, turn up the heat & add chicken livers and sage. Cook for a few minutes, until the liver has turned pale. Remove from pan & keep hot. Add the wine and boil briskly until reduced by half, stirring in the bits from the pan. Return the livers to the pan, stir quickly, add salt & pepper & remove from heat. Turn the sformato out onto a dish (it should now have a crunchy golden crust) & pour the livers into the middle. Serve immediately.

• GINESTRATA •

Chicken and wine cordial (4)

In the spring in Tuscany the perfume of wild broom, ginestra, is overpowering and the roads are lined with huge bushes covered in the brilliant yellow blossoms. These flowers give their name to a famous Tuscan soup that was once endowed with miraculous powers. It could supposedly increase potency, cure disease and improve the powers of the brain (essential after too much Chianti the night before). Although it was & is a recipe particularly associated with the Chianti region where the ginestra blooms most profusely, they make a similar soup at the Buca di San Francesco called 'cordiale'. It lays equal claims to renew vigour & health in just one bowlful.

- 4 EGGS
- 2 OZ/50 G BUTTER
- 1 WINEGLASS OF MARSALA OR VIN SANTO
- 3/4 PINT / 1/2 LITRE GOOD HOME MADE CHICKEN STOCK
- 1/2 TSP CINNAMON
- PINCH OF SAFFRON
- PINCH OF NUTMEG
- JUICE OF 1/2 LEMON
- SUGAR

Beat the eggs and while mixing steadily, slowly add marsala, chicken stock, cinnamon & saffron. Heat gently and add butter cut in small pieces. Continue to mix and when it begins to thicken remove from heat and pour into pretty cups. Stir in lemon juice and sprinkle with sugar and nutmeg.

· FOCACCIA ·

Savoury flat bread (4~6)

This dimpled salty bread is popular not only in Tuscany and its origins would probably be hotly contested by every baker in Italy. It is particularly good with crispy pieces of bacon or onion worked into the dough.

8~10 OZ/225~275 G RISEN BREAD DOUGH (SEE RECIPE PAGE 65)
COARSE SEA SALT
OLIVE OIL

Pour a thin layer of oil into a large flat baking sheet. Roll the dough out to ½ in/1cm thickness and place on the baking sheet. Every 2½ in/6 cm make a dimple by pressing your finger well down into the dough. Pour 4~5 tbsp of oil over and sprinkle on lots of salt. Bake for 20~25 minutes until deep golden & crusty in an oven preheated to 200°C/400°F/Gas Mark 6. Serve warm.

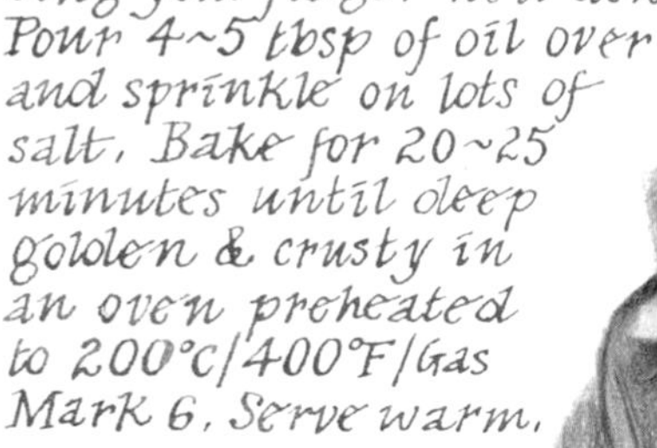

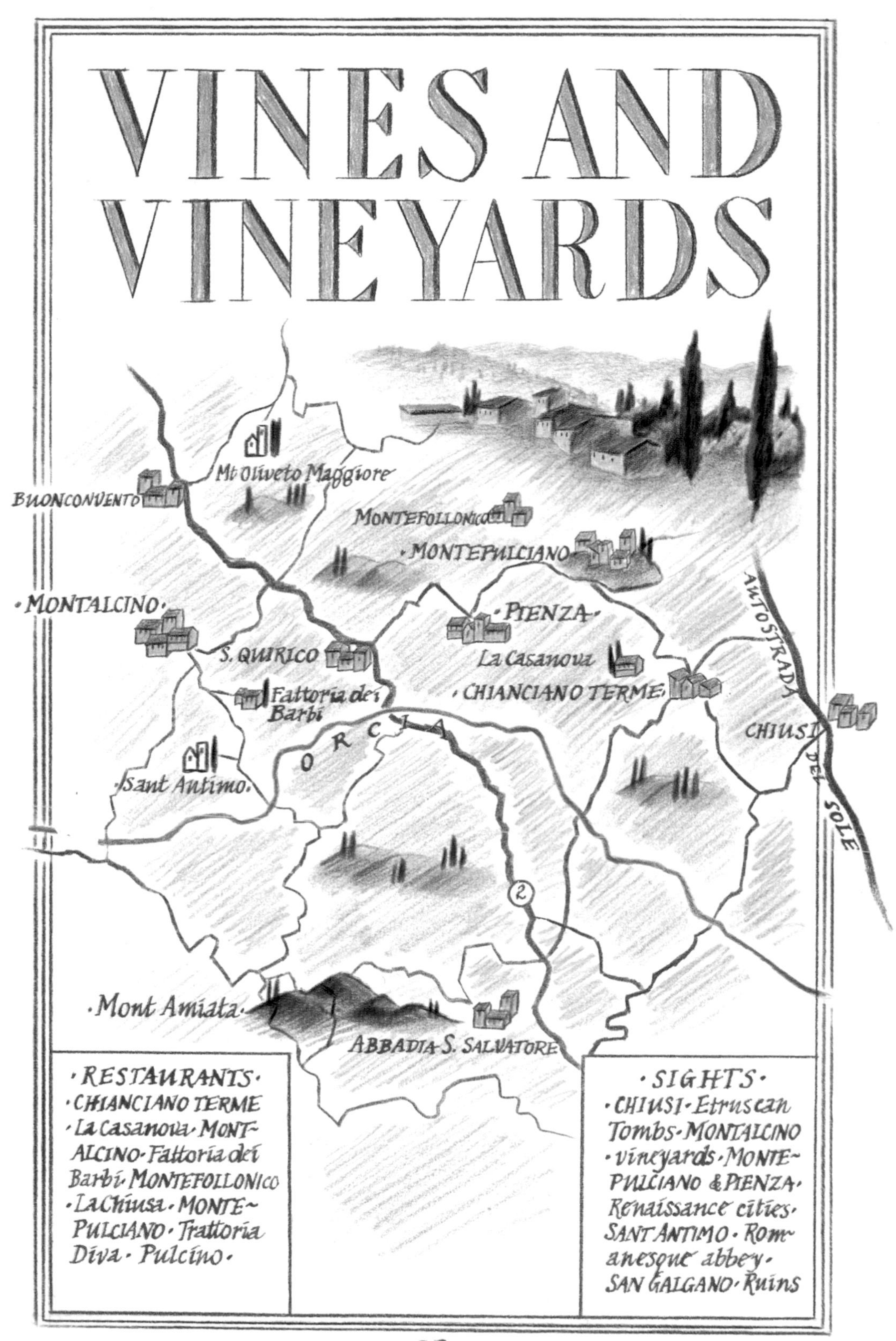
VINES AND VINEYARDS
Mt Oliveto Maggiore
BUONCONVENTO
MONTEFOLLONICO
MONTEPULCIANO
MONTALCINO
PIENZA
S. QUIRICO
La Casanova
Fattoria dei Barbi
CHIANCIANO TERME
AUTOSTRADA DEL SOLE
CHIUSI
ORCIA
Sant Antimo
2
Mont Amiata
ABBADIA S. SALVATORE
RESTAURANTS
CHIANCIANO TERME · La Casanova · MONTALCINO · Fattoria dei Barbi · MONTEFOLLONICO · La Chiusa · MONTEPULCIANO · Trattoria Diva · Pulcino
SIGHTS
CHIUSI · Etruscan Tombs · MONTALCINO · vineyards · MONTEPULCIANO & PIENZA · Renaissance cities · SANT ANTIMO · Romanesque abbey · SAN GALGANO · Ruins

·INTRODUCTION·

The area between Montalcino and Montepulciano, south of Siena, is notable not only for the beauty of its countryside and fine Renaissance towns but also for the quality of its wines. Vino Nobile di Montepulciano, an elegant Chianti-style wine, has had its praises sung by poets for centuries. In the seventeenth century the poet-physician Francesco Redi wrote 'Montepulciano d'ogni vino è re' ~ Montepulciano of all wines is king. If modern vino nobile is less the king than one of the crown princes of traditional Tuscan wines, it is still worthy of its title. One of the best vino nobiles comes from the little estate of Poderi Boscarelli, lying on the south-eastern slopes of the hill that is crowned by the lovely city of Montepulciano.

Together with its neighbour Pienza, Montepulciano is a model of fifteenth-century town planning. Walk up the main street, the Corso, on a windy spring day and panoramic views of distant vineyards are glimpsed around the corners of impressive baroque palaces. Small balconied piazzas are conveniently designed to open up these views off each of the cobbled streets that climb steeply to the Piazza Grande, the wide and splendid central square that is the highest point in Montepulciano, as well as the focus of the annual music and mime festival every August.

Nine miles to the west of Montepulciano lies Pienza, the ideal city of Piccolomini (Pope Pius II 1458~64), who virtually created the city out of his birthplace, Corsignano. In 1459 he commissioned the Florentine architect Bernardo Rossellino to rebuild the town and make it, and its cathedral, 'the finest in all Italy'. He almost succeeded. Although Piccolomini died before his dream could be realized, he left behind him a beautiful miniature city, complete enough to inspire the director Franco Zeffirelli to use it as the setting for his film of Romeo and Juliet.

Pienza is on the road leading to Montalcino, home of one of the costliest and most prestigious red wines in Italy, Brunello di Montalcino. It has become so in a relatively short time, largely due to the efforts of the Biondi-Santi family. From 1865, when the family first won a citation for a 'Brunello', they have been steadily improving its quality until today it has achieved almost legendary status as a wine whose flavour can outlive some of the longest aged wines in the world. A bottle of Biondi-Santis' Brunello takes years, even decades, to come to full maturity, and if the end result is superb, the cost is prohibitive. Fortunately there are other vineyards producing Brunello at more accessible costs. One of the pleasantest ways to pass a warm autumn afternoon is at Montalcino's elegant little open-air 'Caffe Fiaschetteria Italiana' sampling and discussing vintage Brunellos with the local experts. Or drive through olive and vine-clad hills of matchless beauty to one of the vineyards open to visitors. The Fattoria dei Barbi is one which has the added advantage of its own excellent trattoria serving local recipes and products from the estate.

The food in the area can vary from Sienese-inspired cuisine at the country restaurant La Chiusa (that also sells olive oil pressed in its own antique 'frantoio' or oil press) to the more robust home-cooking of ribollita and grilled meats at the Fattoria Pulcino near Montepulciano's main gate. There is frequent use of local herbs like tarragon and of the giant porcini mushrooms (BOLETUS EDULIS) picked wild from the slopes of nearby Mont Amiata, an extinct volcano. And the beautiful Ristorante La Casanova near Chianciano Terme has fresh lake fish and imaginative game dishes in season.

· TRATTORIA · DIVA ·

· MONTEPULCIANO ·

The Trattoria Diva, named after the owner's wife, is a small jolly family~run trattoria near the main gate in Monte~pulciano. The specialities are simple unpretentious dishes, always accompanied by an excellent selection of local wines from the owner's next door wine enoteca.

·· PICI ··
Tuscan eggless pasta (6)

Pici is/are an amazingly time~consuming, completely hand~rolled pasta with no eggs, originally made only by and for the very poor in the area around Montepulciano. They consist of just flour, salt and water. The following is a very approximate recipe.

- 12 OZ / 350 G PLAIN FLOUR, SIFTED
- PINCH SALT
- SEVERAL TBSP WATER

Knead all the ingredients together to form a stretchy pasta dough. Leave covered for 20 minutes. Roll out until the dough is ¼ in / 5mm thick and cut into strips of ½ in / 1 cm wide. Then work and twist each piece by hand into extremely long and wiggly spaghetti. Keep each string of pasta covered until ready to use. Cook in boiling water in the usual way.

· SALSA di SALSICCIE ·
Sausage sauce (6)

If you can be bothered to make pici, they are an excel~lent and chewy vehicle for this traditional sauce which comes from the foothills of Mont Amiata. And near Chiusi south of Montepulciano pici are eaten tossed in a sauce of 'caviar' from pike caught in the nearby lake.

- 12 OZ / 350 G SPICY ITALIAN SAUSAGE, SKINNED AND CRUMBLED IN PIECES
- 14 OZ / 400 G RIPE TOMATOES, PEELED AND MASHED WITH A FORK
- 8 OZ / 240 G FRESH BOLETUS EDULIS OR
- 1 OZ / 25 G DRIED 'FUNGHI' MUSHROOMS SOAKED IN TEPID WATER 30 MINS
- 1 LARGE ONION, FINELY CHOPPED
- 2 TBSP OLIVE OIL
- RED WINE (OPTIONAL)

Heat the oil in a shallow flame~proof casserole. Cook the onions in it, and when starting to turn transparent, add the sausages and the mushrooms (squeezed out and sliced if dried). Cook, stirring occasionally, for about ten minutes and then add the tomatoes, salt and pepper to taste and a generous splash of red wine if you like. Cook for another 30 minutes on a low heat. Serve over the cooked, drained pici ~ or any other pasta.

· PICI con CONIGLIO ·

Pasta with rabbit sauce (4)

This, one of the most traditional sauces to serve with pici, can also be used as a sauce with more readily available pastas such as spaghetti or penne.

- 1 OZ / 25 G PANCETTA OR BACON, FINELY CHOPPED
- 1 LARGE RABBIT, CUT IN PIECES, WITH GIBLETS
- 1 SMALL ONION, FINELY CHOPPED
- 1 CARROT, FINELY CHOPPED
- 2~3 SPRIGS FRESH THYME
- 1 LB 2 OZ / 500 G TOMATOES, PEELED, SEEDED AND CHOPPED
- ½ BOTTLE CHIANTI
- 3 TBSP OLIVE OIL
- SALT
- PEPPER

Saute the pancetta, onion and carrot until softened in the oil. Add the rabbit pieces (except the giblets) and brown on all sides. Then add the wine and when nearly evaporated the tomatoes and the thyme. Cover and simmer gently until the rabbit is tender ~ about 1~1½ hours. After about half an hour, add the giblets, finely chopped, and a few tablespoons of warm water or beef stock to ensure that the sauce stays quite liquid. About 10 minutes before the end of cooking remove the rabbit and keep hot. Add the pici and cook through. Or, if using dried pasta, cook the pasta until softened but still firm in boiling water and then add to the sauce. Serve the pasta as a first course with the rabbit to follow, served with spinach and olive oil.

*** FUNGHI SECCHI ~** (Boletus edulis / Porcini / Ceps) These huge mushrooms are widely available throughout Tuscany in the late spring & autumn, both in markets & growing wild in woodland clearings (especially on the slopes of Mont Amiata). Their rich flavour is used to enhance everything from peasant stews & simple pasta sauces to elegant veal dishes. Where fresh porcini are not available it is still possible to capture some of their fragrance using dried funghi, 'funghi secchi' (available in packets from many speciality stores).

MACELLERIA

· FATTORIA · DEI · BARBI ·

In the restaurant of the Fattoria dei Barbi near Montalcino there is an English cook from Bournemouth who makes one of the best bean soups in Tuscany. Even the Tuscans will admit this, which shows how good it must be. It helps that she has been in the country for 20 years, is married to a Tuscan and, even more importantly, has a Tuscan mother~in~law. And it also helps to have the Fattoria products to cook with, herb~flavoured ricotta, fresh pecorino, olive oil, peppery prosciutto, pork steaks for the grill and the famous Barbi/Columbini Brunello wine. It is a good place to go on a hot summer's day, to sit at a check~cloth covered table in the middle of a vineyard and hear the history of Brunello and to follow this with a visit to the beautiful old wine cellars, where you may also taste some of the wines.

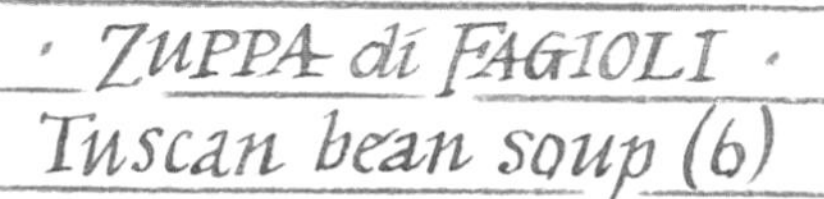

· ZUPPA di FAGIOLI ·
Tuscan bean soup (6)

This bean soup, a version of the famous 'ribollita' (meaning re~boiled), may well have an even longer history than Brunello wine, & is best made the day before.

2 LB 2 OZ / 1 KG FRESH CANNELINI (SMALL HARICOT) BEANS OR 14½ OZ / 420 G DRIED ONES, SOAKED OVERNIGHT
3~4 RIPE TOMATOES, PEELED, SEEDED AND MASHED
2 STICKS CELERY, FINELY CHOPPED
2 CARROTS, FINELY CHOPPED
2 LEEKS, FINELY CHOPPED
11 OZ / 300 G CAVOLO NERO (TUSCAN BLACK CABBAGE) OR YOU CAN SUBSTITUTE SWISS CHARD, SPINACH BEET OR ANY DARK GREEN CABBAGE

(Continued)

7 OZ/200 G SAVOY CABBAGE (SAUTED SEPARATELY & KEPT FOR TOPPING)
2 CLOVES GARLIC, CRUSHED
2 SPRIGS FRESH THYME
6~8 TBSP OLIVE OIL
STOCK
SALT & PEPPER
6 PIECES HARD STALE BREAD

Boil the beans in plenty of water until slightly softened. Cover, leave for an hour & drain. Sieve 3/4 into an equal amount of fresh water & reserve the rest. Put the oil in a large saucepan & cook the carrots, celery & leeks. When soft add the tomatoes, garlic & thyme. After 5 minutes add the cabbage, salt & pepper. Cook about 10 minutes & add the bean puree & the bean water. Cook slowly for an hour, adding tepid water if the soup becomes too solid, although it should be fairly thick. About 5~10 minutes before end of cooking, stir in the whole beans to heat through & ladle some of the hot soup over the bread in each bowl. Serve with cooked cabbage on top, a bowl of sliced red or spring onions and a jug of good green olive oil.

RISOTTO PRIMAVERA
· Spring Risotto (6) ·

This is a very festive looking risotto.

1 LB 2 OZ/500 G ITALIAN ARBORIO RICE
11 OZ/300 G GREENISH TOMATOES, DICED
12 OZ/350 G SMALL COURGETTES (ZUCCHINI), DICED
7 OZ/200 G GREEN PEPPER OR ASPARAGUS, DICED
4 OZ/100 G CARROT, DICED
1 ONION OR LEEK, CHOPPED
BEEF STOCK
5 OZ/150 G BUTTER
2 TBSP OLIVE OIL
SALT & PEPPER

Cook the onion in oil in a saucepan & when beginning to brown, add all the vegetables except the tomatoes. Cook 10 minutes over moderate heat & add tomatoes, salt & pepper. Cook for 15 minutes & then pour in the rice & a little hot stock. Continue adding tablespoons of hot stock every few minutes as the rice absorbs the liquid. It should take 20~30 minutes for the rice to cook to the 'al dente' stage. Then stir in butter & serve.

Tuscany is justifiably famous for the quality of its meat & fresh vegetable dishes, but less well-known (outside Italy) for the variety of ways in which wild herbs are used for anything from pasta filling to souffles or sformati, a Tuscan cross between a souffle and a vegetable mold. These two recipes come from an old lady encountered picking a basket of nettles near Montepulciano.

SFORMATO di ORTICA

• Souffle of Nettles • or spinach (4)

2 LB 2 oz/1 KG TENDER SPRING NETTLE LEAVES (OR SPINACH)
4 EGGS, BEATEN
4 oz/100 G PARMESAN CHEESE, GRATED
PINCH GRATED NUTMEG
4 oz/100 G BUTTER
CLOVE GARLIC, CRUSHED
SALT
PEPPER

Wash the nettles under running water for at least half an hour. Boil (save water for soup) for 10 ~ 15 minutes until tender, drain well and chop. Melt the butter in a medium~sized pan and saute the nettles, garlic and salt for 5 minutes. Add pepper and nutmeg and put through a food processor or vegetable mill. Stir in the eggs and cheese and pour into a buttered souffle dish. Place in a bain marie or roasting tin with water about ½ in/1 cm deep and bake in an oven pre~heated to 400°F/200°C/Gas 6 for about 30 minutes or until it has risen and is golden brown. Serve immediately.

MINESTRA di PISCIALETTO

• Tuscan Dandelion • greens soup (4)

Translated literally, piscialetto means pissbed, a Tuscan ref~erence to the colour of the dandelion flowers and its proximity to passing dogs. Elsewhere, however, it is trad~itionally regarded as having medicinal properties for humans.

9 oz/250 G TINY DANDELION LEAVES
2 CLOVES GARLIC, CRUSHED
1¾ PT/1 LTR WATER OR STOCK
LEEK, FINELY CHOPPED
STICK CELERY, FINELY CHOPPED
OLIVE OIL
SALT
BLACK PEPPER

Saute the onion, garlic and celery in oil in a medium~sized pan. When softened, add the dandelion leaves (keep a few for garnishing the soup), washed well and chopped. Cook for 5 minutes and then add water or stock, salt and pepper. Cook for half an hour and then put through a food processor or vegetable mill. It can then be re~heated and served over toasted bread.

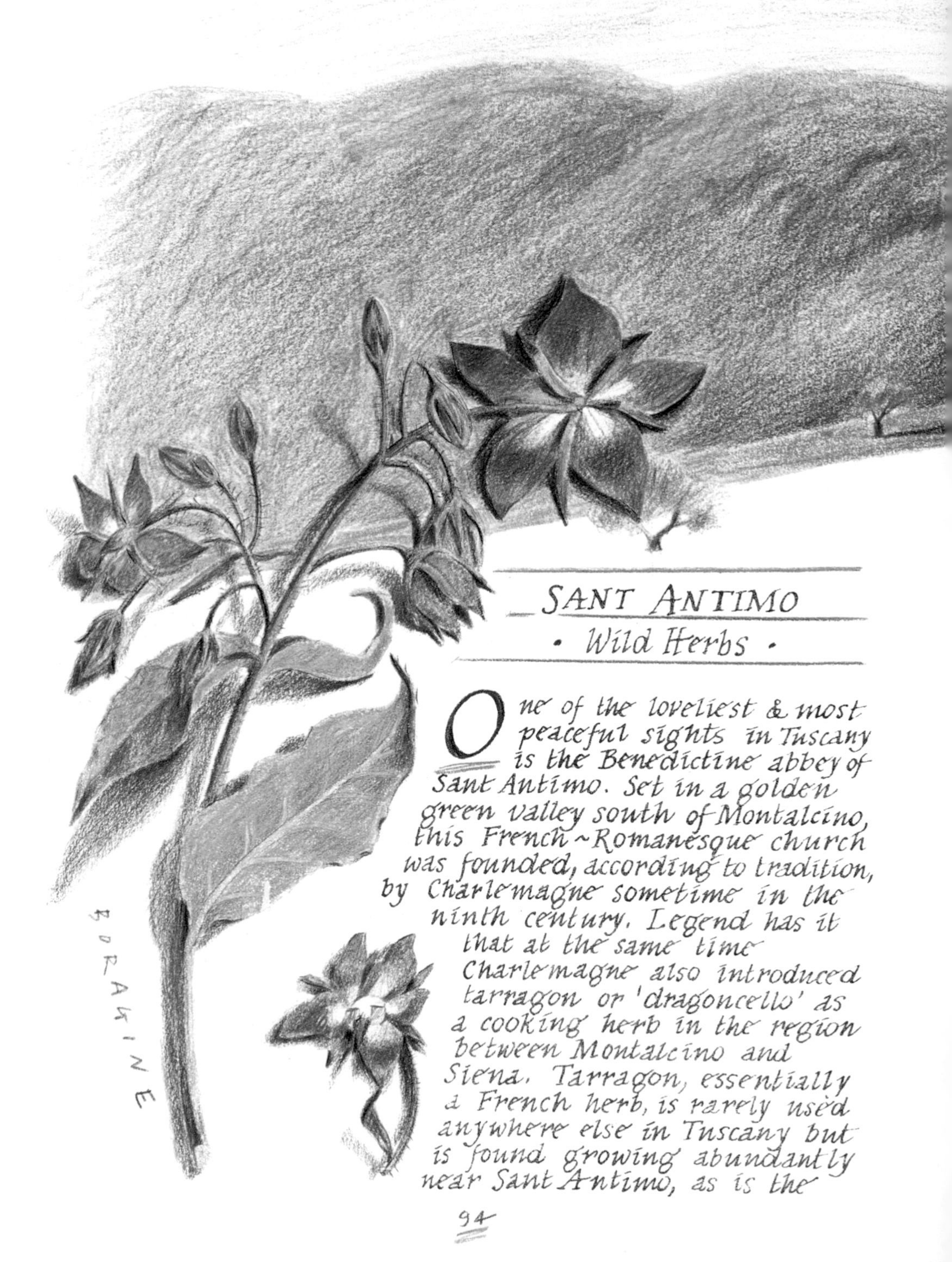

SANT ANTIMO

• Wild Herbs •

One of the loveliest & most peaceful sights in Tuscany is the Benedictine abbey of Sant Antimo. Set in a golden green valley south of Montalcino, this French~Romanesque church was founded, according to tradition, by Charlemagne sometime in the ninth century. Legend has it that at the same time Charlemagne also introduced tarragon or 'dragoncello' as a cooking herb in the region between Montalcino and Siena. Tarragon, essentially a French herb, is rarely used anywhere else in Tuscany but is found growing abundantly near Sant Antimo, as is the

more common wild borage. The young tender leaves and vivid blue flowers of borage can be cooked as fritters (like the zucchini flower fritters on page 70), tossed in salads with other wild greens such as dandelions or sauted gently in oil and added to beaten eggs to make a borage frittata. Tuscan frittatas, although similar in some ways to French omelettes, differ in that they are cooked slowly until firm over a low heat and are then usually grilled quickly to set the top side. They are often served as a light evening meal with a selection of antipasti, but also make an interesting alternative to sandwiches when served cold on a picnic.

· PAN CO' SANTI ·

Saint's bread

Just outside Montepulciano is the farm estate and trattoria PULCINO, selling its own Vino Nobile as well as sausages, home cured hams, sweet breads and cakes made from old local recipes by aunts, uncles and other relatives of the owner. One of these recipes is for Pan co' Santi (bread with saints), an ancient sweet bread that is traditionally eaten on All Soul's Day. It can be adapted from most bread recipes (or use the recipe page 65). To make it knead 17oz/510g of risen bread dough with the following ingredients:

- 2 TBSP MELTED HONEY
- 2oz/60G WALNUTS, TOASTED & CHOPPED
- 2 oz/60G DRIED FIGS OR PEARS, FINELY CHOPPED
- 2 oz/60G DATES, CHOPPED
- 1 TSP ROSEMARY, CHOPPED
- 2 oz/60 G PINENUTS,
- GENEROUS HANDFUL RAISINS
- 3 TBSP OLIVE OIL

When well amalgamated shape into an oval & leave to rise for 30~40 minutes. Brush the top with beaten egg and bake the loaf in an oven preheated to 400°F/200°C/Gas 6.

THE ETRUSCAN MAREMMA
Mont Amiata
TIRLI
GROSSETO
SORANO
SOVANA
SATURNIA
Da Laudomia
PITIGLIANO
MANCIANO
TALAMONE
Lago di Bolsena
CAPALBIO
ORBETELLO
MAREMMA
Mediterranean
1
2
·RESTAURANTS· ·SATURNIA· Da Laudomia· SOVANA·Taverna Etrusca·TIRLI· Tana del Cinghiale·
·SIGHTS· ·PITIGLIANO· wine ·SATURNIA· Roman baths· SORANO· Medieval hilltop town·SOVANA· Etruscan Tombs· TALAMONE· coast wildlife park·

· INTRODUCTION ·

Driving through the wide meadows and gently rolling low hills that are the Tuscan Maremma today, it is almost impossible to believe that less than a hundred years ago much of this now fertile countryside was malaria-ridden marshland. During Etruscan times the area northeast of the principal city of Grosseto was a navigable gulf. By the middle ages this had become a freshwater lake, which in turn became a swamp, causing widespread disease and famine. Many unsuccessful efforts were made to reclaim the land but it was not until the early years of this century that the Maremma was effectively rid of the malaria that had wiped out whole towns. In the 1950s a systematic government programme of agricultural incentives and repopulation was begun and the area's past prosperity virtually restored. Today the Etruscan-red soil produces abundant flowers, vegetables, grains and grapes.

The word 'Maremma' means coastal plain and, apart from the modern resorts along the coast, the area was probably more densely populated in Etruscan times, 2000 years ago, than it is now. Certainly evidence of these earliest settlers of Tuscany is everywhere. They left behind their name for the country, 'Tuscia', as well as many of their tombs and burial sites. At the lonely semi-abandoned village of Sovana the single-story medieval houses seem less inhabited than the Etruscan necropolis set in a cool birch gulley a mile away. Five miles to the south-east, Sovana's gloomy & forbidding neighbour, Pitigliano, grows out of a magnificent rocky mountain-top whose base is riddled with caves that were once Etruscan and Roman tombs but now serve as cellars for the excellent Pitigliano white wine. The three deep ravines around the town formed a natural moat when this town was the seat of the Roman Orsini barons during the thirteenth century.

The Etruscans were not the only settlers to leave their mark on the land. During the mid-1500s, when Orbetello was the capital of the Spanish Garrison States, pirates from the Barbary coast were a constant hazard along the coast and close to the sea are the crumbling remains of a few towers from which watch was kept for the invaders. Despite these precautions however, one night in April 1543, the beautiful young daughter of a local family, the Marsilis, was kidnapped by Barbarossa's pirates and survived to become the favourite wife of Sultan Solimani. And at Orbetello many of the present-day inhabitants still retain the swarthy good looks of Moorish forbears.

Much of the Maremman coast has been ruined by expensive resort developments but fortunately some of the original terrain is protected by the Monti dell' Uccellina, the Maremman Nature Reserve. In this long stretch of wood & scrubland wildlife flourishes and the huge umbrella pines, so typical of the area, shade miles of white deserted beaches. It is possible to see hare, deer and porcupines, and most unexpectedly, herds of long-horn cattle & wild horses rounded up by 'butteri', the cowboys of the Maremma. At the medieval town of Capalbio these cowboys have their own riders fair in October.

Capalbio is the main centre of horse breeding in southern Tuscany and also an excellent place to sample wild game prepared in appetizing local recipes. But throughout the Maremma game is readily available. During the autumn hunting season small family restaurants, Da Landomia near Saturnia and the Taverna Etrusca in Sovana, serve hearty toe-warming dishes that make use not only of the plentiful wild boar and roebuck but also of fresh local herbs, tomatoes and wild mushrooms. Garlic is used here far more than in the rest of Tuscany, perhaps because it is a cheap way of adding flavour to a simple dish. The Maremman people do not easily forget that their region has only very recently become agriculturally rich after centuries of much hardship.

TANA DEL CINGHIALE

For centuries the Tuscans, some of the world's most avid hunters, shot anything that moved: wild boar, deer, pheasant, thrushes, porcupines and even hedgehogs. And then it usually reappeared on the table. Now there is an increasing reluctance to wipe out songbirds. There is much less reluctance, however, to halt the hunting of wild boar, or cinghiale, which, being large and quite fierce, provides more sport than a songbird. All over Tuscany you can buy delicious hams and sausages made from this tasty meat, particularly in the Maremma where the broom-covered hills provide excellent cinghiale cover. The recipes below come from the cook at the Tana del Cinghiale, a remote hunting lodge at the tiny village of Tirli in the Maremman hills.

CINGHIALE alle MELE
Wild boar with apples (6)

Wild boar, unless very young and tender, needs to be marinated, but before that it should have been hung for a few days. Ask your butcher or game dealer, he should know its history.

- 2½ LB/1.2 KG WILD BOAR ~ THE RIB MEAT FOR PREFERENCE
- 3~4 LARGE COOKING APPLES, PEELED, CORED & SLICED
- 1 ONION, CHOPPED
- 2 GLASSES RED WINE
- SMALL PIECE CHILI PEPPER
- CARROT, CHOPPED
- CELERY STICK, CHOPPED
- SALT
- FRESH ROSEMARY
- FRESH THYME
- OLIVE OIL
- ABOUT 1¾ PT/1 LTR BEEF STOCK

· MARINADE ·

1 3/4 PT/1 LTR RED WINE
1/4 PT/150 ML VINEGAR
3 1/4 PT/1.75 LTR WATER
5~6 BAY LEAVES
1/2 TSP CINNAMON
6 WHOLE PEPPERCORNS
4 LEAVES FRESH MINT
2 OZ/50 G SEA SALT
3~4 SPRIGS FRESH ROSEMARY
3~4 SPRIGS FRESH THYME

Combine all the ingredients for the marinade. Cut the meat into chunks and completely cover in the marinade. Add more wine if the meat is not covered. Leave for three days in a refrigerator and stir often. If it begins to give an unpleasant smell, change the liquid ~ this is not a 'cucina povera' dish. After three days rinse well in warm water. Heat the oil in a heat~proof casserole and add the onion, carrot, celery, chili and herbs. When soft add the meat, salt and pepper, and brown well. Pour in the red wine and when slightly evaporated lower the heat and add a cup of beef stock. Cover and cook gently for 2~3 hours, until tender, adding stock as necessary to prevent it drying out. Half an hour before the end of cooking, pack the apples over the meat. Recover and finish cooking. Serve over toasted bread or deep fried polenta (see page 49).

LEPRE in DOLCE e FORTE

· Hare in strong ~ sweet sauce (6) ·

This classic way of cooking both boar and hare requires a strong wild meat. The quantities are for the more readily available hare. The dish has a strange, exotic taste and is much better made the day before it is required. Be sure of your guests' capabilities before serving it ~ it is definitely not nouvelle cuisine.

1 LARGE HARE, CLEANED
2 OZ/50 G PANCETTA, FINELY CHOPPED
3 SPRIGS THYME
GOOD BEEF OR CHICKEN STOCK
OLIVE OIL
11 OZ/300 G TOMATOES
2 TBSP CHOPPED PARSLEY
LARGE WINEGLASS WHITE WINE
2 CRUMBLED BAY LEAVES

· MARINADE ·

1 PT/1/2 LTR WHITE WINE
WINEGLASS OF WHITE WINE VINEGAR
ONION STUCK WITH 4 CLOVES
CELERY STICK, SLICED
CARROT, SLICED
CLOVE GARLIC, CRUSHED
3 JUNIPER BERRIES
6 PEPPERCORNS

(continued...)

SALSA AGRODOLCE

- 2 TBSP GRANULATED SUGAR
- 2 TBSP WATER
- 2 TBSP RED WINE VINEGAR
- 2 OZ/50 G BITTER COOKING CHOCOLATE
- 1½ OZ/40 G RAISINS, SOAKED
- 2½ OZ/60 G PINENUTS
- 2 TBSP MIXED CANDIED LEMON AND ORANGE PEEL

Combine all the ingredients for the marinade. Cut the hare in pieces, wash well and cover with the marinade for 24 hours, stirring often. Drain, wash and dry the hare. Heat a little oil in a flame proof casserole, add the thyme, parsley, bay leaves & finely chopped pancetta & soften. Then add the hare & saute well. Add salt, pour in a glass of wine & when it has evaporated add the tomatoes. Cover & cook slowly over a low heat for at least 2 hours, adding hot stock as needed to stop the stew drying out. About half an hour before the hare has finished cooking, melt the sugar with water over low heat until slightly brown. Add the chocolate melted in the vinegar, and after a few minutes the raisins, pinenuts & peel. Mix well & take from the heat. Remove hare from the liquid, & sieve or liquidize the remaining juices. Return meat & sauce to the casserole & slowly add the agrodolce. Heat through for 10 minutes & serve with a crisp borage salad.

CIPOLLE alla GROSSETANA

· Stuffed onions Grosseto style (4) ·

This recipe has hundreds of variations in the Maremma. Some cooks substitute half a finely chopped chili pepper for the nutmeg & cinnamon, some add ½ oz/15 g dried mushrooms, soaked, squeezed out & chopped. Whatever variation you use, these onions make a good lunch for a cold winter's day.

- 4 LARGE OR 8 SMALL WHITE ONIONS
- 4 OZ/125 G LEAN BEEF, GROUND OR MINCED
- BUTTER
- OLIVE OIL
- SALT & PEPPER
- ¼ TSP NUTMEG
- 4 OZ/125 G GROUND SPICY SAUSAGE
- 1 EGG
- 1 WINE GLASS DRY WHITE WINE
- 4 TBSP GRATED PECORINO OR PARMESAN CHEESE *
- ¼ TSP CINNAMON

Peel the onions and boil until slightly softened in salted water (about 10 minutes). Trim enough off one end so the onions will stand upright. Remove a little of the other end & most of the inside, leaving just a shell. Chop the remaining onion finely & saute in butter with the beef and sausage until brown. Stir in the spices and wine. When the wine has nearly evaporated, turn off the heat and leave to cool. Then mix the sauce with egg and cheese and stuff the onion shells with this. Bake at a moderate heat, 350°F/180°C/Gas 4, in an oiled baking dish for about 25 minutes until brown, moistening with water or stock if the onions seem to be burning.

* It is also good to serve this dish with several tablespoons of bechamel sauce instead of cheese.

CANNELLA
CANNELLA
CANNELLA
CANNELLA
BUSTINA
ITALIA

DA LAUDOMIA

One hundred years ago Da Laudomia was a small posting inn (called Locanda Butelli after the present owner's grand-parents) where tired travellers stopped to eat, change horses and buy anything from trousers to home-made sweets. The store and the horses have gone, but Da Laudomia remains much the same (despite the change of name) and the present patronne, Clara Detti, can tell you more about the history & the

practice of Maremman cooking than can be found in any book on the subject

· ACQUACOTTA ·

Tomato and bread soup (4)

Signora Detti believes that Acquacotta (literally 'cooked water') began when itinerant carbonari or charcoal-burners worked through the winters in the Maremma. They were so poor that they lived in igloos of twigs built around their ever-burning charcoal fires, and over each of these fires hung a pot of simmering water. Any food that could be scrounged or exchanged for charcoal was put in this pot ~ usually garlic, stale bread and onions, but as times got better, tomatoes, celery and an egg or two went in. From these humble beginnings Acquacotta has evolved into this slightly more sophisticated version without losing its original simplicity. There are an almost infinite number of variations to this soup, one of the best is the addition of several dried mushrooms and one spicy grilled sausage per person at the beginning of

(continued...)

(continued from previous page)
cooking. But whatever variation you follow, this soup always tastes best if eaten when you are tired and hungry.

- 2~3 LARGE ONIONS, FINELY CHOPPED
- 1 LB 10 OZ/750 G TOMATOES, PEELED AND DESEEDED (OR A MIXTURE OF 11 OZ/300 G SWEET RED PEPPERS AND 1 LB/450 G TOMATOES)
- 5~6 STICKS CELERY, DICED (INCLUDING THE LEAVES)
- 4 TBSP GOOD OLIVE OIL
- 1 3/4 PT/1 LTR BOILING SALTED WATER
- 4 EGGS
- 8 PIECES STALE BREAD, TOASTED (OR FRIED IN OLIVE OIL IF YOU ARE NOT TOO WEIGHT CONSCIOUS)
- SALT & PEPPER

Heat the olive oil in a medium saucepan and cook the onion & celery over a low heat until just beginning to brown. Add the tomatoes, salt and pepper and cook for 20 minutes. Pour in the boiling water and leave to simmer. Meanwhile toast (or fry) the bread and put on the bottom of a fireproof soup tureen. When the soup tastes good (after about 30 minutes) put the tureen over a low heat and pour the soup over the bread. Then break each egg separately into the soup, spacing them well apart and taking care that the yolks do not break. (For safety's sake you can break the eggs into a cup first.) Serve the soup as soon as the eggs have set, with plenty of freshly grated parmesan or pecorino cheese sprinkled over.

• MAIALE con LATTE •

Pork with milk (4)

As this dish is served at Da Laudomia, the sauce at the end has a slightly curdled appearance. If this offends you, sieve the cooked sauce and reheat gently before serving it.

- 2 LB 2 OZ/1 KG LOIN OF PORK, BONED
- 4 OZ/100 KG BUTTER
- 1 LARGE TOMATO, PEELED, SEEDED AND FINELY CHOPPED
- 3 LEEKS, FINELY CHOPPED
- 1 STICK CELERY, DICED WITH LEAVES
- 2 LARGE SPRIGS FRESH THYME
- 1 3/4 PT/1 LTR MILK
- SALT & PEPPER
- FLOUR
- CLOVE GARLIC, CRUSHED

Melt the butter in a casserole large enough to hold all the ingredients. Put in the celery, leeks, garlic and tomatoes. Cook over a low heat until the celery and leeks have softened. Meanwhile snip the thyme over the pork, roll the meat up with the thyme inside, tie it with string and rub salt & pepper well into the skin. Roll lightly in the flour and brown over a low heat in the casserole with the vegetables. While it is browning, heat the milk almost to boiling and pour over the meat. Cover & cook for about 2 hours, or until the meat is tender, in an oven preheated to 350°F/180°C/Mark 4. Check occasionally to see the milk does not burn. If the meat seems to be drying out, add a few tbsps of water. To serve, slice the meat thickly & pour the sauce over it, after scraping all the meat from the casserole & stirring it in.

• BAR LUPI •

At Mario and Nadia Lupi's bar on the cliffs of Sorano, they make Gli Sfratti, a honey-filled sweet, at Christmas.

• GLI SFRATTI •

Sweet walnut rolls (2 dozen)

This delicious sweet is extremely ancient in origin. As far as it can be traced, the Etruscans enjoyed it as much as the 'Gioca' playing customers in the Lupis' bar.

FOR THE PASTRY

- 4 oz/110 G GRANULATED SUGAR
- 4 oz/110 G COLD BUTTER, CUT IN SMALL PIECES
- 9 oz/250 G PLAIN FLOUR
- 1 EGG, BEATEN
- PINCH OF BICARBONATE OF SODA
- 2 TBSP MILK (APPROXIMATE)
- GRATED PEEL OF ½ LEMON

FOR THE FILLING

- 9 oz/250 G HONEY
- 9 oz/250 G WALNUTS, CHOPPED VERY FINELY
- 1 oz/25 G FINE BREADCRUMBS
- GRATED PEEL OF ½ LEMON

First make the stuffing. Cook the honey over a low heat for 20 minutes. Add the walnuts and continue cooking for a further 10 minutes. Stir in the bread-crumbs and lemon peel very thoroughly and put the mixture in the refrigerator to cool.

Meanwhile make the pastry. Sift the flour and bicarbonate together together onto a pastryboard or worksurface. Mix in the sugar, make a well in the middle & into this put the egg, lemon peel and butter. Rub this in and knead it to form a stiff dough, adding a little milk if necessary to keep it pliable. Put aside and chill for about 30 minutes. Then roll the dough out very thinly and trim to a width of 2 in/5 cm. Spread with a thin layer of the filling mixture. Roll the dough up carefully to form a long finger. Trim to fit onto a greased baking sheet and brush all over with beaten egg yolk. Bake in an oven preheated to 400°F/200°C/Gas 6 for 15 minutes until golden. Cool on a wire rack and serve sliced into 'fingers' or rounds.

L'ETTO L 2000
PECORINO NOSTRALE
L'ETTO L 1200
L'AMATORE
AMADORI
TUTTAPECORA
PECORINO SENESE
PURA PECORA FRESCO

TORTINO di POMODORI
Hot tomato pie (4)

This simple recipe from Tuscany's south bears a strong resemblance to the Basque dish 'piperade' without the ham. It is best cooked in the dish it will be served in and then carried, still sizzling, straight to the table.

- 6 EGGS, BEATEN
- 4 RIPE TOMATOES, PEELED, SEEDED AND CHOPPED
- 1/4 ~ 1/2 HOT CHILI PEPPER, FINELY CHOPPED
- 1 CLOVE GARLIC, CRUSHED
- 4~5 FRESH BASIL LEAVES, TORN IN SMALL PIECES
- 1/2 ONION, FINELY CHOPPED
- OLIVE OIL
- SALT & PEPPER
- GRATED PECORINO CHEESE

Cook the onion, garlic and chili pepper in oil over a low heat. When softened but not brown add the tomatoes and the basil. Cover and leave to cook just until the tomatoes look slightly mashed. Add beaten eggs, salt and pepper to taste and leave to set. When it is firm throughout but still creamy on top, sprinkle on several tablespoons of cheese and put under a hot grill until bubbling. Serve it piping hot with more basil on top and plenty of fresh crusty bread.

*Another simple & good 'tortino' is made by mixing 2 1/2 tbsp flour, 7 tbsp milk, 5 tsp granulated sugar & 2 sliced apples. Fry in butter like an omelette & dust with sugar.

...My dear abbot, twixt cakes and soups
so much cheese have you my body imbued
that should I continue my stay with you
I would Paulo cease to be and a form
of cheese would I assume.

(ATTRIBUTED TO PAULO UCCELLO WHEN HE WAS WORKING ON A FRESCO FOR THE ABBOT OF SAN MINIATO)

It seems likely that Uccello's surfeit was of pecorino, the pungent cheese made of sheeps milk whose origins date back to Roman times. It is still the most popular and widely available cheese in Tuscany. Some people would say too popular. There are over 100 different varieties but when trying them be open-minded. Creamy yellow Maremman pecorino is excellent & may seem more appetizing, but equally good are the small Siena cheeses with hard red rinds, & the mold covered pecorino that has absorbed different flavours from the leaves in which it has been wrapped to mature. All pecorino cheeses change character with age, varying from a Gouda~like consistency when young or 'fresco' to a pungent crumbly Parmesan texture when mature.

OLIO all'ARRABIATA
'Enraged' oil

If you are unsure of your own or your friends' liking for hot chili pepper, fill a small stoppered bottle 3/4 full of olive oil and into it put a couple of whole chili peppers (slightly bruised). Left for several days, the chili will 'enrage' the oil enough to satisfy any hot-blooded person. Serve as a condiment at the table so everyone can add a few drops, or not to their own taste. This is a particularly good idea when serving Fettunta (page 29) or any of the robust Tuscan soups like Pappa al Pomodoro.

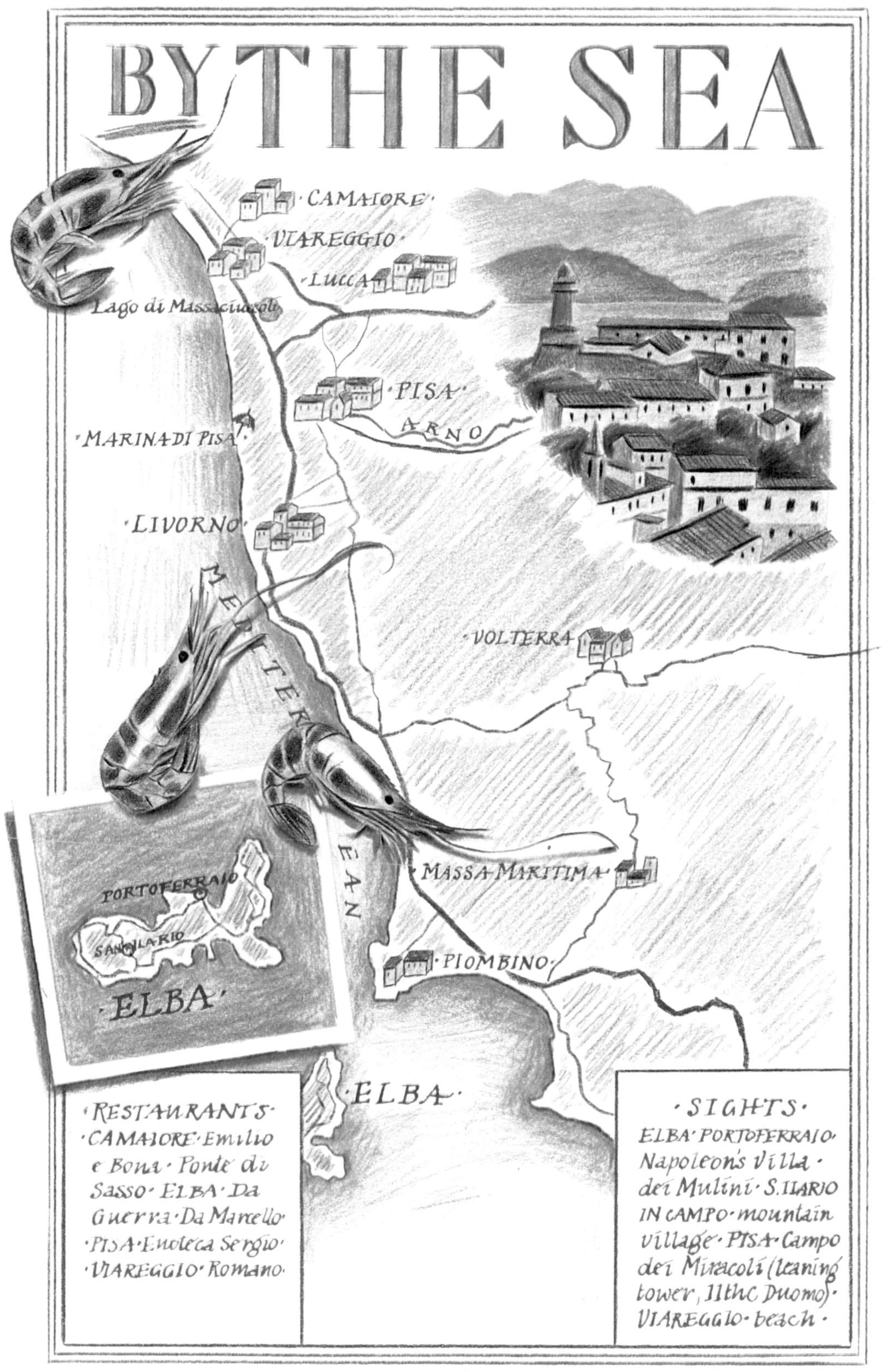

BY THE SEA
CAMAIORE
VIAREGGIO
LUCCA
Lago di Massaciuccoli
PISA
ARNO
MARINA DI PISA
LIVORNO
VOLTERRA
MASSA MARITIMA
PORTOFERRAIO
ELBA
PIOMBINO
ELBA
RESTAURANTS
CAMAIORE · Emilio e Bona · Ponte di Sasso · ELBA · Da Guerra · Da Marcello · PISA · Enoteca Sergio · VIAREGGIO · Romano
SIGHTS
ELBA · PORTOFERRAIO · Napoleon's Villa dei Mulini · S. ILARIO IN CAMPO · mountain village · PISA · Campo dei Miracoli (leaning tower, 11thC Duomo) · VIAREGGIO · beach ·

· INTRODUCTION ·

An hour by ferry from the Tuscan Maremma lies mountainous Elba, the largest island in the Tuscan archipelago. Its huge supply of iron ore provides much of Italy's requirement and has been mined on the island for at least 3000 years. The main port was called Portoferraio (Port Iron) as early as the eigth century and the rich palette of Elba's wines is due to the high iron content in the soil.

Possibly because of this mineral wealth, Elba has been in turn invaded & settled by the Sicilians, Etruscans, Romans, Moors, Spanish, Pisans & finally, of course, by the French under Napoleon. It is not surprising then that the island's cuisine is such a melting pot of cookery styles, each with its own distinctive Elban twist. It is possible to eat 'puttenaio', a ratatouille-like vegetable stew, in Portoferraio, or 'la sburrida', a fish soup of Spanish origin in Capoliveri, where legend has it that Cosimo de' Medici promised sixteenth-century Spanish pirates he would leave their favourite haunt unharassed if they would do the same for his town of Cosmopolia.

Not all past visitors to Elba were military ones. The tourist trade certainly existed in 1914. In a book, Napoleon's Elba, published in that year, an English-woman, Lydia Bushnell Smith, mentions buying '... the obligatory picture card of the island.' But it was not until later in this century that tourists began coming to Elba for its fine sandy beaches instead of its Napoleonic associations.

Livorno, the major Tuscan commercial port, is less likely to suffer change than Elba as a result of the tourist trade. The 'ideal city' created by the Medici grand dukes suffered heavy bombing during World War 2, losing in the process much of its charm along with many of its fine buildings. The sixteenth-century foreigners who knew and loved Livorno under the old English name 'Leghorn' would barely recognize it today. Still one of the greatest ports in the Mediterranean, it is now best known for its famous fish dishes 'alla Livornese', rich with tomatoes, parsley and garlic, a style of cooking whose influence can be appreciated along most of the Tuscan coast.

On the river Arno, a few miles north, lies Pisa, a thriving port when Livorno was still a small medieval fishing village. Thriving, that is, until 1284, when Pisa's navy was destroyed in battle, & its government allowed the harbour to fill with silt. Now Pisa lies miles inland, no longer a port but a university town, one of the most respected in Italy. The university's science faculty is as strong today as it was when Galileo dropped 3 metal balls from the top of the famous leaning bell tower, the Campanile, to disprove Aristotle's theories about the acceleration of falling objects. The Campanile, along with the black & white pyjama-striped Duomo, the lovely Baptistry & the vast cemetery is both the tourist & the ecclesiastical centre of the city. But the heart of Pisa must be the market area sprawling over a maze of streets north of the Arno. Here medieval buildings lean crazily over the pavements to form narrow tunnels linking piazzas. Foreign university students jostle stout Pisan housewives for freshest mullet & tiniest 'Cee', the local name for the tiny eels that are a speciality.

The poet Percy Bysse Shelley lived for years in Tuscany & wrote some of his best poems in Pisa in the 1800s. He described the region as a 'paradise of exiles', a particularly apt description of the coastal resort Viareggio. During the summer the city's famous square, the Piazza Shelley, fills with parties of English tourists, standing mournfully in front of the poet's monument. It records that in 1822 Shelley's drowned body was washed up on Viareggio's beach, a fact that doesn't deter these same mournful tourists from later dining well in one of Viareggio's excellent fish restaurants.

NAPOLEON

When the defeated Napoleon arrived on Elba, he immediately set about turning his island prison into a setting more suitable for an emperor—even if a deposed one. One of the first things he did was to convert two old windmills into the lovely villa 'Palazzino dei Mulini,' which still stands today, surrounded by palm trees and cypresses on top of the hill at Portoferraio.

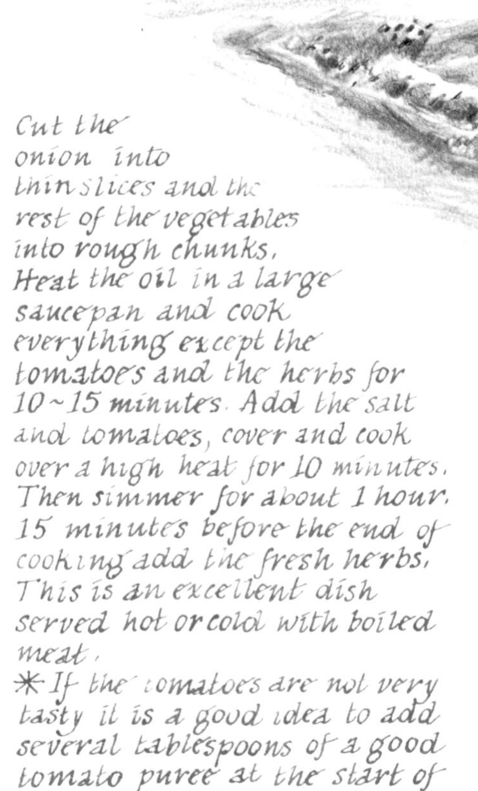

• PUTTENAIO •

Prostitutes' stew (4)

Napoleon's stay, short though it was, brought a decidedly French influence to the island's cooking. Evidence is this vegetable stew, derogatorily called 'Puttenaio' (prostitute's stew) which bears a distinct resemblance to the famous French ratatouille.

1 LB 6 OZ / 600 G GREEN PEPPERS
2 LARGE POTATOES
2 AUBERGINES (EGGPLANTS)
1 STICK CELERY
CARROT
LARGE ONION
1 LB 6 OZ / 600 G RIPE TOMATOES, PEELED AND SEEDED
2 ZUCCHINI (COURGETTES)
1/4 PT OLIVE OIL
SMALL HANDFUL OF FRESH HERBS SUCH AS PARSLEY, ROSEMARY, THYME OR BASIL
COARSE SEA SALT
2 CLOVES GARLIC, CRUSHED

Cut the onion into thin slices and the rest of the vegetables into rough chunks. Heat the oil in a large saucepan and cook everything except the tomatoes and the herbs for 10~15 minutes. Add the salt and tomatoes, cover and cook over a high heat for 10 minutes. Then simmer for about 1 hour. 15 minutes before the end of cooking add the fresh herbs. This is an excellent dish served hot or cold with boiled meat.

* If the tomatoes are not very tasty it is a good idea to add several tablespoons of a good tomato puree at the start of cooking.

· PESCI ARROSTO ·
Grilled fish (4)

There is a story that Napoleon, on one of his frequent restless walks around Portoferraio, stopped to admire a catch brought in by some fishermen. The emperor was known to like simple people and simple food. After a chat with the men he invited them back to dinner at the Villa Mulini. And the dinner that night was their own fish! This recipe for grilled fresh sardines comes from Signora Pierangela Piras' excellent book L'ISOLA D'ELBA IN CUCINA, but it is such a

(continued...)

(continued from previous page...)
classic way of cooking fish that it could well have been served that night.

- FRESH SARDINES, THE NUMBER PER PERSON DEPENDING ON WHETHER THEY ARE BEING SERVED AS A STARTER OR A MAIN DISH
- TSP SEA SALT
- CLOVE GARLIC
- 3 TBSP OLIVE OIL
- 4 OZ/100 G FENNEL BULB & LEAVES, FINELY CHOPPED
- 1/2 HOT CHILI PEPPER
- 1 TBSP WHITE WINE VINEGAR

Clean, scale and thoroughly wash the fish. Make a marinade by crushing all the remaining ingredients together in a mortar, adding more oil if necessary. Put fish in the marinade and leave it for 30~40 minutes, turning often. Grill the fish, turning once only and basting frequently with the marinade oil. If using a grilling rack, wipe it with oil first so the fish don't stick.

Quite understandably, these fish taste best cooked over a wood fire (the Tuscans use chestnut which is particularly aromatic) but if you must use charcoal, try throwing fresh herbs on it to scent both the air & the fish.

· Zucchini Ripieno ·

Stuffed zucchini/courgettes (4)

This delicious Elban method of cooking the first young spring zucchini is equally good using small aubergines (eggplants) instead. Or serve a big mixed plateful with whole zucchini flower fritters.

- 8 TINY ZUCCHINI
- 7 OZ / 200 G GROUND LEAN BEEF
- 4 OZ / 100 G CHOPPED MORTADELLA
- OLIVE OIL
- OIL FOR DEEP FRYING
- 4 EGGS, BEATEN
- 4 TBSP GRATED PARMESAN
- 2 TBSP FRESH THYME, CHOPPED
- 2 CLOVES GARLIC, CRUSHED
- 1½ CUPS (APPROX) FINE BREAD CRUMBS

Boil the whole zucchini for 2~3 minutes until just tender. Cut in half lengthwise and remove the pulp. In a frying pan heat the olive oil and cook the beef and garlic until browned and then mix with mortadella, zucchini pulp, cheese, thyme and 2 eggs. Stuff the zucchini with this mixture and tie the two halves together with thread. Dip each stuffed zucchini into beaten egg and then roll in breadcrumbs until well covered. Deep fry or bake in a hot oven preheated to 450°F/230°C/Gas 8 until crisp and brown. Remove the thread before eating.

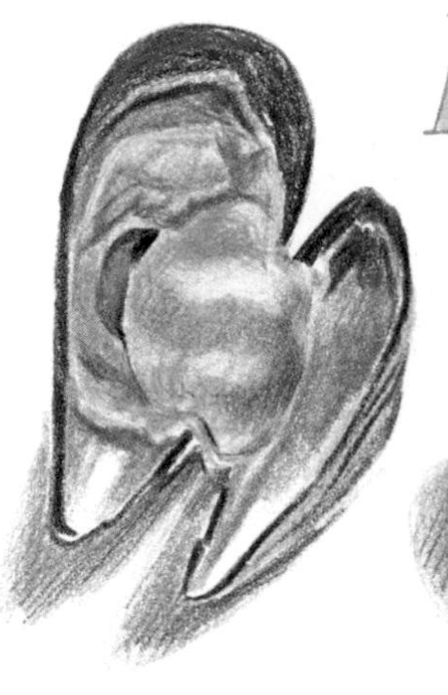

People come from all over Elba to eat at Marcello's small and cosy fish restaurant on the waterfront in the fishing village of Marciana Marina. There he serves fresh fish and regional specialities to both regular customers and discerning visitors.

SPAGHETTI alla MARINARA
Spaghetti & seafood sauce (4)

This is a loose interpretation of Marcello's delicious recipe, but it can be varied according to the season and individual taste, including crab and lobster, although that seems rather an extravagance.

- 1 LB/450 G THINNEST SPAGHETTI
- 4 OZ/100 G OCTOPUS
- 4 OZ/100 G CUTTLEFISH WITHOUT THE INKSAC
- 1 LB 2 OZ/500 G MUSSELS
- 1 LB 2 OZ/500 G ARSELLE (BABY CLAMS), SOAKED OVERNIGHT IN SALT WATER
- 3 TBSP FRESH CHOPPED PARSLEY
- 2 CLOVES GARLIC, CRUSHED
- 1~2 GLASSES DRY WHITE WINE
- 6 TBSP OLIVE OIL
- SALT
- 1 ONION, FINELY CHOPPED

Cook half the mussels in a little water until just beginning to open. Keep half the mussels and all the clams aside. Clean the cuttlefish and octopus and chop finely. Remove the cooked mussels from their shells and chop finely. Heat the oil in a medium~sized pan and saute the onion. When soft add the octopus, cuttlefish and chopped mussels. Cook for about 5 minutes and then add the wine. When partially evaporated, put in the garlic and parsley. After 10 minutes add the clams and mussels in their shells, adjust salt and cook for another 5~10 minutes or until they have all opened. Discard any that remain closed. Meanwhile put the spaghetti on to cook in boiling salted water. When just cooked, drain and toss with the sauce. Serve with more chopped parsley sprinkled on top.

· DA · MARCELLO ·

FONTE
APOLEONE
RENDEZ-VOUS
DA MARCELLO
grissini
tipo torinesi
FIORAVANTI

· DA GUERRA ·

The Elbans claim it never rains in summer. Don't believe them, it can and it does. But if you, too, are unlucky, don't mourn those lost days on the beach, enjoy instead long leisurely meals, for Elban cooking has much to offer. Da Guerra in Portoferraio is a large family-run trattoria, serving excellent fish as well as other specialities.

· RISO NERO ·
Black Rice (4~6)

Riso nero was originally a Florentine dish, but it could have travelled to Elba with anyone from Cosimo de' Medici onwards. Don't be put off by its appearance ~ riso nero means black rice and black it is (made so by the cuttlefish ink-sac). But it's also a wonderful dish.

- 1 LB 8 OZ/700 G SMALL CUTTLEFISH OR BABY SQUID
- ½ ONION, FINELY CHOPPED
- 3 HEAPED TBSP FINELY CHOPPED PARSLEY
- 2 CLOVES GARLIC, CRUSHED
- 1 LB 2 OZ/500 G TOMATOES, PEELED, SEEDED AND PUT THROUGH A FOOD PROCESSOR OR VEGETABLE MILL
- ¼ CRUSHED CHILI PEPPER
- ¼ PT/120 ML OLIVE OIL
- 1 LB/450 G ITALIAN ARBORIO RICE
- SEA SALT
- BLACK PEPPER
- ½ PT/300 ML DRY WHITE WINE

Wash the cuttlefish very well, taking care not to break the ink-sacs which should be cut off and kept aside. Chop the fish, including the tentacles, quite finely. In a deep saucepan heat the oil and cook the onion gently until soft, then add the cuttlefish. Simmer for about 10 minutes, then add the white wine. When this has evaporated put in the tomatoes, parsley, garlic, chili and salt & pepper to taste. Cook for another 15 minutes, adding water if necessary, as the sauce must be quite liquid to cook the rice. Add the rice and the 'ink' from the fish and stir well. Continue as for any other risotto: adding a little water at intervals as the rice absorbs the liquid. Once the rice is added the cooking time should be approximately 20~30 minutes. Serve hot, as a starter or light dinner.

TRIGLIA alla LIVORNESE

• Red mullet as cooked in Livorno (4) •

Livorno may not be a city that most tourists would choose to visit, but from its substantial port area come many of Tuscany's most famous fish recipes. If you encounter them far from Livorno, their heavy use of tomatoes, garlic and parsley is a clue to their origins.

- 12 SMALL CLEANED RED MULLETS
- 1 LB 2 OZ/500 G TOMATOES, PEELED, SEEDED & CHOPPED
- 2 CLOVES GARLIC, CRUSHED
- 2 SPRIGS FRESH THYME
- SEA SALT
- BLACK PEPPER
- 4 TBSP CHOPPED PARSLEY
- FLOUR
- OLIVE OIL FOR FRYING
- ½ HOT CHILI PEPPER, CRUSHED

Dust the fish liberally with flour and put in a large frying pan in which the oil has been heating. Fry for about 3~4 minutes on each side. Remove fish from pan and keep warm. Add garlic, 3 tablespoons of the parsley, thyme, and chili and cook until the garlic begins to brown. Then add tomatoes, salt and pepper and cook over a low flame for 20~30 minutes or just until the sauce begins to thicken. Return the fish to the pan, taking care not to break them and cook for a further 5 minutes. Sprinkle with remaining parsley and serve immediately.

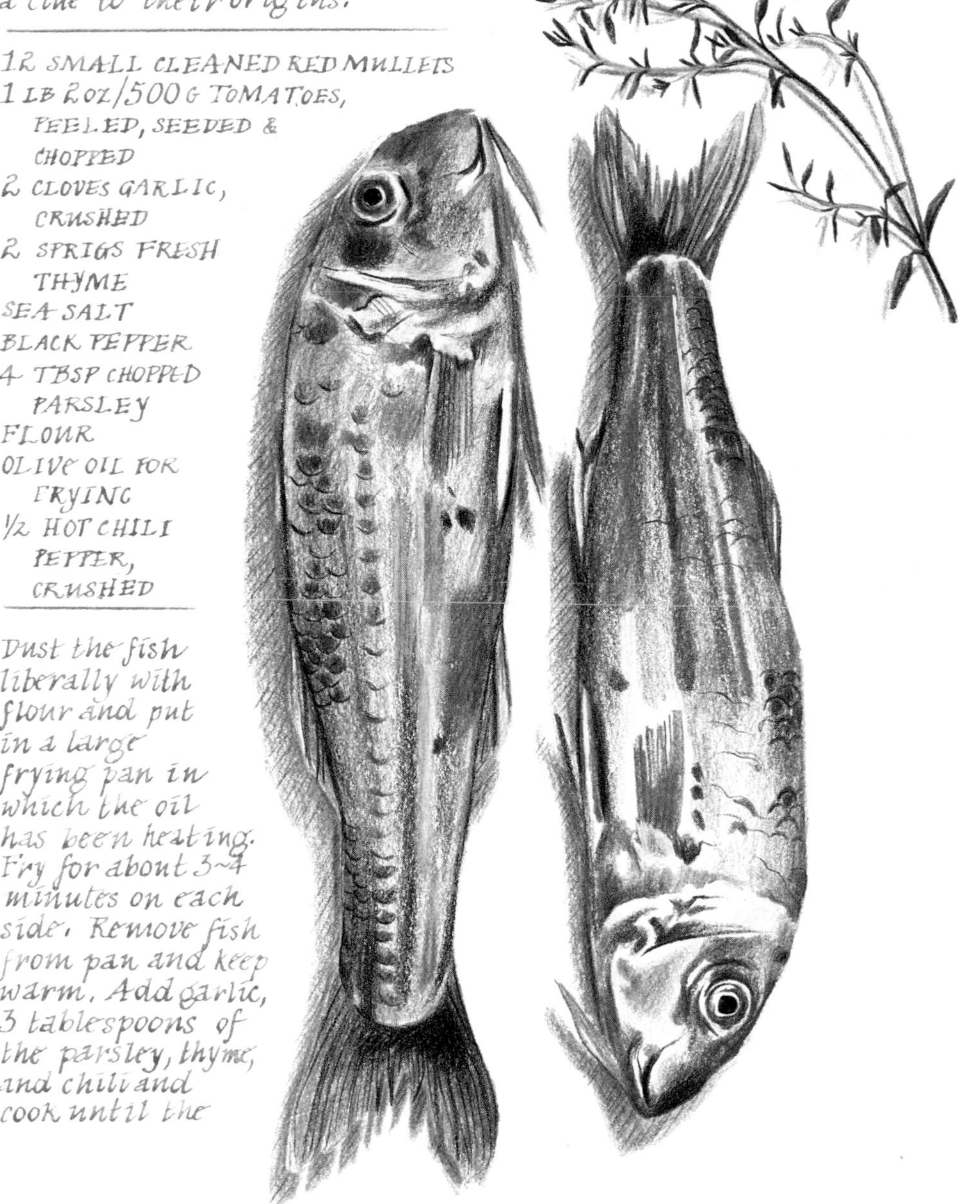

PILES OF CHEESE & SALAMI IN A PISA SHOP

· PISA MARKET ·

One of the nicest and fastest ways to find the 'real' Pisa (not the easiest thing to do) is to wander the rabbit warren of narrow streets leading off Piazza S. Uomobuono, the main market square. Here there are vendors selling every imaginable, and some unimaginable, type of produce. At Tuttovo, 1 Piazza Donati, you can watch through a glass wall while they make a startling variety of pasta: everything from wild nettle ravioli to bitter chocolate tagliatelle. And there are almost as many different types and ages of Tuscan pecorino cheese at the Casa del Formaggio, where an astute enquiry may yield a free taste.

POLLO all'ARRABIATA
'Enraged' chicken (4)

This recipe is best made with the excellent free-range chickens sold at the butcher's shop in the main piazza, but is almost as good with a more ordinary bird.

- 1 CHICKEN, ABOUT 2½ LB / 1 KG, CUT IN PIECES
- 1 LARGE ONION, FINELY CHOPPED
- ½ HOT CHILI PEPPER, SLIGHTLY CRUSHED
- 2 CLOVES GARLIC, CRUSHED
- 4~5 TOMATOES, PEELED, SEEDED AND ROUGHLY CHOPPED
- ½ PT / 275 ML CHIANTI WINE
- 3 TBSP OLIVE OIL
- SALT & PEPPER

Heat the oil in a large heavy saucepan and saute the onion and garlic until golden (but not brown). Add the chicken pieces and brown well on all sides. Then add the wine, chili pepper, salt and pepper and cook over a low heat, turning frequently, until the wine is half evaporated. At this point add the tomatoes, cover and continue cooking for another 25 minutes or until the chicken is tender. Delicious when served with plain tagliatelle tossed in a little olive oil and lots of freshly chopped parsley.

* Other popular and delicious variations on this recipe are: the addition of 4 tsps of finely chopped capers (soaked in water to remove some of the vinegar) and 1 finely chopped anchovy fillet 10 minutes before the end of the cooking; the addition of two large finely sliced red or green peppers 15 minutes before the end of cooking; the addition of a generous handful of small green olives (previously rinsed in cold water) at the start of cooking the chicken pieces.

· CECI alla PISANA ·
Chickpea stew (4~6)

This is a hearty peasant stew that is even better cooked in advance, reheated and served in the same dish.

- 11 oz/300 G DRIED CHICKPEAS
- 2 LARGE RIPE TOMATOES, PEELED & CHOPPED
- 2 TBSP FRESH CHOPPED ROSEMARY
- 4~6 SLICES OF BREAD
- 2 LARGE TINNED SARDINES, WASHED UNDER RUNNING WATER & MASHED
- 1 MEDIUM ONION, FINELY CHOPPED
- 3 CLOVES GARLIC
- 11 oz/300 G BEET TOPS OR DARK GREEN CABBAGE
- OLIVE OIL
- COARSE SEA SALT
- FRESHLY GROUND BLACK PEPPER

Cover the chickpeas with water and soak overnight in a warm place. Drain, cover with fresh water, bring to boil and cook for 1½ hours or until tender. Drain, but keep the cooking liquid. Saute the onion, sardines and garlic in oil over medium heat in a heavy saucepan. Meanwhile briefly blanch the beet tops in some of the water used to cook the chickpeas. Remove the garlic (or not, as desired) from the onion and sardines and add the chickpeas, beet tops (with half a cup of their water), tomatoes, salt and pepper. Cook covered for about 3 hours on a low heat, adding several tablespoons of chickpea liquid if the stew seems to be drying out. Put a slice of grilled or toasted bread in each soup bowl, pour the stew over and serve with a jug of cold olive oil in which the rosemary has previously been heated for 10~15 minutes. A large bowl of bitter greens such as curly endive, chicory & dandelions makes a good accompaniment to this dish, especially if the greens are tossed with lemon juice and herb-flavoured olive oil.

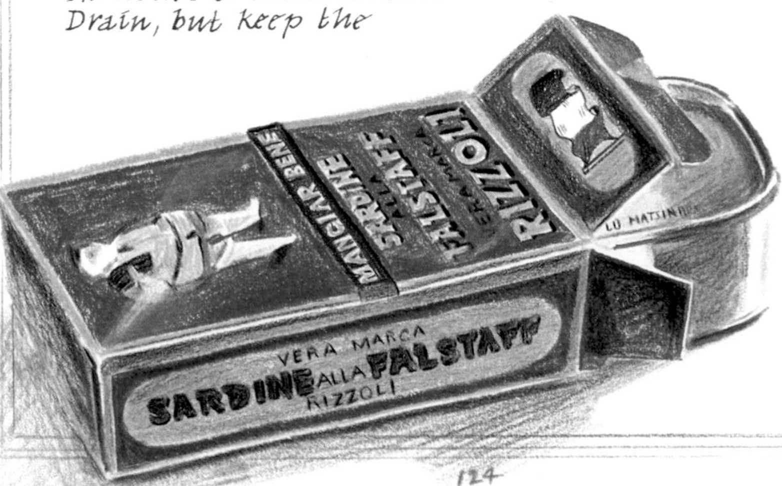

INSALATA di TONNO e PATATE

Tuna & potato salad (4)

The Tuscan salad of tuna and beans is not so much famous as infamous but when there are fresh white cannelloni beans available it is still a delicious summer dish. An alternative, suggested by a fishmonger in Pisa's market, is to substitute tiny new potatoes for the beans. He uses fresh tuna, barbecued over a chestnut fire, but the dish is still tasty when made with good tinned tuna.

8 SMALL NEW POTATOES
7 OZ/200 G TUNA FISH (IN OLIVE OIL)
1 MEDIUM RED ONION, SLICED PAPER THIN
2~3 TBSP WHITE WINE VINEGAR, TO TASTE
HANDFUL FINELY CHOPPED PARSLEY
1 CLOVE GARLIC, CRUSHED
4~5 TBSP OLIVE OIL
SALT & PEPPER

Boil the potatoes in their skins until tender but still firm. Cut in halves or quarters depending on their size. While still warm season with garlic, oil, vinegar and onions. Break up the tuna with a fork and add to the potatoes. Sprinkle with parsley and salt and pepper to taste.

***TONNO e FAGIOLI**
To make the classic bean salad, substitute 7oz/200g dried white beans for potatoes. Soak the beans overnight. Rinse and boil in fresh water until tender (1~1¼ hrs). Drain and follow the recipe above. If using fresh cannelloni beans boil in water for 40 minutes. This makes a lovely summer meal when served with chilled Pappa al Pomodoro.

· RISTORANTE · SERGIO ·

Sergio Lorenzi was not born a cook. Or perhaps he was just late in discovering his vocation. Although these days he is better with food, he worked first as a mechanic and still has a gruff straightforward manner that belies his rather more delicate touch in the kitchen. His lively and fashionable restaurant on the river Arno in Pisa is one of the best in the city, specializing in elegant versions of the local cuisine like 'Cee alla Pisana' (see page 140) and Trippa, spicy with nutmeg and fresh herbs. He serves (and sells) oil made from his own olives and swears it is some of the best in Tuscany for raw vegetables and salads because of the salty sea breezes that blow in from the coast.

ZUPPA del TARLATI VESCOVO

· Chicken soup · alla Bishop Tarlati (8~10)

Shortly after opening his own restaurant in 1976 Sergio wrote a cookbook with everything in it from tips on how to organise a good kitchen, to recipes retrieved from rare sixteenth-century notes found in a Tuscan library. Among the recipes was this one from Arezzo for Zuppa del Tarlati Vescovo which Bishop Tarlati may well have brought with him from the papal court in Avignon. Its creamy richness bears a close resemblance to the French 'Soupe à la Reine'.

2 OZ/50 G BUTTER
2 OZ/50 G PLAIN WHITE FLOUR
3½ PT/2 LTRS GOOD CHICKEN STOCK
2½ LB/1.3 KG BOILING CHICKEN
1 ONION, COARSELY CHOPPED
1 STICK CELERY & LEAVES, COARSELY CHOPPED
½ TSP WHOLE PEPPERCORNS
3~4 CLOVES
2 BAY LEAVES
100 G DOUBLE CREAM
4 PIECES OF BREAD, CUT IN HALF & TOASTED OR FRIED IN OIL
SALT

In a heavy saucepan, melt the butter and mix in the flour to make a roux. Very slowly add the chicken stock, stirring well with a wooden spoon to avoid lumps. Bring slowly to a boil, still stirring. In the meantime wash the chicken and stuff with the onion, celery, peppercorns, cloves and bayleaves. Sew up the cavity to prevent anything escaping. Put the chicken in the broth already prepared and simmer for 45 minutes to an hour. Take the chicken out, remove skin and chop the breast meat finely. Pound the thigh meat into a paste in a mortar and mix thoroughly with the cream. Skim the original broth and add slowly to the mixture to obtain a smooth velvety soup. Stir in the breast meat, salt to taste, reheat and serve over the bread.

MINESTRA di PESCE

· Fish soup (4~6) ·

Sergio originally comes from Camaiore, between Lucca and Viareggio, an area that probably has more soup recipes per square mile than anywhere in Tuscany. This is one for a fish soup that unlike Caccinco, is very simple to prepare. A speciality of the trawling fishermen of the river Serchio, it should, if

(continued...)

(continued...)
possible, have eel in it to make a good traditional soup.

- 1½ LB/700G SALT WATER FISH (ANCHOVIES, BRILL ETC) CLEANED & CUT INTO LARGE CHUNKS
- 11 OZ/300G FRESH-WATER FISH (EEL, TROUT ETC) CLEANED & CUT INTO LARGE CHUNKS
- 3~4 CLOVES GARLIC, CRUSHED
- HANDFUL ROUGHLY CHOPPED FRESH PARSLEY
- 1 ONION, CHOPPED
- 1 STICK CELERY, CHOPPED
- 1 CARROT, CHOPPED
- 2 TOMATOES, CHOPPED
- PEEL OF 1 LEMON
- RIND (LEFTOVER) OF PECORINO OR PARMESAN CHEESE
- 6 TBSP OLIVE OIL
- SALT & PEPPER

In 3½ pints/1½ litres water boil the onion, carrot, celery, tomatoes, lemon peel and cheese rind for about 20 minutes. In the meantime put the oil and garlic in a large heavy pan until the garlic slightly browns. Add the chopped parsley and stir 2 or 3 times, then add the fish. Brown slightly on both sides, then add to the broth and continue to boil for about 20 minutes. Ad~just salt and pepper and put everything through a food processor or vegetable mill (not too fine as the soup should have a chunky texture). Pour the soup into a tureen into which you have put 2 large slices of bread fried in oil & rubbed with garlic.

SORBETTO al VINO ROSSO con PROFUMO di LAMPONE

Red wine sorbet with raspberries (4~6)

Like so many other excellent ideas, the making of fresh fruit sorbets was invented in Tuscany, taken to France in the sixteenth century and made famous there. However, it still remains a very Italian skill. At Sergio's a light sorbet like this one is often served between courses to provide a refreshing pause, particularly between dishes of fish and meat.

- 1 PINT/½ LTR YOUNG RED WINE, PREFERABLY FIZZY
- 7 OZ/200 G FRESH RASPBERRIES, SLIGHTLY CRUSHED
- 5 OZ/150 G SUGAR
- 5~6 FRESH MINT LEAVES (AND MORE FOR GARNISH)

Boil the sugar, mint leaves and wine together for 2 minutes or until the sugar is dissolved. Add to the raspberries and allow to sit for at least 1 hour, stirring occasionally. Remove the mint and put the mixture through a food processor. Freeze in an ice tray in the freezer (normal ice~making setting) for about 3 hours, stirring frequently until no more ice crystals form. Serve with more mint leaves (dipped in sugar & water, then frozen) as a garnish.

A variation on this basic red wine sorbet is to add the finely grated peel (using only the outside skin, not the white pith) of ½ an orange or ½ a lemon just before freezing. Or, for a more delicately coloured sorbet, use one of the new pale Tuscan rosés or spumante-style sparkling wines instead of the red wine suggested, and white seedless grapes instead of the raspberries.

· DA ROMANO ·

Walk around the rather seedy streets of Viareggio now and it is possible to chart the gradual decline over the decades of this once grand old dame of Italian coastal resorts. Her heyday was the turn of the century when most of the still remarkably beautiful Art Nouveau hotels and casinos were built. Then came the slightly less elegant, but still sleek 1920s and 1930s, with their ocean liner facades and Art Deco neon signs. Then, finally, the inevitable 1960's and 1970's plasticized consumerism. Viareggio today is more deserving of a place in her own outrageous spring carnival than in a polite drawing room. But if the pearls are a bit tarnished, the oysters and clams are still fresh, and it is possible to find hidden in the back-streets some of the best fish restaurants in Tuscany. One is Romano Franceschini's, where he and his wife Franca, who is the cook, serve excellent versions of local seafood specialities.

SPAGHETTI al CARTOCCIO

Spaghetti with seafood cooked in a bag (4)

This is one of Franca's special recipes. When the 'cartoccio' is opened at the table it gives off a delicious aroma that is one of the highlights of the dish.

11 OZ/300 G SPAGHETTI
20 BABY SQUID, CLEANED *
4 GIANT PRAWNS
10 BABY CLAMS, CLEANED
8 LARGE CLAMS, CLEANED
6 MUSSELS, CLEANED
1 RED MULLET, CLEANED & BONED
1 CLOVE GARLIC, CRUSHED
6~8 BASIL LEAVES
6 TBSP OLIVE OIL
4 RIPE TOMATOES, PEELED, SEEDED & FINELY CHOPPED
1/4 CHILI PEPPER, FINELY CHOPPED
2 TBSP PARSLEY, FINELY CHOPPED
SALT

Put 5 PT/3 LTR water in a large saucepan and bring to the boil. Meanwhile heat the oil in a cast-iron pan and in it cook the chili, garlic and all the fish. After 5~10 minutes, add the tomatoes, basil and parsley. Cook over a low heat for another 5~10 minutes. When the water in the big pot is boiling add salt and the spaghetti. When half cooked, drain and add to the fish. Adjust seasoning. Take a large piece of aluminum foil and fold it in half. Open it out flat and place on a large plate or serving dish. Put the fish and spaghetti on half the foil. Fold the edges of the foil together on all three sides so no juices or steam can escape. Place the dish in an oven preheated to 475°F/250°C/Gas 9 for 5 minutes or until the foil puffs up. Take immediately to the table and serve.

* To clean clams & mussels, scrub the shells with a stiff brush under cold running water until clean. Cut off the mussels' beards (the stringy tufts that protrude from the shells) and discard any of the shellfish that are not tightly

(continued...)

Le Penne
martelli
artigiani pastai
caponi caponi
Pasta all'uovo
PASTA ALL'UOVO
PENNE
PAPPARDELLE
RAVIOLI ROLLING PIN

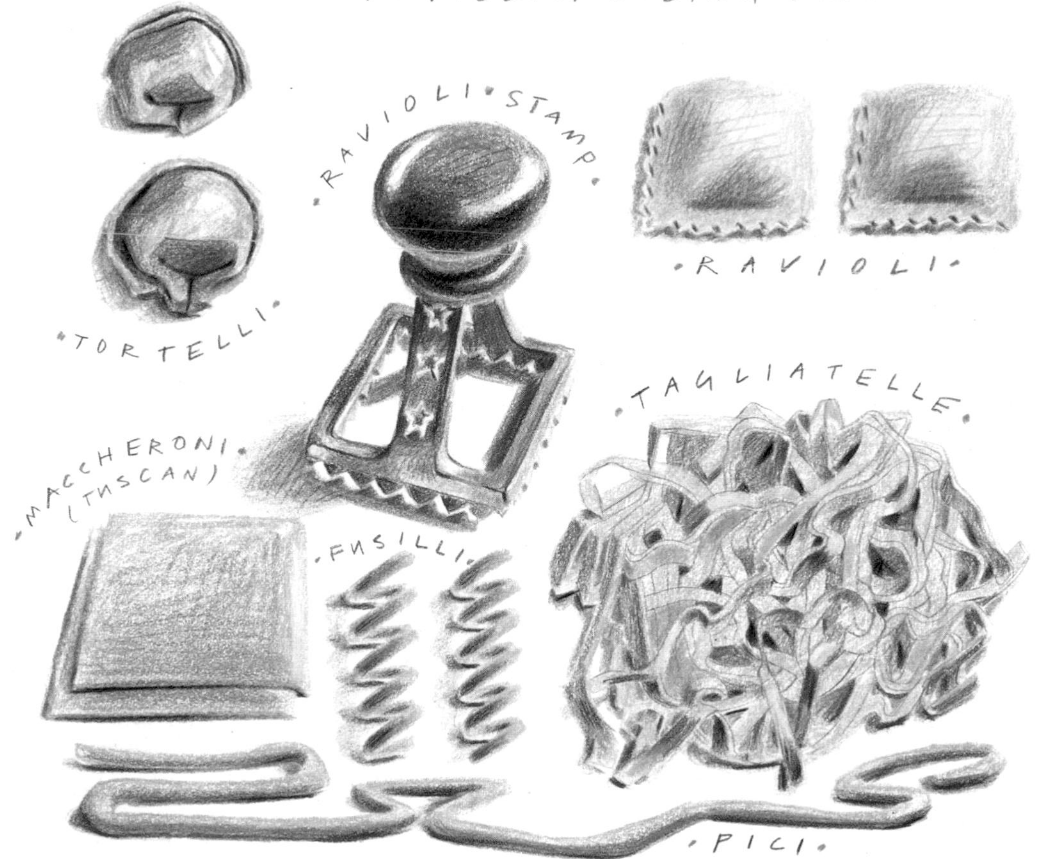
TORTELLI
RAVIOLI STAMP
RAVIOLI
TAGLIATELLE
MACCHERONI (TUSCAN)
FUSILLI
PICI

(continued from previous page...)

closed, or rather that do not close up again when lightly tapped. Continue to rinse the shellfish under running water until no more sand or grit appears.

ROMBO al FORNO con ASPARAGI

• Turbot baked with asparagus (6) •

This is another of Franca Franceschini's modern adaptations of a regional fish dish.

1 LB 12 OZ/800G TURBOT
6 SCAMPI
1 OZ/20 G BUTTER
2 TBSP OIL
20 ASPARAGUS TIPS
2 WINE GLASSES FISH STOCK
SALT & PEPPER

Clean & wash the turbot. Shell the scampi & remove the black intestinal track but not the heads. Pat fish dry and flour lightly, only flouring the white part of the turbot. Arrange the fish in a greased baking dish with the asparagus tips, salt & freshly ground black pepper. Dot with butter and pour over the oil & about 2 wine glasses of good fish stock. Bake in an oven preheated to 400°F/200°C/Gas 6 for 20 minutes. Serve hot.

*Make good fish stock by boiling together the following ingredients: 4 or 5 fish heads, ½ onion, 1 bay leaf, 1 stick celery, 5 peppercorns, 1 tsp sea salt, 1 clove garlic, 5 wine glasses water & 5 tbsp dry white wine. After 20 minutes, remove the bay leaf & pass other ingredients through a food processor or mouli.

MARTINELLI
MARTINELLI
UMBRELLA CASES
OFF SEASON
· VIAREGGIO ·

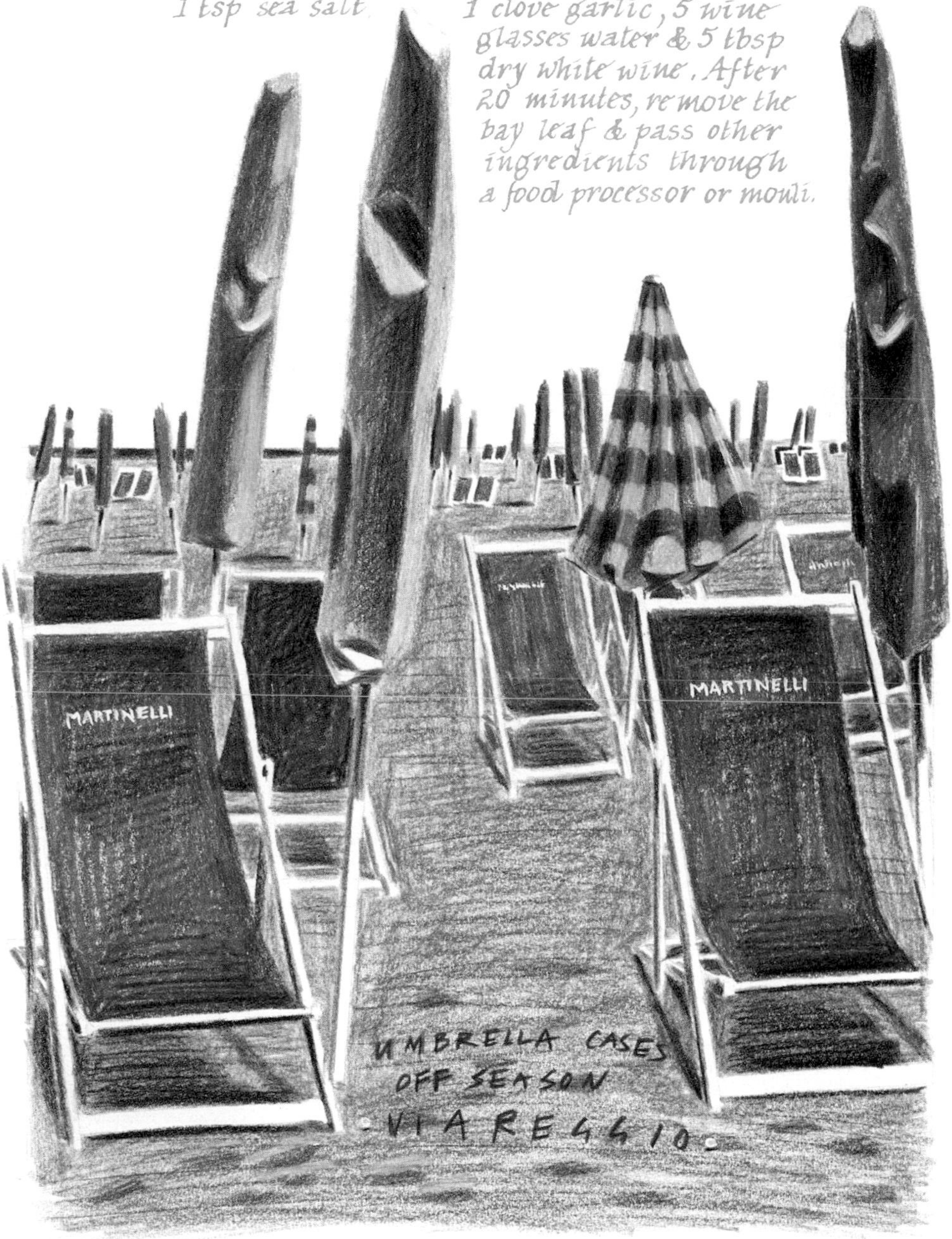

· THE CERRAGIOLI FAMILY ·

Drive up into the hills between Camaiore and Lucca and keep going until you run out of road. If you have taken the right road you will probably be at the village of Greppolungo. Park your car and walk to the only alimentari shop there. You will find Paulo Cerragioli and his wife selling their own excellent olive oil and, if you are lucky and have had the sense to ring before hand, they will be ready and willing to cook you an excellent meal. They serve only a few dishes, and theirs is the real 'casalinga' ~ the home cooking that is almost impossible to find in restaurants.

LA GALLINA RIPIENA
Stuffed chicken (6)

This recipe for stuffed boiled chicken is one of the best and most typical of the Camaiore area. At Greppolungo they splash rough red wine into the chicken broth just before serving, an interesting Tuscan variation on sherry in consommé.

1 LARGE BOILING FOWL WITH GIBLETS
2 CARROTS
1 STICK CELERY
1 ONION
SALT
1 LEEK
OLIVE OIL

FOR THE STUFFING

2 SLICES HAM OR MORTADELLA SAUSAGE, CHOPPED
2 SPRIGS FRESH THYME, CHOPPED
3 SLICES BREAD, SOAKED IN MILK
6 TBSP PECORINO CHEESE, GRATED
8 OZ/225 G GROUND (MINCED) VEAL OR LEAN BEEF
1 ~ 2 EGGS
2 CLOVES GARLIC, CRUSHED
4 TBSP OLIVE OIL
3 TBSP PARSLEY, FINELY CHOPPED
½ ~ ¾ TSP NUTMEG

First make the stuffing. In a large frying pan gently cook the chicken giblets in the oil until they change colour. Chop finely and reserve. Add the sausage, meat and garlic to the pan and cook just until the meat starts to brown. Mix with the giblets, herbs, bread, cheese and 1 beaten egg. If this does not bind the stuffing, add another beaten egg.

Clean, wash and dry the inside of the chicken. Pack loosely with the stuffing ~ the stuffing tends to swell in cooking and you don't want an exploding chicken. Sew up both ends of the chicken so that nothing can escape. Put in a large flame~proof casserole with the carrots, celery, onion, leek and salt and cover with water. The water should be about 1in/2.5cm over the chicken. Bring to a boil and then simmer over a low heat for about 2½ hours, until the chicken is cooked. Remove it from the pan, cut the threads, carefully lift out the stuffing, which should be quite solid, and serve both the chicken and the stuffing sliced thinly and garnished with either fresh thyme or Tuscan salsa verde (see page 75). To make a complete meal of this, remove the vegetables from the broth and boil fresh tortellini or ravioli gnudi (page 78) in it to serve as soup before the chicken.

· PONTE DI SASSO ·

Of course Caccincco is a Mediterranean fish soup, originally from Livorno, as the Livornese will proudly tell you; and the cooks in Viareggio will disdainfully say that no good ever came from Livorno, and certainly not Caccincco. Its a subject for endless, inconclusive debates. Certainly one of the best versions of caccincco must be that served at the Ponte di Sasso restaurant outside Camaiore. A good caccincco is a joy to behold, like fine wine first enjoy its rich colour, then its bouquet and finally the time the rich flavour remains on the tongue.

· CACCIUCCO ·

Fish soup (6)

Caccincco is a poor man's dish, at least theoretically, so most of the fish should be cheap, saltwater scaled ones ~ not salmon or sole! There should also be at least five different types of fish, preferably more. Franco, the brilliant chef at Ponte di Sasso, used twelve.

10 LB 10 OZ/5 KG ~½ ORDINARY SCALED FISH SUCH AS DOGFISH, NON BONY PIECES OF EEL, ½ A MIXTURE OF SQUID, CUTTLEFISH, OCTOPUS, SHRIMP, CLAMS AND MUSSELS
3 CLOVES GARLIC, CRUSHED
4 TBSP TOMATO PUREE
2 TBSP RED WINE VINEGAR
4 TBSP FRESH PARSLEY, CHOPPED
SMALL HOT CHILI PEPPERS (1~2)
½ BOTTLE ROBUST RED WINE (DRY)
6 PIECES WHOLEMEAL BREAD
2~3 TOMATOES, PEELED AND CHOPPED ROUGHLY
COARSE SEA SALT
BLACK PEPPER, FRESHLY GROUND
OLIVE OIL

Clean and scale the fish, cut off and save the heads and tails for stock. Remove the beak and insides of the squid and the cuttlefish's ink sac. (Your fishmonger may do this for you if you ask, but be sure that you ask him for the heads and tails.) Put the fish heads and tails, 1 clove garlic, 2 tbsp parsley, the tomatoes and tomato puree in a large pan with 1 pint/600 ml of water and bring to the boil. Cover and simmer for 20 minutes.

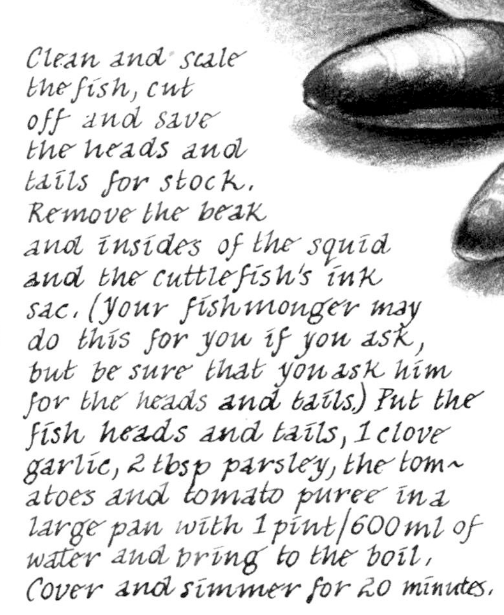

Discard the fish heads and tails. Add the fish, beginning with the boniest variety (ask your fishmonger's advice), cover and simmer for 20 minutes. Rub through a sieve and continue cooking the various more tender fish for a further 15 minutes. Meanwhile, saute the other two crushed cloves of garlic in a large pan. When just turning brown add salt, chili pepper, pepper and remaining parsley. Put in the shellfish, squid and cuttlefish and when the water they release has evaporated, add the vinegar. Swirl around the pan and pour in the red wine. When this has almost evaporated add the extra tomatoes (if desired) and continue cooking for 15 minutes. Toast the bread, rub thoroughly with fresh garlic and put in bowls. Pour the rest of the fish, in their rich tomato sauce, over the top. Serve immediately.

Cacciucco is meant to be a complete meal in a dish rather than just a first course. It should be served with plenty of crusty bread and look more like a hearty fish stew than a soup, its wide variety of fish and crustaceans only just covered by a thick binding of hot and garlicky sauce.

· POLENTA MATUFFI ·

Sausage & polenta stew (6)

This is a sturdy, old-fashioned peasant dish, redolent of cheese and spicy sausages. It should be eaten with a spoon and a minimum of good table manners, and of course plenty of equally

(continued...)

In Viareggio there is a tradition that in addition to the healthy quantity of whiting, hake, red mullet, John Dory, gurnard and crawfish, a good cacciucco should always contain one stone from the ocean. Perhaps this is because cacciucco is a dish that was eaten originally only by Tuscan fishermen. Whatever they scooped up with their nets and lines went in the cooking pot.

Although the origins of cacciucco are thus very humble, it can be made as elegant as the fish used. The only absolutely essential ingredient (apart from the stone) is the hot chili pepper.

(continued from previous page.) sturdy young red wine should be available to wash it down.

- 1 LB 2 OZ/500 G FINE GRAIN CORN MEAL, SIFTED
- 6 BIG LEAN TUSCAN SAUSAGES
- 1/4 PT/120 ML OLIVE OIL
- 2 LB 2 OZ/1 KG TOMATOES, PEELED AND CHOPPED
- 3/4 OZ/15 G DRIED MUSHROOMS, SOAKED FOR AT LEAST 10 MINUTES IN WARM WATER, DRAINED & CHOPPED
- 1 SMALL CARROT, CHOPPED
- 1 SMALL STICK CELERY, CHOPPED
- 1 ONION, CHOPPED
- BAY LEAF
- 1/2 BOTTLE RED WINE
- GENEROUS QUANTITIES OF GRATED PECORINO OR PARMESAN
- SALT & PEPPER

Heat the oil in a medium-sized saucepan. Saute the carrot, onion and celery in it until softened. Mash the sausages with a fork, add to the pan and brown with the vegetables. Skim off 1/2 the fat (if there is any) and add the red wine. When it has almost evaporated add the mushrooms. Brown and put in the tomatoes and bay leaf. Simmer gently for 20 minutes. Meanwhile bring 1 3/4 pt/1 ltr of salted water to the boil in a large pan. Add the corn meal very slowly, stirring constantly with a wooden spoon to prevent lumps forming. Continue cooking and stirring for 20 minutes. Then put a ladleful of polenta into each bowl, followed by a ladleful of sauce & lots of cheese. Continue in layers with each bowl until the sauce is finished.

· IL GIARDINETTO ·

Scarpaccia is a zucchini pie without pastry from the region around Camaiore. At the beautiful Art Nouveau hotel Il Giardinetto in northern Tuscany they serve a delicious version called Torta di Zucchini, as well as another delicious Tuscan side dish, Panzerotti. These are golf~ball size pieces of raw bread dough that are wrapped around chunks of cooked sausage or pecorino cheese and then deep~fried to a crisp golden brown and sprinkled with coarse sea~salt.

SCARPACCIA
Zucchini pie (6)

The name Scarpaccia means 'old, flat battered shoe' and refers to the fact that the pie should have a similar appearance. There are two versions, a sweet one somewhat like Lucca's Torta di Verdure (page 148) and this savoury one, an ideal side dish with summer roasts and salads.

- 14 OZ / 400G SMALLEST ZUCCHINI / COURGETTES (WITH THEIR FLOWERS IF POSSIBLE)
- 3 LARGE SPRING ONIONS, FINELY CHOPPED
- 1/2 CLOVE GARLIC, CRUSHED
- 1/2 CUP MILK & WATER, MIXED
- 4 TBSP FLOUR, SIFTED
- 2 EGGS
- 4 TBSP GRATED PARMESAN
- SALT & PEPPER
- OLIVE OIL

Finely chop the zucchini. Salt them and allow to drain for 20 minutes. In the meantime, beat together the eggs, flour, milk and water to form a smooth batter. Rinse salt off the zucchini and dry with kitchen paper towels. Mix the zucchini, onions, cheese and garlic into the batter and pour into 2 greased 8in / 20.5cm baking tins. (You can use 1 large one, but the batter should not be more than 1/2 in / 1cm deep.) Drizzle several tablespoons of olive oil on top and bake in an oven preheated to 425°F / 220°C / Gas 7 until set and golden brown on top ~ about 30 minutes. Serve with more grated cheese on top if desired.

· CEE alla PISANA ·

Probably the most famous dish in Pisa is 'Cee alla Pisana'. Cee is Tuscan slang for 'cieche' meaning blind, and also for the tiny baby eels ('elvers' in England) that are caught at the mouth of the Arno during the winter months. In Pisa the eels (4 oz/100g per person), are first washed several times and dried very well. Then they are put into a frying pan with lots of very hot oil in which have been browned 2 cloves of garlic, 3~4 sage leaves and ½ hot chili pepper finely chopped. The little eels, no more than 3in/7.5cm long, are stirred rapidly for about 15 minutes until they turn white, then mixed with 2 beaten eggs, the juice of a lemon and 3 tablespoons grated parmesan. This is stirred until just barely set and served still creamy, looking rather like spaghetti carbonara.

OLIVES & CHESTNUTS
GARFAGNANA
SERCHIO
BARGA
BAGNI di LUCCA
PISTOIA
PESCIA
PONTE a MORIANO
COLLODI
MONTECATINI TERME
LUCCA
MONTECARLO
PISA
RESTAURANTS
Lucca · da Giulio in Pelleria · Vipore ·
PESCIA · Cecco ·
PONTE A MORIANO ·
Trattoria La Mora ·
SIGHTS
BAGNI DI LUCCA · Victorian spa ·
BARGA · mountain top town ·
LUCCA · medieval city ·
PISTOIA · sculpture

• INTRODUCTION •

The Garfagnana and Pistoian mountains, high foot~hills of the rugged Appennines, are divided lengthwise by the river Serchio. Tiny villages, where rocks hold red roof tiles in place, cling perilously to steep hillsides, their bars and outdoor cafes dropping away to the valleys below. Because this is a relatively poor region of Tuscany, the best cooking makes good use of available local products ~ trout fresh from the rivers, porcini the size of t~bone steaks and a stunning variety of other wild mushrooms, simple flat cakes made with sweet chestnut flour and smeared with honey and creamy ricotta cheese, and everywhere near Lucca, the famous Luccan olive oil, considered the best in the world.

Perhaps because of its remoteness and its history of poverty, the wild Garfagnana region north of Lucca remains unspoilt, in fact almost undiscovered, by the tourists that have overrun the Tuscan coast. Hill towns like beautiful Barga, with steep cobbled streets and honey~coloured buildings, have sweeping views of pine forests, castles and distant snowy mountains. West of Barga, straggling along rivers a startling shade of turquoise, are towns whose streets rise almost vertically from the river bank into high mountain fields. During World War 2 many of these moun~tain villages were havens for the Italian resistance, their remoteness making them almost impossible for the government troops to control. Memories of those war years are still fresh and many stories are told in the bars of escaped prisoners hidden for months in cellars or shepherds' huts.

On the southernmost edge of the Garfagnana moun~tains lies walled Lucca, birthplace of the opera composer Giacomo Puccini, and the only city in Tuscany to resist Florence successfully. It remained an indep~endant city state until becoming part of the Grand Duchy of Tuscany in the nineteenth century and even today preserves an air of aloofness.

Lucca, with Siena, is one of the loveliest small cities in Italy. The poverty of the Garfagnana seems not to have penetrated the massive sixteenth~century walls. John Ruskin, writing in the nineteenth century, claimed to have begun his study of architecture after seeing Lucca's beautifully preserved twelfth-century buildings, built '... in material so incorruptible, that after 600 years of sunshine & rain, a lancet could not now be put between their joints.' Narrow medieval streets between these buildings lead quietly to huge windy piazzas and past elaborate Romanesque churches like tiered marble wedding cakes.

From the plane tree-shaded pathway that tops the city walls living trees growing on the high tower of the Palazzo Guinigi are clearly visible, as are private and public gardens hidden from city streets by the red brick facades of palaces built during the fourteenth and fifteenth centuries ~ Lucca's richest period. The Palazzo Pfanner is one of the most elegant with symmetrical rows of white marble statues and lemon trees in terracotta pots, but it cannot match for splendour the summer palaces outside Lucca, built by Lucchese nobility between the sixteenth and eighteenth centuries. Three of them, Villa Imperiale at Marlia, Villa Mansi at Segromigno & Villa Torrigiani at Camigliano, lie in magnificent gardens in cool hills to the north of the city. At the Villa Imperiale, summer residence of Napoleon's sister Elisa Baciocchi, Paganini (said to have been one of her many lovers) gave his first musical performance.

It is not only Lucca's past that is attractive. Like Siena the city is famous for its sweet breads and pastries, and where better to sample them than sitting in one of the many sunny cafes, set in flowered courtyards, distracted only by the occasional (and inevitable) moped buzzing past?

·PALAZZO·PFANNER·
144

· LUCCA ·

Lucca is an elegant little city rather than a town and the pleasures to be enjoyed there are naturally rather more sophisticated than in the villages of the Garfagnana. The lovely, well~preserved turn~of~the~century shop fronts and signs are particularly pleasing. If you're exploring the city walls on a hot day, a glass of the local white wine, Montecarlo Buonamico, at the beautiful Antico Caffe della Mura, is a certain reviver. Or, in less auspicious weather, find your way to Puccini's favourite cafe, Cafe di Simo, for cups of frothy cappucino and Torta di Verdure, Lucca's great speciality.

· TORTA di VERDURE ·
Sweet spinach pie

This sweet is sold in most of Lucca's delicatessans & tastes something like a Tuscan version of American pumpkin pie.

FOR THE PASTRY

11 oz/300g PLAIN WHITE FLOUR
3¼ oz/80g SUGAR
4 oz/100g BUTTER, SOFTENED
2 EGG YOLKS
PINCH SALT

· FOR THE FILLING

7oz/200g ZUCCHINI/COURGETTES
11 oz/300g SPINACH OR SWISS CHARD
3 oz/75g SUGAR
2 oz/50 g PINE NUTS
1¼ oz/30 g RAISINS
1 EGG, BEATEN
2 TBSP GRATED ORANGE PEEL
2 TBSP GRATED PARMESAN
½ TSP CINNAMON
½ TSP NUTMEG
PINCH SALT
1~1¼ oz/25~30 g BUTTER

To make the pastry, sift the flour on to a pastryboard or work~surface. Make a hole in the middle and put in the butter, sugar, salt and egg yolks. Work into a soft smooth dough with your fingertips. Cover and leave for 2 hours in a warm place.

To make the filling, first chop the zucchini and spinach finely, discarding any tough stalks. Wash and drain well, then simmer in the butter until soft. Let cool and then mix well with the other ingredients.

When the dough is ready, cut off about a quarter and keep aside to make a lattice top for the pie. Roll the remainder out into a large circle and place in a greased, floured flan dish. Pour in the filling. Roll out the remaining pastry and cut into strips for the lattice top. Brush with beaten egg yolk and bake for 25~30 minutes in an oven preheated to 375°F/190°C/Gas 5 (until a toothpick put into the centre of the pie comes out dry).

DA GIULIO IN PELLERIA

Lucca and olives are synonymous. In fact some gastronomes consider the delicate Luccan olive oils to be among the world's best, although there is stiff competition from i colli senesi oils ~ the green gold of the hills around Siena. When the olives are plump and ideal for eating, they are pickled with lemon, cinnamon, salt and hot chili peppers ~ a particular speciality at the Ristorante Vipore, west of Lucca. Or else they are used to add bite to fatty rabbit or lamb stews, as in the recipe below.

AGNELLO con OLIVE NERE

Lamb and black olive stew (4~6)

Variations on this recipe are served in many of the restaurants of the area, but it is particularly good at the Buca di San Antonio as well as at the little cafe Da Giulio, both in the back streets of Lucca.

You can give this dish something of the tang provided by fresh olives if you add a tablespoon of grated lemon peel during the cooking.

- 2 LB 2 OZ / 1 KG STEWING LAMB
- 14 OZ / 400 G RIPE TOMATOES, PEELD & SEEDED
- 30 PLUMP BLACK OLIVES (OR MORE ACCORDING TO TASTE)
- 6~8 TBSP OLIVE OIL
- 2 SPRIGS FRESH ROSEMARY
- 2 (GENEROUS) WINE GLASSES OF DRY WHITE WINE
- 2 CLOVES GARLIC, CRUSHED
- SEA SALT
- BLACK PEPPER

Put the oil in a big frying pan and gently cook the garlic and rosemary. When the garlic is golden add the lamb cut in bite size chunks and brown it. Add the wine and when it has almost evaporated, the tomatoes (and the lemon peel if desired). Stir, cover and cook over a low heat for 15 minutes. If using fresh olives boil them for several minutes; if using pickled ones (tinned, bottled etc) rinse them well. Add to the lamb, cover and cook very slowly until the meat is tender, about 1½ hours, adding warm water or stock if the stew seems to be drying out. For a less rich stew skim off any visible fat that rises during cooking. Serve poured over polenta or with tiny boiled potatoes to soak up the sauce.

* When buying olive oil, be sure to get 'cold pressed extra virgin' from the first pressing. It is the best, expensive even in Italy, but well worth the price. Olive oils are classed by their acidity level; the less acidic they are, the better and more costly. During oil-pressing time (Nov-Feb) around Lucca you may come across a soup called 'Zuppa alla Frantoiana' or 'oil-press soup'. It is basically a form of Ribollita. Where Ribollita is usually yesterday's minestrone re-heated today, Zuppa alla Frantoiana has zucchini, carrots, celery, onions and cabbage cooked freshly, mixed with pre-cooked beans & ham, & served with a jug of the newly pressed olive oil.

some of 'La Cucina' Povera' ~ dishes that might have otherwise disappeared, if not from Tuscan homes, at least from Tuscan restaur~ ant menus.

· GRAN FARRO ·

Grain and bean soup (4)

Gran Farro is traditional wheat soup made in Tuscany from raw spelt (hard wheat) but if unavailable you can make a similar soup using buckwheat (kasha) boiled for about an hour.

- 5 OZ/150 G RAW SPELT OR GERMAN WHEAT, BOILED FOR AT LEAST 3 HOURS
- 9 OZ/250 G DRIED OR 1 LB 6 OZ/600 G FRESH KIDNEY BEANS
- ½ ONION, SLICED THINLY
- 3 TBSP OLIVE OIL
- STICK CELERY, DICED WITH LEAVES
- CLOVE GARLIC, CRUSHED
- 4 OZ/100 G PROSCIUTTO OR FATTY HAM, FINELY CHOPPED
- 8 OZ/225 G TOMATOES, PEELED, SEEDED & FINELY SIEVED
- 3~4 SAGE LEAVES
- 1 TSP MARJORAM
- ½ TSP NUTMEG
- SALT & PEPPER

TRATTORIA LA MORA

Some restaurants serve food. Others serve atmos~ phere ~ a taste of a place, of its people, its countryside and its history. Sauro Brun~ icardi's Trattoria La Mora, north of Lucca, is one of these. The wine (from his own enoteca) is excel~ lent, the food delicious and creative, but almost more important is the warmth & generosity of Signor Brunicardi and his staff. Sauro Brunicardi is one of the small group of Italian restauranteurs who in 1980 formed 'La Linea Italia in Cucina' to pre~ serve the traditional reg~ ional cooking of Italy, and to serve carefully researched and prepared dishes from their own areas. As a result of this fidelity to tradition, with additional ingenuity because not all traditional food is necessarily good, it is still possible to find

Boil fresh beans in water until tender (about 1~1½ hrs). If using dried beans, soak them overnight, rinse and then boil in fresh water for about 45 minutes. Drain and put through a food processor or mouli, reserving the water & ¼ of the whole beans. Heat the oil in a deep saucepan & add the onion, ham, celery, garlic, sage, marjoram and nutmeg. Saute gently and when the onion starts to brown, add the tomatoes, salt and pepper to taste. Simmer for about 15 minutes until the mixture is well blended. Add the bean puree with a little of its own water. Mix well before adding the wheat. Simmer for about 40 minutes, adding more bean water if the soup seems to be drying out. About 10 minutes before the end of this time, add the whole beans and allow to heat through. Serve with a jug of olive oil to pour over.

GARMUGIA alla LUCCHESE

· Spring vegetable ·
soup as made in Lucca (6)

This is a soup made only in the spring when the tiniest fresh vegetables are available. The cooking times given are approximate ~ the vegetables should be just barely cooked and served while they are still a bright clear green.

4 SPRING ONIONS, FINELY CHOPPED
1LB 2OZ/500G GROUND (MINCED) LEAN BEEF
4 OZ/100G PROSCIUTTO OR BACON
7OZ/200G FRESH BROAD BEANS, SHELLED
TENDER LEAVES FROM 3 ARTICHOKES, TRIMMED
9OZ/250G FRESH PEAS, SHELLED
2 CLOVES GARLIC
7OZ/200G TENDER ASPARAGUS, CHOPPED
3~4 CUPS BEEF STOCK
5 TBSP OLIVE OIL
SALT & PEPPER

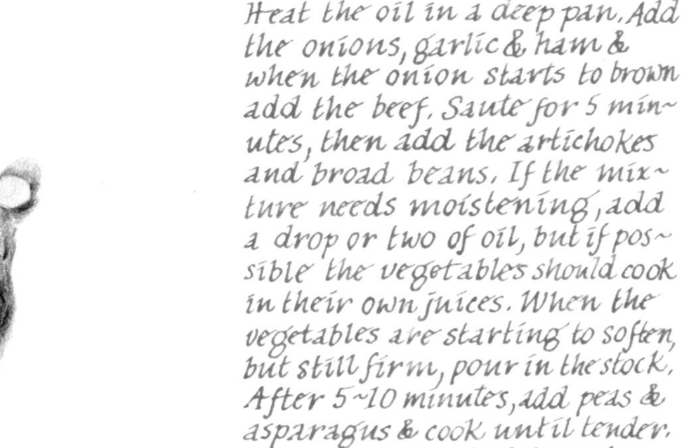

Heat the oil in a deep pan. Add the onions, garlic & ham & when the onion starts to brown add the beef. Saute for 5 minutes, then add the artichokes and broad beans. If the mixture needs moistening, add a drop or two of oil, but if possible the vegetables should cook in their own juices. When the vegetables are starting to soften, but still firm, pour in the stock. After 5~10 minutes, add peas & asparagus & cook until tender. Serve over toasted bread.

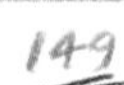

CRESPELLE alla FIORENTINA

Spinach crepes

This dish is of questionable Tuscan origin, but Beppe the chef makes crepes with such verve and expertise it would be a pity to leave them out. You can toss the pancakes if you do not possess the asbestos fingertips needed to turn them by hand as Beppe does.

FOR THE BATTER

- 3½ OZ/90 G PLAIN WHITE FLOUR
- 3 EGGS, BEATEN
- 2 WINEGLASSES MILK
- SALT
- OIL

FOR THE FILLING

- 14 OZ/400 G RICOTTA
- 1 LB 6 OZ/600 G FRESH SPINACH
- 1 EGG, BEATEN
- ½ TSP NUTMEG
- SALT
- FRESHLY GROUND BLACK PEPPER

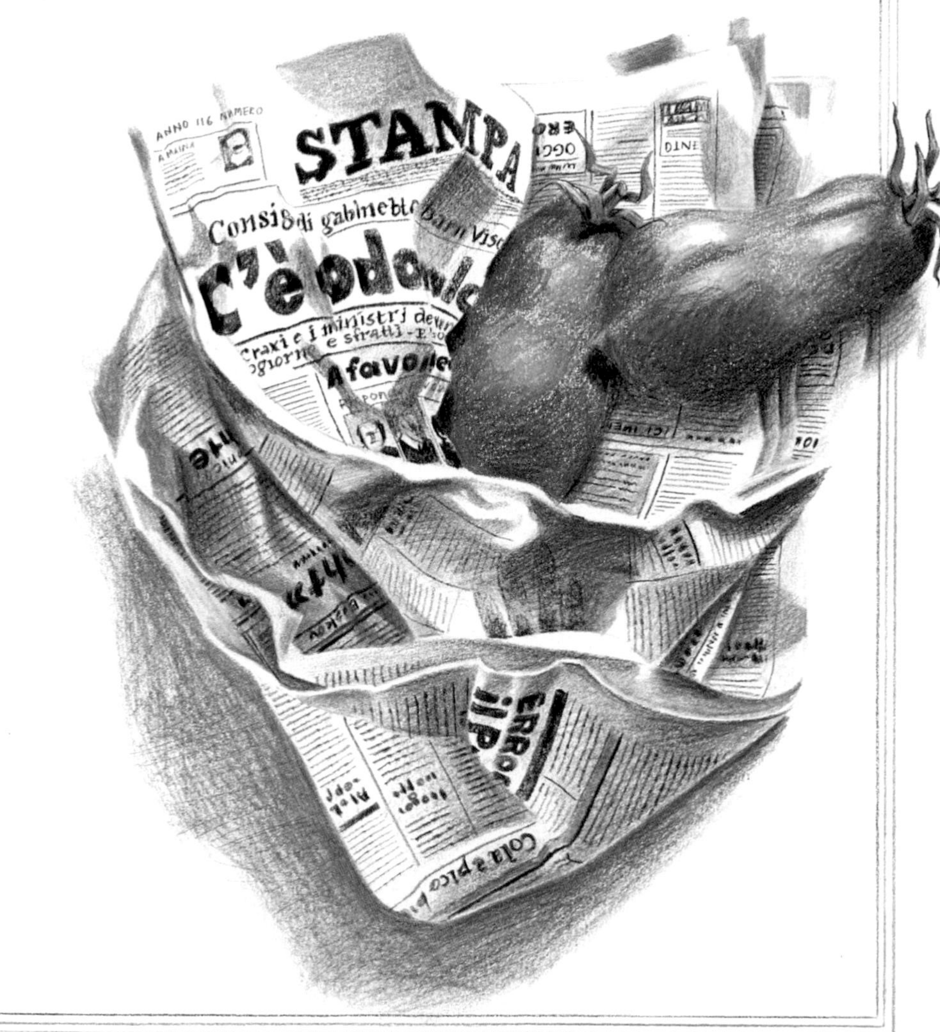

· FOR THE SAUCE ·

- 3 OZ/75 G FLOUR PLAIN WHITE
- 3 OZ/75 G BUTTER
- 1¼ PT/¾ LTR MILK
- SALT & PEPPER
- 5 TBSP OF A HOMEMADE TOMATO SAUCE (AS A GARNISH) OR 3 VERY TASTY TOMATOES, PEELED, SEEDED & FINELY CHOPPED
- 3 TBSP GRATED PECORINO OR PARMESAN CHEESE

To make the filling, trim & clean spinach, remove any tough stalks and cook, covered, in a little water until tender. Drain well through a fine-mesh sieve or strainer, pressing with the back of a wooden spoon to get out all the water. Chop very finely and mix with the other ingredients.

To make the sauce, melt the butter in a pan, add the flour and once blended with the fat, cook for a few minutes over a low heat. Add the milk gradually, stirring all the time to prevent lumps forming. When all the milk has been added, raise the temperature and bring sauce to the boil. Cook for 2~3 minutes, continuing to stir. Remove from the heat and add salt and black pepper to taste.

To make the crepes, sift the flour into a basin, make a well in the middle and put in the eggs and salt. Beat in the milk gradually, using either a wooden spatula or a small sauce whisk. Stir rapidly at first, then more slowly while mixing the flour from the sides of the bowl. The batter must be quite liquid and never thick or doughy. Leave for 30 minutes. Heat a crepe pan or else a smooth frying pan with round sides and when very hot wipe with a cloth or pastry brush dipped in oil. Immediately ladle or pour in just enough batter to make a paper thin covering over the bottom of the pan ~ swirl the batter around the pan as you pour because it will set quickly. When bubbles form and the edges curl away from the sides of the pan, gently lift the pancake with your fingertips or a spatula and flip it over to cook the other side. Continue with the rest of the batter. Spread each pancake with some of the stuffing, roll up and put in a greased baking dish. Cover with the sauce, the tomatoes and the grated cheese. Bake in an oven preheated to 350°F/180°C/Gas 4 for 15~20 minutes and then under a grill for a minute or two to make the top bubbling and golden. Serve with a crisp salad as a starter or light main course.

LESLI
- 2 -
152

·SANTUARIO·EREMO·DI·CALOMINI·

Driving to the Eremo di Calomini it is increasingly clear why it is obligatory to sound the car horn. A narrow mountain road with snake-like bends and recent worrying evidence of landslides leads slowly but persistently upwards to the final breath-taking view from this isolated monastery, that at weekends has an open-air restaurant. It serves some of the best trout in Tuscany ~ if not the world ~ caught in the stream running beside the restaurant.

TROTA alla GARFAGNANA

Grilled trout as cooked in the Garfagnana

- 1 TROUT PER PERSON
- COARSE SEA SALT
- BLACK PEPPER
- LEMON JUICE
- FRESH ROSEMARY
- OLIVE OIL

First prepare the fire. In Tuscany they use chestnut wood which gives a characteristic sweet taste to the fish. Failing this use a charcoal grill or the grill of your cooker. Clean, scale and rinse the trout under cold running water. Sprinkle the inside cavity with coarse sea salt, pepper and lemon juice and stuff with plenty of fresh rosemary (or if necessary use dried). Brush olive oil all over the fish & on the grill rack to prevent sticking. Cook the fish about 4~5 in/10~12.5 cm from the wood or charcoal, turning only once. The fish is cooked when the juices run out clear and the flesh is opaque, about 10 minutes for a 2 lb/450 g fish. This is very good served with a simple salad of finely sliced tomatoes, red peppers and onions.

For a more substantial meal cook small potatoes and tomatoes together as they do in the Garfagnana. Take 1~2 potatoes per person (cut in pieces if they are large) & 1 tomato, peeled & chopped for each potato. Put in a lidded flameproof casserole with 5~6 tbsp of olive oil per 6 small potatoes, 1~2 cloves of garlic, crushed, 1 carrot, 1 stick of celery and 1 large onion, all finely chopped. Add salt and black pepper to taste and cook over a low flame until the juice from the tomatoes has evaporated & potatoes are tender.

· PISTOIA · MARKET ·

A particularly soft sweet flour is made from the chestnuts that grow so abundantly in the mountains north of the city of Pistoia. From it the local cooks make a strange, aromatic flat cake called castagnaccio. It is an acquired taste ~ difficult for non-Italians unused to sweets made with olive oil and rosemary, but certainly a taste that is very reminiscent of Tuscany.

Ricotta Pura

£460

CASTAGNACCIO

· Chestnut cake ·

This recipe comes from the big alimentari shop in Pistoia's permanent central market. The buxom proprietress was quite clearly amused that a foreigner should be asking for 'farina di castagna', chestnut flour, out of season (as the flour doesn't keep well it is only available from late autumn to spring, after the chestnut harvest) & also clearly concerned that it should be used properly.

1LB 4OZ/550G SIFTED CHESTNUT FLOUR
1PT/550 ML WATER
4~5 SPRIGS ROSEMARY, COARSELY CHOPPED
5 TBSP OLIVE OIL
GENEROUS HANDFUL RAISINS
2½ OZ/60G PINENUTS
PINCH SALT
2 TBSP GRANULATED SUGAR

Mix chestnut flour and water carefully with wooden spoon or spatula so as not to form lumps. It should be quite a liquid batter. Add raisins, pinenuts, salt and sugar. Pour into a greased baking tray not more than ¾ in/2 cm deep. Sprinkle with the rosemary and drizzle the oil over the top. Bake in an oven preheated to 400°F/200°C/Gas 6 until brown and, as the Pistoian lady described it, 'cracked like dry earth' or, more accurately, about 40 minutes. It is delicious straight from the pan either hot or cold, dredged with icing sugar or smeared with honey and fresh ricotta cheese.

• PISTOIA • EARLY MORNING MARKET •

CECCO

The town of Pescia is famous for its flowers, its proximity to Pinocchio's home town of Collodi and its local Asparagi giganti, although to those of us used to small tasty green stalks, these giants of the asparagus world are not so impressive.

ZUPPA di FUNGHI
Wild mushroom soup (4)

This delicious and delicate soup is made at Cecco's with an amazing quantity of fresh porcini mushrooms (BOLETUS EDULIS).

Commercial mushrooms are no substitute but you can use other wild mushrooms such as morels and chanterelles or, and only if pressed, use cultivated mushrooms and add 3/4 oz/15g of packaged dried porcini.

- 1 LB/450G SMALL CLEAN PORCINI (OR MORE IF YOU CAN AFFORD IT)
- 3~4 CUPS GOOD BEEF STOCK
- CLOVE GARLIC, CRUSHED
- 2 TBSP PARSLEY, FINELY CHOPPED
- 5~6 LEAVES NEPITELLA (THIS IS CATMINT, IF IT IS NOT AVAILABLE USE ANY FRESH GARDEN MINT)
- 4 SLICES BREAD
- OLIVE OIL
- SALT & PEPPER

Heat a little olive oil in a medium~sized saucepan, cut the porcini into small pieces & saute gently with the nepitella, adding salt and pepper to taste. When browned add the stock and then simmer for 10~15 minutes (with the dried mushrooms if using). After about 7 minutes stir in the garlic and parsley pounded together in a mortar. Toast the bread and rub with a garlic clove, freshly cut. Put the bread in bowls and pour the soup over.

POLLASTRINO al MATTONE

Chicken under a brick (2)

A mattone is a terracotta housebrick and the chicken in this recipe gets its characteristic crispy texture from the weight of a heavy glazed terracotta plate pressed down on it all through the cooking. You can buy traditional mattone plates in Lucca, or use any clean, heavy glazed terracotta brick.

- 1 SMALL CHICKEN, CUT IN HALF DOWN THE BREASTBONE AND POUNDED FAIRLY FLAT
- JUICE OF 1 LEMON
- CLOVE GARLIC, CRUSHED
- FRESH ROSEMARY
- 3~4 TBSP OLIVE OIL
- COARSE SEA SALT
- COARSE GROUND BLACK PEPPER

Rub all the ingredients well into the chicken's skin and then put the chicken in a frying pan. Place the brick on top and fry (in plenty of olive oil) over a low heat for about 20 minutes on each side until the skin is crunchy. Or put the chicken in a marinade made of the same ingredients. Leave for several hours, turning occasionally, and then fry as above.

RESTAURANTS

Restaurants mentioned in the text

THE VALE of FLORENCE

BORGO ANTICO ~ Piazza Santa Spirito, Florence

LA CARABACCIA ~ Via Palazzuolo, Florence

LE CAVE DI MAIANO ~ Via delle Cave 16, Maiano

CIBREO ~ Via de' Macci 118/R, Florence

COCO LEZZONE ~ Via del Parioncino 26r, Florence

DA GANINO ~ Piazza de Cimatori, 4, Florence

MASHA INNOCENTI (cookery school) ~ Via Trieste 1, Florence

SOSTANZA ~ Via del Porcellana 25, Florence

THE CHIANTI HILLS

ALBERGO LOCANDA GIOVANNI DA VERRAZZANO ~ Greve

CASTELLO DI SPALTENNA ~ Gaiole

IL FEDINO ~ San Casciano in Val di Pesa

TRATTORIA DEL MONTAGLIARI ~ near Panzano

MEDIEVAL CITIES

BUCA DI SAN FRANCESCO ~ Via di San Francesco 1, Arezzo

LOCANDA DELL'AMOROSA ~ Sinalunga

PONTE A RONDOLINO ~ Via Sevestro 32, San Gimignano

VINES & VINEYARDS

LA CASANOVA ~ Strada della Vittoria 10, Chianciano Terme

DIVA ~ Via Gracciano nel Corso 92, Montepulciano

FATTORIA DEI BARBI ~ 4 Km from Montalcino on the road to Castelnuovo dell'Abate

FATTORIA LA CHIUSA ~ Via della Madonnina 88, Montefollónico

FATTORIA PULCINO ~ Località Fonte Castagno, Montepulciano

THE ETRUSCAN MAREMMA

BAR LUPI ~ Sorano

DA LAUDOMIA ~ Poderi di Montemerano

TANA DEL CINGHIALE ~ Tirli

BY THE SEA

DA GUERRA ~ Portoferraio, Elba

RENDEZ-VOUS DA MARCELLO ~ Marciana Marina, Elba

RISTORANTE ENOTECA SERGIO ~ Lungarno Pacinotti 1, Pisa

PONTE DI SASSO ~ Località Ponte di Sasso, Viareggio

DA ROMANO ~ Via Mazzini 122, Viareggio

OLIVES & CHESTNUTS

LA BUCA DI SANT'ANTONIO, Via della Cervia 3, Lucca

CECCO ~ Viale Forti 84, Pescia

DA GIULIO IN PELLERIA ~ Via San Tommaso 29, Lucca

TRATTORIA LA MORA ~ Località Sesto di Moriano 104

VIPORE ~ Località Pieve Santo Stefano

· INDEX ·

Recipes are indexed according to their English names

SAUCES, SOUPS & STARTERS

· BREAD, PASTA & RICE ·

· FISH ·

· POULTRY, MEAT & GAME ·

· VEGETABLES ·

GRAZIE
ARRIVEDERCI
GOOD-BYE